T0244596

Inspiring Cooperation
and Celebrating Organizations

Genres, Message Design, and Strategies
in Public Relations

THE HAMPTON PRESS COMMUNICATION SERIES
Communications and Social Organization
Gary L. Kreps, *series editor*

Inspiring Cooperation and Celebrating Organizations

Genres, Message Design, and Strategies in Public Relations

Peter M. Smudde

Jeffrey L. Courtright

Illinois State University

HAMPTON PRESS, INC.
NEW YORK, NY

Printed in the United States of America

Library of Congress Cataloging-in-Publication Data

Smudde, Peter M.
    Inspiring cooperation and celebrating organizations : genres, message design, and strategies in public relations / Peter M. Smudde and Jeffrey L. Courtright. — 1st ed.
        p. cm. — (The Hampton Press communication series)
    Includes bibliographical references and index.
    ISBN 978-1-61289-058-6 (hardbound) — ISBN 978-1-61289-059-3 (paperbound)
    1. Public relations. 2. Communication in organizations. 3. Industrial sociology. I. Courtright, Jeffrey L. II. Title.
    HD59.S58 2012
    659.2—dc23   2011038331

Hampton Press, Inc.
307 Seventh Ave.
New York, NY 10001

Contents

List of Illustrations

Figures

Table

Acknowledgments

This book grew out of our mutual interests in and observations about the intersections among public relations, genres, rhetoric, and strategy. A number of people helped us with this project, to whom we would like to publicly express our heartfelt appreciation.

We express our gratitude to Gary Kreps, Hampton Press' series editor, for his support and sage counsel about our project. We also wish to thank the graduate students in Pete's Spring 2010 class and Jeff's Spring 2011 class, when they "test drove" the manuscript and, in particular, engaged in discussions about and made applications of our work. We also deeply appreciate the work of Karla Huffman for reviewing our manuscript and giving us feedback; Jim Ellis for giving us his fine preface to our book and a practitioner's perspective, as well as reviewing the manuscript; and Heather Jefferson for copyediting. We also want to thank the following people who have been especially supportive of us during this project: Peggy Simcic Brønn, Mark Comadena, Vince Hazelton, Larry Long, Finn Frandsen, Bob Heath, Øyvind Ihlen, Winni Johansen, Dean Kruckeberg, Fraser Likely, Bonnie Dostal Neff, Doug Newsom, Tom Watson, and Debra Worley.

We also wish to thank our families for their continued support, interest, and tolerance of us as we worked through our ideas and made this project come to life.

Preface

My 25 years as a corporate public relations manager was a rewarding and fulfilling time in my life. I had the great good fortune to work for companies that recognized the value of communication and trusted their public relations professionals to do their jobs. That is not to say that every assignment was a happy one.

For example, I continue to feel the agony that accompanied having to go into pleasant, usually small, communities as the "messenger of doom" about layoffs and, in a couple of instances, plant closings. One such occasion remains particularly vivid for me.

Despite the best efforts of company managers, a plant had to be closed. The final decision was made in October. With Thanksgiving Day the very next month and Christmas a month later, the question for the managers was when to close the plant. For those of us in the public relations department, the questions were multiple: After telling the employees, what was the order in which we went to our other audiences and who did the job? What tools and techniques did we use? For example, did we go first to the local newspaper or to the radio station, both of which had mid-day deadlines? Did we rely on a prepared release or, in the case of the radio station, did we want to do an on-air interview? If it was the latter, was it to be the plant manager or the out-of-town "hired gun?"

We managed to answer the questions before us, we were able to handle a difficult situation in as satisfactory a manner as it could have been handled and the company preserved its reputation in that community. Still, I wish I had been able to study this book when all of that was taking place—as well as other times as a reporter and editor in the Carolinas and Pennsylvania and as a Journalism professor in Louisiana and Nevada.

Pete and Jeff describe what they've done here as "the beginning of a long conversation."

They want that conversation to be about effective communication, specifically the manner in which the process and product of discourse relate and converge. After all, they tell us, "Organizations and societies are made up of people who act with others, principally through communication."

For these two scholars, the foundation for that long conversation is to approach the way we do public relations plans and programs in terms of types or categories—the *genres*—of public relations discourse we create. They lay out 39 individual genres that belong to seven "families" that practitioners at every level of expertise, accountability and authority are expected to use effectively.

It's not that those 39 categories include surprises. They don't. Rather, it's that they are appropriately grouped in a way I've not previously seen. They are described and discussed in terms of characteristics described by Pete and Jeff as celebratory, epistemic, performative and preservative, and the relative importance of each of those characteristics to each of the seven "families."

True to their calling, the scholars occasionally wander into semantic thickets with academic and technical terminology. But the way out of that is easily solved by following my own advice: "Get out the dictionary." That doesn't happen often enough to be a concern, however, and the standards they recommend come across as matter-of-fact, friendly counsel.

For example, they make it clear that good writing is basic. So, too, is the demand that, regardless of genre, there is a fundamental insistence that we seize the opportunities to be perceived as being similar to our target audiences. They want us to understand that honest, ethical behavior is not an option, and that everything comes together only when we think and create critically, strategically and tactically.

In an interesting and appealing way, Pete and Jeff describe the final chapter of the book as "the introduction" to the hoped-for long conversation. It is just that, they say, for the central question in their writing has been concerned with how thinking about and enacting public relations plans, programs and other activities can make better the practice and serious study of what we do. They believe, and I agree, the reward can be shaping our work as more forward-looking and strategic.

James B. Ellis, APR, Fellow PRSA
Emeritus Professor of Journalism
University of Nevada, Reno

1

A Foreword About "Generic" Public Relations

Public relations is known primarily for what its practitioners create—texts. The types of texts that public relations professionals plan, create, and evaluate are, in fact, numerous and ubiquitous, and they can be oral, printed, or symbols-based. From press releases to social media, public relations' role in society is a discursive one.[1] Sadly, the focus on literal texts is limiting. So much more is demanded of effective communication than the mere final product of one's or a group's work to bring a text into being for specific audiences and particular purposes. Effective communication (i.e., effective public relations) requires sound process *and* product, the latter being the result of the former. At the same time, however, the type of public relations discourse that is the focus of the process of bringing it into being plays a role in its creation. This push-me pull-you of communication is at the heart of this book. It is the stuff of "generic" public relations.

We do not mean to use the term *generic* in the colloquial sense—something devoid of differentiation. We mean to use the term in a specialized way that is, after all, familiar to people—a categorization (i.e., genre) of things that share important similarities. Generic public relations (GPR), then, places emphasis on the types or categories—the genres—of public relations discourse that practitioners and students strategically create. For us the term *discourse* refers to instances of texts that include both their form *and* content, not the more restricted sense of discourse as only verbal utterances in the tradition of Habermas (1985a, 1985b), or that of Austin (1974), and Searle (1969).

Public relations is the measured and ethical use of language and symbols to inspire cooperation between an organization and its publics (Smudde, 2001, 2011; also see Courtright & Smudde, 2007). This view places human communication at the nexus of public relations as a purposeful (i.e., strategic), contextual, and valuable organizational and societal function. The thesis for this book is that competence in the genres of public relations discourse is the real driving force in the process of planning, developing, enacting, and evaluating effective communication between an organization and its publics. This idea means basically that discourse competence is the reason that public relations professionals and students can strategize about and accomplish what they must to be successful at their work for both their organizations and their publics. The ultimate question this book answers is: How much may thinking about and enacting GPR change the practice and study of public relations for the better—to be more *prospective* (i.e., forward-looking and strategic) than retrospective (i.e., backward-looking and a matter of 20/20 hindsight)?

Overview of Genre and Discourse Studies

The basis for a generic view of public relations is two prominent fields of study: linguistics and rhetoric. Work in both of these fields has yielded many useful insights under the headings of "discourse analysis" and "generic criticism," for example. Indeed, these fields and the public relations field have much in common, and this book demonstrates how they integrate into a useful and usable framework that can be used in the practice and study of public relations.

Genre concerns have been with us since Aristotle, who argued that three specific types of situations (forensic, deliberative, and epideictic) necessitated the use of specific forms and types of argument. (These broad genres are explained in Chapter 2.) Logical appeals also exhibited a concern for form, with the syllogistic reasoning and a particular type of argument (i.e., enthymemes; see Chapter 4) associated with them. Rhetorical use of genres thus began as guidelines for the creation of messages. Although Aristotle's ideas are noted in general treatments of organizational discourse today (Cheney, Christensen, Conrad, & Lair, 2004; Heracleous, 2004), most uses of genres in organizational rhetoric serve as post hoc methods of rhetorical and literary criticism. We applaud (and have used) such methods because there is much to be learned from examples of corporate practices done well or gone awry. Critical discourse analysis of the kind covered in this book, as Fairclough (1995) argues, entails "analysis of the *texture* of texts, their form and organization, and not just commentaries on the 'content' of texts which ignore texture" (p. 4). In this way, we maintain that genres and their attendant writing conventions may be used in the same way that the Greeks used rhetoric: prospectively to address audiences as discourse communities.

Genre studies within the speech communication tradition are tied in part to Bitzer's (1968) "Rhetorical Situation" article because many studies have treated speech types or genres as responses to the constraints posed by situations and those related to audience characteristics or expectations. Chief among these has been the work of Campbell and Jamieson (n.d.), who argued that genres are a "constellation of forms," a unique fusion of style, substance, and situation, recurring over time. Studies using this perspective include eulogies (Goldzwig & Sullivan, 1995; Jamieson & Campbell, 1982), various forms of discourse associated with the U.S. presidency (Campbell & Jamieson, 1986, 2008), the diatribe (Windt, 1972), and messages prophetic in tone (e.g., apocalyptic rhetoric [Brummett, 1984] and the jeremiad [Johannesen, 1985]). Each of these genres has been shown to have specific audience needs, situational constraints on the message source, style and tone, and identifiable message strategies (specific content may vary, but the broader message strategies remain the same).

A generic approach "aims at understanding rhetorical practice over time by discerning recurrent patterns that reflect the rules that practitioners follow. . . . Those rules outline the parameters within which symbolic action will express the rhetor's motives, will be acknowledged by the audience as a form or recognized as a convention for expressing intention, and will be capable of satisfying audience expectations" (Campbell & Jamieson, 1986, p. 295). This approach to generic analysis "aims to illuminate rather than classify" (Swales, 1990, p. 43). Identifying a text as a genre is but the first step to understanding its rhetorical value. So we can think of corporate messages as fitting specific genres of discourse that can be studied for their rhetorical and social dimensions. Approaches to genre found in linguistics, and in applications found in the technical communication literature, emphasize the latter.

From a linguistic perspective, genres of discourse may be defined not only in terms of the *forms* they take—the discourse conventions that have been used time and time again—but by the *purposes* they accomplish (Miller, 1984) and the *audiences* for whom they are useful toward those ends. Regarding this latter point, audiences who use and respond to a common set of genres and discourse conventions may be said to constitute a discourse community. For example, as Smudde (2011) demonstrates, a large community upholds conventions about enacting public relations discourse for external and internal audiences. Such social agreement about texts gets at the heart of discourse genre. A genre's communicative purposes "are recognized by the expert members of the parent discourse community, and thereby constitute the rationale for the genre. This rationale shapes the schematic structure of the discourse and influences and constrains choice of content and style. . . . In addition to purpose, exemplars of a genre exhibit various patterns of similarity in terms of structure, style, content and intended audience" (Swales, 1990, p. 58). Swale's perspective thus unites rhetorical and linguistic approaches to genres.

In short, multiple audiences use—and respond to—genres and discourse conventions. As Smudde (2011) argues, categories of public relations discourse derive from conventions for discursive action that are upheld by members of the large community of people in the field of public relations (and other disciplines) in both industry and academe. That is, the broad community of people (e.g., professional organizations for public relations, university curricula, scholars/researchers, publishers, practitioners, news media, and organizational departments such as marketing, sales, legal, and human resources) who are competent in or work with public relations means that the genres of public relations discourse are institutionalized, but they also allow people to adapt them to specific organizational needs and communication situations.

The social process of creating any public relations discourse type is governed by contextual cues about the order of things reflected in the text, which is shared among diverse publics to induce cooperation with them. As Killingsworth and Gilbertson (1992) observe, "In selecting appropriate genres, writers model appropriate actions. They tell the audience something about the action implicit in the discourse and something about how they want the audience to respond. . . . Genres are shorthand codes for describing typical kinds of communal actions" (pp. 73, 87). The categories of public relations discourse, then, are major genres of public relations that practitioners create and members of a discourse community respond to because they exhibit formal appeal: As Burke (1968) puts it, "form is the creation of an appetite in the mind of the auditor, and the adequate satisfying of that appetite" (p. 31) by reflecting certain discursive patterns (see Burke, 1968, pp. 124–149), that is, genres.

What is striking to us is how little has been done, particularly in the public relations and organizational rhetoric literatures, to take what is known about genres and discourse conventions and apply them to the creation of organizational messages. There are at least two reasons for this. First, the majority of what we know in the organizational rhetoric literature comes, as referred to earlier, from post hoc, retrospective studies of organizational crisis communication. Granted, the research programs of Benoit (1995a, 1995b; Benoit & Brinson, 1994; Benoit & Czerwinski, 1997; Blaney, Benoit, & Brazeal, 2002; Brinson & Benoit, 1996, 1999) and Hearit (e.g., Courtright & Hearit, 2002; Hearit, 1995, 1997, 1999; Hearit & Brown, 2004) have generated multiple studies of corporate *apologiae* (for a review, see Hearit, 2001), no rhetorical studies to our knowledge have proposed that typologies such as Benoit's (1995a, 1995b) are to be used in *propter hoc*, prospective scholarship to move beyond the logistics of crisis plans to scenarios to develop standby statements grounded in an understanding of apologia as a genre. We recognize that this is somewhat problematic because apologia does not conform to the generic parameters set by theorists such as Campbell and Jamieson (n.d.) because not all crisis situations have the same type of exigence, constraints, or audience needs. (For further discussion of this problem and an explanation of why this may occur, see Rowland & Jerome, 2004.)

Second, there may be resistance to applying genre theory more generally to all types of organizational discourse because some forms (e.g., memos, news releases, public service announcements, etc.) may at first blush appear mundane and even uninteresting. Orlikowski and Yates (1994) argue that genres shape—and are shaped by—social actors, and they are adapted in response to community norms, specific events, time pressure, and media channel capabilities. In the field of rhetorical studies, Campbell and Jamieson (n.d.) maintain that genres are interactions of substance and style in response to recurrent situations. ("Substance" includes strategies and form; in 1992, linguists Yates and Orlikowski stated a similar position, though expressed as substance and form.) In contrast, Rowland (1991) posited that genres are best understood as a set of strategic constraints created by needs, purposes, and societal limitations related to the situation. Regardless of the source, strategy is central to using genres.

Some of us may resist the idea of applying genre theory to organizational discourse because there are handbooks and writing textbooks that have presented any genre or discourse convention as merely following a formula or recipe for format, style, and basic content. Some industry articles (e.g., McClenaghan, 2005; Ryan, 1995) offer writers' preferred recipes for news releases, for example, but at best display an implicit and incomplete understanding of the reasons behind the discourse conventions they invoke. As we explained earlier, however, there are theoretical reasons behind the expected patterns that are valuable to anyone desiring to be competent in public relations discourse. Yet despite a call for studies of corporate communication that employ discourse conventions, genres, and other rhetorical concepts in a prospective manner (e.g., Smudde, 2004b, 2007, 2011), we have found no studies of corporate communication criticism that led to concerns for message design (for one exception, see Courtright & Slaughter, 2007). Only one experimental design (Coombs & Schmidt, 2000), has tested Benoit's (1995a, 1995b) image repair typology of apologetic strategies, but the study stops short of offering recommendations (see Smudde & Courtright, 2008).

With the exception of corporate apologia, the academic literature also tends to treat public relations genres as tacit assumptions of form, messages to be analyzed from perspectives other than a generic one or not at all. This last position treats the particular genre into which a type of writing falls as a subject not worthy of consideration. We contend that it is. In public relations, books that have been published have appealed to various audiences but are dated, and none of them seems to adequately address the issues valued by *both* scholars and practitioners equitably enough. Indeed, there are no books in the communication, technical writing, and management literatures that approach public relations messages as genres to be studied. This gap is not due to a lack of interest but one of misunderstanding.

The lack of focus on a strategic, prospective message design, let alone attention to the genre theory and discourse conventions associated with it, thus pervades both the public relations literature. Taken together, the work of linguists, rhetoricians, and communication scholars has provided us with tools for making sense of and planning for public relations discourse. There is much to be gained by addressing the various theories that underlie the need for genres and human responses to them. As Northup Frye (1957) wrote, "The purpose of criticism by genres is not so much to classify as to clarify . . ." (pp. 247–248). We maintain that an understanding of how genres function can help practitioners, academics, and students create more powerful messages. So there is a major hole in the literature that our book, *Inspiring Cooperation and Celebrating Organizations*, fills. In addition to the scholarly research done on public relations, examples of actual public relations efforts are important to examine. There is at least one archive of such examples.

Archive of Public Relations Genres

When it comes to ready examples of public relations discourse—"excellent" examples—the Public Relations Society of America (PRSA) has an archive of all Silver Anvil Award winners, dating back to the first winners in 1947. The archive is kept at the Wisconsin Historical Society in Madison, Wisconsin, which was arranged in 1963 by the late Scott Cutlip, who was on the faculty at the University of Wisconsin and very involved with the PRSA (J. Nelson, personal communication, June 16, 2010). As part of our work for this book we felt this archive would be a natural place to look for examples—even standards—of discourse that were judged by public relations professionals as "excellent," because the Silver Anvil Award is considered the top award recognizing excellence in public relations.[2] Specifically, we believed Silver Anvil winners would provide us with "best practices" for public relations discourse—that we could divine from them discourse categories and, especially, discourse conventions because they were the best of the best of public relations practice.

We had two objectives for our archival research: (a) to identify patterns of excellence based on judging criteria and actual winners' examples for each classification of public relations work, and (b) to define an initial taxonomy about discourse practices per genre from the award winners. Our sampling frame was the entire archive of all Silver Anvil winners, and our data were the actual texts in all archived Silver Anvil winners. Our approach, after becoming familiar with the archive's cataloging system, was to conveniently select multiple winners from each decade and examine them for their contents and, especially, discourse examples.[3]

As we examined the winners, we found the archive organized the winners by year and category, and the archive only contained the entries themselves. There were no documents about how judges evaluated any entries (i.e., feedback on score sheets or evaluation forms). Also missing in the archive are the calls for entries for each year of the Silver Anvil Award. However, we did happen to find two calls for entries from 1979 and 1980. Indeed, these two calls for entries revealed that the judging criteria changed in 1980 from three (i.e., research, planning, and execution) to four (i.e., research, planning, execution, and evaluation). Prior to this change, evaluation was merely part of the execution criterion. Interestingly, the PRSA does not have records about past calls for entries (and thereby judging criteria) and only retains documentation about preparing entries (also called "study guides") for the Silver Anvil Awards since 2002 (G. Gressley, personal communication, July 16, 2009).

Our observations of the archives suggest that these campaigns indeed demonstrate the tactics used as the *sine qua non* of discourse conventions in use by public relations practitioners. But in the end, we could not fulfill our objectives through our archival research. We expected that the award winners would reveal consistency with discourse conventions, and we expected documentation of message and discourse effectiveness from judging, ratings and comments. Without feedback from the judges, there is nothing to indicate what made any Silver Anvil entry "excellent" or award worthy. The dearth of judging criteria (at least per a call for entries) also made it difficult to infer on what grounds any discursive practices could be determined to be better than any other. Best practices are therefore not defined directly through any award winner.[4] We can, however, at least rest assured that the entries are examples of the best of public relations practice for a given year, if only because they won a Silver Anvil Award and the winners are a matter of record with the PRSA. In this way the winning entries can be used no differently than any other examples of public relations discourse (e.g., those used in the chapters that follow): Generic characteristics must be inferred from them as discourse exemplars that exhibit similar patterns of structure, purpose, content, style, and audience.

During our process, we hoped there was an archive of PRSA's Bronze Anvil Award winners as well. After all, this award is meant to recognize annually the best individual examples of public relations discourse by type (e.g., press release, speech, newsletter, etc.). Although there is a record of winners of the award, we found that no archive of winning entries exists, and, if we would like to see any award winners' entries, we would have to contact the winners themselves and ask for permission to see their work (R. Mason, personal communication, July 15, 2009). There is also no guarantee of seeing any judges' feedback about the winners, if such feedback was given.

In the end we are left with two conclusions about these award winners. First, the Silver Anvil winners reveal best practices and professionalism based on campaign inputs, throughput, outputs, and outcomes, which is consistent with the RACE model and similar theory-based approaches. We also expected to see more of a business case made for the quality of any campaign's performance, but that was not found, even for winners from the last two decades. Second, the Silver Anvil winners do not give us information about (a) the specific characteristics necessary for any public relations discourse to be identified as one kind of discourse over any other, and (b) how to best ensure that the use of any public relations genre can be used effectively to fulfill the objectives for a particular situation. Our book, then, is all the more important as it fills this gap above and beyond the gap in the scholarly research because we detail the genres of public relations discourse, the conventions that are necessary to make them work, message design matters that befit each genre, and strategy implications for broader public relations action. Practitioners, scholars, and students of public relations alike should find this book useful.

Target Readers

Inspiring Cooperation and Celebrating Organizations bridges insightfully theory with practice for its readers. It also follows up with our previous book, *Power and Public Relations* (Courtright & Smudde, 2007), and extends Smudde's (2011) work, *Public Relations as Dramatistic Organizing.* To be sure, this book offers a broad range of appeal to key groups of target readers. Those readers break into the following three categories, admittedly with some overlap among them but with enough uniqueness to secure individual appeal:

1. Professionals—practitioners in graduate school looking for a way to enhance their credentials to move up in careers with a master's degree in the field but not to go on for a doctorate; also practitioners wanting to build their knowledge about public relations through independent reading on the subject.

2. Academics—professors and practitioners who teach, research, and serve in public relations education.

3. Students—graduate students plus motivated, advanced undergraduate students in public relations, communication, organizational studies, and marketing.

Based on this breakdown, we envision the ideal audience for this book to cover two similar yet different audiences: scholar-practitioners and practitioner-scholars. The relative position of either term, "scholar" or "practitioner," suggests the respective audience's primary area of emphasis. Scholar-practitioners are those who have been public relations professionals for some length of time in their careers and have chosen a more academic path so that they can *help build knowledge* about the field. Practitioner-scholars are those who are employed as public relations professionals (including consultants, freelancers, etc.) and *seek to apply specific knowledge* about the field to their public relations projects and programs.

Both scholar-practitioners and practitioner-scholars enjoy intellectual examinations of the field and how it works, seeking more than mere recipes about how to make a particular communications effort more effective, measurable, defensible, and so on. Both audiences are inspired by the epistemological and ontological dimensions to public relations literature, and they see utility of any scholarship that befits their needs appropriately (Smudde, 2004a). There is a keen cross-pollination of ideas that these people value reflection and experience, as practice informs theory and theory informs practice. (Indeed, this dynamic rings true to one of the authors, who has been a practitioner-scholar for 16 years and has been a scholar-practitioner for 9 years, and his co-author has come to appreciate the interplay between theory and praxis in teaching undergraduate public relations majors for 18 years.) Both audiences engage in research, teaching, and service to differing degrees that meet the professional requirements and personal interests for their respective careers in academe and industry.

What This Book Is and Is Not

As with any project, we made some deliberate choices about what we want this book to "do" for its readers. From what we have seen in the development of public relations literature, and as we already described, this book fills some important gaps. Accordingly, there are a number of things this book is not. This book is not another how-to textbook on public relations writing. A bevy of books exist about public relations writing, and many are updated in new editions on an almost annual basis. These books tend to be formulaic in their approaches, presenting recipes for discourse creation and use. This book goes beyond those books because we want people to look beyond the end product and see public relations discourse genres more purposefully (which requires *vision* about long-range outcomes) rather than merely means to ends (which favors immediate or short-term results). In this way, our book is the first of its kind that focuses on public relations discourse genres in terms of purpose and strategy rather than mere writing recipes and process.

This book is not an exercise in examining past cases of good and bad public relations tactics and campaigns. This book also does not go into an exhaustive review and analysis of all public relations genres because they are amply addressed in other sources, such as public relations writing texts, and as a matter of practically, we cannot obtain and analyze all instances of each genre. Indeed, this book does not focus on public relations genres at the campaign level (e.g., crisis communication as corporate apologia or even new-product introductions). This book, then, presents sufficient statements about what constitutes public relations genres by employing a conceptual approach grounded in linguistics and rhetorical theory that is a starting point to encourage people to think about genres and apply them in different ways beyond their taken-for-granted structures. But this book does use numerous examples of those genres and past cases to illustrate points to be made about the strategy behind public relations discourse. The examples serve as touch points for prospective message design and strategic business planning. Indeed, as Chapter 3 shows, the biggest mistake that practitioners and students make is "jumping to tactics" when a public relations problem or opportunity arises, rather than examining it more systematically and within the larger, strategic business context. Although seasoned veterans may seem to do this, we contend that they use a kind of cognitive shorthand to process contextual information quickly and arrive at a sound, strategic decision based on much experience. Our approach in this book is to draw out new, salient details about this process and anchor them in the context of organizational business, not just the isolated organizational function of public relations.

This book can and should supplement any case study-based approach to learning and applying public relations principles to "real-world" opportunities. The flow of chapters purposely uses groupings or "families" of genres so they may be more effectively addressed in their shared message design and strategic lights that have not been covered in the literature previously (see Appendix 1). This chapter has set the book's place in the public relations literature and argued for its value. The next chapter presents our method for analysis and, most important, message design and strategic planning with public relations discourse. The seven chapters that follow present particular groupings of public relations genres (i.e., news, summaries, features, conversations, showcases, collections, and reports) that allow us to (a) present the rationales that facilitate their being put into purpose-related groups and summarize discourse conventions that make them up individually, (b) address the message design matters that they share collectively based on the method presented in Chapter 2, and (c) explain the strategic implications for the public relations discourse genres in each chapter. Readers who feel very familiar with public relations discourse can choose to skip the summaries of their discourse conventions and go into the message design and strategy implications. The final chapter ends the book literally but is the beginning metaphorically (thus the title, "Introduction") of the long-term practical and academic discussion and action about the strategy behind public relations discourse genres used to inspire cooperation and celebrate organizations.

Notes

1. In this book social media are not addressed as one medium, as it seems is so often mistakenly done. Social media comprise many separate web-based technologies and media channels that facilitate interpersonal interaction, collaboration, and community development among Internet users who create and share their own content, and such channels include blogs, podcasts, wikis, virtual worlds, Internet forums, networking sites, and so on. To this end there are numerous social media channels, and we do not address all of them because few of them are used in public relations. Additionally, those channels' particular technological parameters pose an interesting conundrum for discourse form and function, which we address in Chapter 10. So, it is important to understand that we do not address social media as a single discourse type, but instead address discourse conventions and epideictic characteristics of selected social media where they apply in our taxonomy (see Appendix 1). Doing so allows for deeper understanding of the discourse and, especially, strategic planning of social media and other public relations discourse in optimum combinations to meet specific objectives.

2. This archival research was supported by a 2009 University Research Grant from College of Arts and Sciences at Illinois State University, for which we are grateful. We also are grateful to Helmut Knies at the Wisconsin Historical Society (WHS) for giving us access to the archive, Jonathan Nelson at the WHS for information about the archive's history, and Randi Mason and Gladiss Gressley at PRSA headquarters for helping us with answers to questions and other matters for this project.

3. It is important to note that, although all Silver Anvil winners from 1947 to 2002 are in the archive, the winners from 2003 onward are not yet formally cataloged, but they are accessible as unsorted and noncataloged records (see the Wisconsin Historical Society's online catalog at http://arcat.library.wisc.edu/).

4. We also observed two other important characteristics among Silver Anvil Award winners. First, there appears to be little or no connection or parallel with APR requirements, especially for the most recent years for with APR requirements are accessible. This point is important because, if excellence is to be understood at the practitioner *and* the practice levels, they ought to be in sync. And second, the

emphasis in winning submissions seems mostly to be on tactics overall. In other words, it seems, even for the most srecent entries, the flashier an entry's tactics, the better.

References

Austin, J. L. (1974). *How to do things with words* (2nd ed.). Cambridge, MA: Harvard University Press.

Benoit, W. L. (1995a). *Accounts, excuses, and apologies: A theory of image restoration strategies.* Albany, NY: SUNY Press.

Benoit, W. L. (1995b). Sears' repair of its auto service image: Image restoration discourse in the corporate sector. *Communication Studies, 46,* 89–105.

Benoit, W. L., & Brinson, S. L. (1994). AT&T: Apologies are not enough. *Communication Quarterly, 42,* 75–88.

Benoit, W. L., & Czerwinski, A. (1997). A critical analysis of USAir's image repair discourse. *Business Communication Quarterly, 60,* 38–57.

Bitzer, L. (1968). The rhetorical situation. *Philosophy & Rhetoric, 1,* 1–14.

Blaney, J. R., Benoit, W. L., & Brazeal, L. M. (2002). Blowout! Firestone's image restoration campaign. *Public Relations Review, 28,* 379–392.

Brinson, S. L., & Benoit, W. L. (1996). Dow Corning's image repair strategies in the breast implant crisis. *Communication Quarterly, 44,* 29–41.

Brinson, S. L., & Benoit, W. L. (1999). The tarnished star: Restoring Texaco's damaged public image. *Management Communication Quarterly, 12,* 483–510.

Brummett, B. (1984). Premillennial apocalyptic as a rhetorical genre. *Central States Speech Journal, 35*(2), 84–93.

Burke, K. (1968). *Counter-statement.* Berkeley, CA: University of California Press.

Campbell, K. K., & Jamieson, K. H. (n.d.). Form and genre in rhetorical criticism: An introduction. In K. K. Campbell & K. H. Jamieson (Eds.), *Form and genre: Shaping rhetorical action* (pp. 9–32). Falls Church, VA: Speech Communication Association.

Campbell, K. K., & Jamieson, K.H. (1986). Introduction (Special issue on genre criticism). *Southern Speech Communication Journal, 51,* 293–299.

Campbell, K. K., & Jamieson, K. H. (2008). *Presidents creating the presidency: Deeds done in words.* Chicago: University of Chicago Press.

Cheney, G., Christensen, L. T., Conrad, C., & Lair, D. J. (2004). Corporate rhetoric as organizational discourse. In D. Grant, C. Hardy, C. Oswick, & L. Putnam (Eds.), *The Sage handbook of organizational discourse* (pp. 79–104). Newbury Park, CA: Sage.

Coombs, T., & Schmidt, L. (2000). An empirical analysis of image restoration: Texaco's racism crisis. *Journal of Public Relations Research, 12,* 163–178.

Courtright, J. L., & Hearit, K. M. (2002). "The good organization speaking well": A paradigm case for institutional reputation management. *Public Relations Review, 28,* 347–360.

Courtright, J. L., & Slaughter, G. Z. (2007). Remembering disaster: Since the media do, so must public relations. *Public Relations Review, 33,* 313–318.

Courtright, J. L., & Smudde, P. M. (Eds.). (2007). *Power and public relations*. Cresskill, NJ: Hampton Press.

Fairclough, N. (1995). *Critical discourse analysis: The critical study of language*. New York: Longman.

Frye, N. (1957). *Anatomy of criticism*. Princeton, NJ: Princeton University Press.

Goldzwig, S. R., & Sullivan, P. A. (1995). Post-assassination newspaper editorial eulogies: Analysis and assessment. *Western Journal of Communication, 59*, 126–150.

Habermas, J. (1985a). *The theory of communicative action: Reason and the rationalization of society* (Vol. 1) (T. McCarthy, Trans.). Boston: Beacon Press.

Habermas, J. (1985b). *The theory of communicative action: Lifeworld and system: A critique of functionalist reason* (Vol. 2) (T. McCarthy, Trans.). Boston: Beacon Press.

Hearit, K. M. (1995). From "we didn't do it" to "it's not our fault": The use of apologia in public relations crises. In W. N. Elwood (Ed.), *Public relations inquiry as rhetorical criticism: Case studies of corporate discourse and social influence* (pp. 117–131). Westport, CT: Praeger.

Hearit, K. M. (1997). On the use of transcendence as an apologia strategy: The case of Johnson Controls and its fetal protection policy. *Public Relations Review, 23*, 217–231.

Hearit, K. M. (2001). Corporate apologia: When an organization speaks in defense of itself. In R. L. Heath (Ed.), *Handbook of public relations* (pp. 501–511). Thousand Oaks, CA: Sage.

Hearit, K. M., & Brown, J. (2004). Merrill Lynch: Corporate apologia and business fraud. *Public Relations Review, 30*, 459–466.

Heracleous, L. T. (2004). Interpretivist approaches to organizational discourse. In D. Grant, C. Hardy, C. Oswick, & L. Putnam (Eds.), *The Sage handbook of organizational discourse* (pp. 175–192). Newbury Park, CA: Sage.

Jamieson, K. H., & Campbell, K. K. (1982). Rhetorical hybrids: Fusions of generic elements. *Quarterly Journal of Speech, 68*, 146–157.

Johannesen, R. L. (1985). The Jeremiad and Jenkin Lloyd Jones. *Communication Monographs, 52*, 156–172.

Killingsworth, M. J., & Gilbertson, M. K. (1992). *Signs, genres, and communities in technical communication*. Amityville, NY: Baywood.

McCleneghan, J. S. (2005). PR practitioners and "issues" in the early millennium. *Public Relations Quarterly, 50*(2), 17–22.

Miller, C. R. (1984). Genre as social action. *Quarterly Journal of Speech, 70*, 151–167.

Orlikowski, W. J., & Yates, J. (1994). Genre repertoire: The structuring of communicative practices in organizations. *Administrative Science Quarterly, 39*, 541–574.

Rowland, R. C. (1991). On generic categorization. *Communication Theory, 1*, 128–144.

Rowland, R. C., & Jerome, A. M. (2004). On organizational *apologia*: A reconceptualization. *Communication Theory, 14*, 191–211.

Ryan, M. (1995). Models help writers produce publishable releases. *Public Relations Quarterly, 40*(2), 25–27.

Searle, J. R. (1969). *Speech acts: An essay in the philosophy of language*. New York: Cambridge University Press.

Smudde, P. M. (2001). Issue or crisis: A rose by any other name. . . . *Public Relations Quarterly, 46*(4), 34–36.

Smudde, P. M. (2004a). Concerning the epistemology and ontology of public relations literature. *Review of Communication, 4,* 163–175.

Smudde, P. M. (2004b). Implications on the practice and study of Kenneth Burke's idea of a "public relations counsel with a heart." *Communication Quarterly, 52,* 420–432.

Smudde, P. M. (2007). Public relations' power as based on knowledge, discourse, and ethics. In J. L. Courtright & P. M. Smudde (Eds.), *Power and public relations* (pp. 207–238). Cresskill, NJ: Hampton Press.

Smudde, P. M. (2011). *Public relations as dramatistic organizing: A case study bridging theory and practice.* Cresskill, NJ: Hampton Press.

Smudde, P. M., & Courtright, J. L. (2008). Time to get a job: Helping image repair theory begin a career in industry. *Public Relations Journal, 2*(1). Retrieved February 1, 2008, from http://www.prsa.org/prjournal/Vol2No1/SmuddeCourtright.pdf

Swales, J. M. (1990). *Genre analysis: English in academic and research settings.* New York: Cambridge University Press.

Windt, T. O., Jr. (1972). The diatribe: Last resort for protest. *Quarterly Journal of Speech, 58,* 1–14.

Yates, J., & Orlikowski, W. J. (1992). Genres of organizational communication: A structurational approach to studying communication and media. *Academy of Management Review, 17,* 299–326.

2

Framework

Reasons for a Generic Perspective

Human beings are captivated by categories. The eras of classical music are marked by styles: baroque, classical, romantic, and so on. Oscars and Tony Awards are given for Best Actor, Best Actress, Best Supporting Actor, Best Supporting Actress, Best Director, and so on. We have the need to make distinctions of hierarchy, classifying things by their similarities and differences. It's actually pretty useful. The entertainment industry's use of genre conventions to create works of art depends on the audience's understanding of how a play, movie, book, or song fits the characteristics of a particular type. Some of this is a matter of taste, but the functional power of genres enables people to make sense of these and other types of communication without having to think hard about it. Not only this, but they have been adapted for audiences with particular needs (e.g., the visually and aurally impaired).

It is this basic ability or need to create and use categories that is at the heart of this book about public relations. We believe public relations can become both more understandable and more effective for all parties through a genre-based view. More important, we believe a stronger grasp of the theoretical and practical dimensions of public relations discourse genres is vital to successful strategic planning. In this chapter, we lay the foundation for these contentions by grounding the theory of genres in past and contemporary times. We also explain the prevalence of discourse genres in today's organizations and how they function. Finally, we present our view of the "generic" nature of public relations as a method for analysis and practice.

A Historical Perspective on Genre and Discourse Conventions

The practice of public relations and the development of rhetoric in Ancient Greece have a common starting point: democracy. Democracy arose after the overthrow of the last Athenian tyrant, Cylon, and the codification of oral standards into written laws (Raaflaub, Ober, & Wallace, 2007). Those in power established courts of law and a legislature and therefore depended on successful message strategies to avoid a repeat of the uprising, affected in part by the sheer number of citizens that brought about Cylon's downfall. Because civil strife is common, people use symbols and forms—genres of discourse—to forestall the need for physical conflict and, of course, to pick up the pieces after wars when they occur.

With the creation of written law, courts to apply it, and public assembly to extend or modify it, oral rhetoric blossomed in Athens. To debate laws, adjudicate them in court, and inspire citizens to respect the rule of law, Greek leaders and landowners learned to engage in public argument, and teachers arose to help them improve strategies of developing, organizing, framing, and expressing ideas so that audiences could be persuaded (Murphy, Katula, Hill, & Ochs, 2003). What is most important to understand here is that rhetorical genres arose because of the *practice* of rhetoric. Aristotle (1954/1984) merely organized what we might call a book of "best practices" of rhetoric, and he organized his ideas according to broad, common situations that any speaker might encounter.

Aristotle was the most renowned of the Athenian teachers. Perhaps this is because he wrote on so many topics: rhetoric, politics, ethics, and biology—and others. We don't know in what order he wrote his different works, but his *On Nature* is the epitome of category systems. What high school graduate does not know that animals and plants are divided into genus and species? From that word, *genus,* we have the related word, *genre.* Just as he divided all knowledge into the various disciplines, and flora and fauna into categories based on their similarities and differences, Aristotle (1954/1984) divided public speaking situations into three broad categories: one for legal argument, another for public debate, and a third for special ceremonies. He also suggested that some arguments were more appropriate in the courtroom than they were in the legislature or a community event.

Likewise, public discourse today has its genres. The average person may not know that there are five components to creating a suitable tribute at a funeral, for example, but he or she recognizes when a speaker has given a poor eulogy. Violations of style are obvious: We should not speak ill of the dead or dwell on matters not directly related to the deceased, for example. Eulogistic strategies are less obvious on a surface level (see Kunkel & Dennis, 2003), but sometimes violations of these implicit audience expectations are obvious. Consider the eulogies at Richard Nixon's funeral. California Governor Pete Wilson focused too much on himself and his positive connections to what Nixon stood for. In contrast, Robert Dole came closest to fulfilling the expectations of the situation. Dole emphasized the loss to the nation that had occurred. He eulogized Nixon as a consummate politician who was as complex as the average person: He was "one of us." Dole met the difficulties of the situation, eulogizing a man whose greatness in conducting foreign policy was eclipsed by scandal and resignation from office. Dole's word choices ("style") and strategies (or "substance") were, overall, appropriate to the situation.

Corporate discourse also has its genres (see Figure 2.1), and we can think about them at various levels. The layperson knows that organizations use memos, quarterly and annual reports, and so on to conduct business—what management communicates. Students, however, learn the patterns of organization required to create news releases, public service announcements, and other genre conventions—the craft of what public relations practitioners do. At a deeper level, genres are grounded in the situations they address and the purposes organizations bring to their use. They are strategic because they rely on linguistic and rhetorical principles that suggest the style, form, and function appropriate to the situation—the reasons *why* all organizational communicators create discourse and *how* they do so. It is at this deeper level that we focus primarily throughout the rest of the book.

Although in everyday parlance we talk about organizations issuing statements, news releases, and the like, the messages are not merely the product of an organization's various departments. Discourse genre conventions are co-created through interactions with publics: media contacts, consumers, communities, investors, legislators/regulators, and so on. Audience understandings of recurring situations and expectations that arise from those perceptions impinge on what the organization says and how it says it. Some situations provide greater flexibility than others. News releases have an obvious, standard form (the inverted pyramid) and strategies that frame a story's main point and build the organization's image. Additional strategies for them vary, however, depending on the situation (e.g., investor news, personnel announcements).

Our field-dependent approach to public relations *discourse genres* stands in relation to the field-independent approach of *rhetorical genres*. The latter realm of rhetorical genres concerns use of any discourse—including public relations discourse and beyond—for specific rhetorical purposes. Core rhetorical genres include but are not limited to these:

- Apologia—discourse enacted in self-defense when faced with or to preempt accusations of wrong-doing. Examples of this rhetorical genre include individuals' asking for forgiveness for transgressions and corporations' communication during crises.

Formal letters
Memos (printed & electronic)
Meetings (e.g., team, department, company)
Shareholder meetings
Project/progress/trip reports
Research reports
Proposals
Formal presentations
Public speeches
Strategic planning documents
Employee handbooks
Training manuals
Owner's manuals
Periodic financial reporting documents
Fliers

Posters
Annual corporate reports (e.g., financial and public-interest)
Tax forms
Corporate image pieces (e.g., brochures, websites, advertisements)
Prepared statements
Press releases
Video news releases (VNRs)
Photo news releases (PNRs)
Audio new releases (ANRs)
Fact sheets
Backgrounders
FAQs (frequently asked questions)
Biographical statements
Press conferences
Press kits

Interviews
Articles
Matte releases
White papers
Case studies
Public service announcements (PSAs)
Advertorials
Newsletters
Video programs
Pitch letters
Pitch calls
Conversations (telephone, face-to-face, or real-time video conference calls)
Blogs
Podcasts (video & audio)
Wikis

Figure 2.1. Representative genre set for corporate discourse, including those for public relations.

- Apocalyptic—discourse enacted to prophesy end-times. Examples of this rhetorical genre are, as in the national healthcare debate in the United States, the proclamations that society as we have known it will be forever changed for the worse.

- Jeremiad—discourse enacted to appeal to first principles that inspire people to return to their core values that made them great. Examples of this rhetorical genre include sermons from religious leaders that call on people to repent and embrace the values of their faiths, or corporate chief executives who call on employees to reapply their organization's original, core values to attain greater performance and regain market dominance.

- Utopian—discourse enacted that envision an ideal state of affairs. Examples of this rhetorical genre include communication to employees about how major organizational changes will make the company better than ever.

- Introduction—discourse enacted to present someone or something for the first time or at the outset of some occasion. Examples of this rhetorical genre include the presentation of a speaker at an event, a new-product unveiling, an author at a book signing, or some other occasion.

- Appreciation—discourse enacted in thanksgiving. Examples of this rhetorical genre include thank-you statements in various forms.

- Award—discourse enacted in the presentation of special recognition. Examples of this rhetorical genre include formal recognitions of success, excellence, or outstanding accomplishment.

- Tributes—discourse enacted to extol someone or something. Examples of this rhetorical genre include events celebrating someone's lifetime achievements in a field of specialization.

The important point to remember about rhetorical genres is that they do not subsume and are not restricted to given discourse genres. Rhetorical genres are, as we said, field-independent (i.e., they transcend subjects and occasions) and allow for certain arguments to be presented in any discourse type as long as they fulfill their rhetorical purpose as outlined earlier. This field independency of rhetorical genres explains how apologia, for example, functions well for individuals and organizations while relying on specific discourse genres to enact an effective self-defense. Effectiveness of rhetorical genres, stated simply, depends on how well any enacted discourse fulfills both the requirements for the selected rhetorical genre *and* the conventions for the discourse genre(s) used.[1] Note that our use of the word *genre* is done specifically to refer to discourse genres. Other contexts, such as rhetorical genres, will be made plain as needed.

Because Aristotle's (1954/1984) categories are so broad, all corporate discourse genres fit within his three situations: law courts (forensic), government (deliberative), and celebrations (epideictic). The most recognizable for publics and practitioners alike is a specific type of courtroom discourse, although today it also takes place in the court of public opinion. Crisis communication, in part, employs the Greek rhetorical genre of self-defense, the *apologia*. Although it may include an apology, when corporate apologia is used, the organization has an array of strategies to choose from when it does not admit to wrongdoing (or only partially takes the blame). In the case of *Dateline NBC*'s 1992 test of C/K pickups (with the alleged exploding gas tank), in 1993, General Motors relied on counterattack to show that NBC News had rigged its tests of the vehicle. During its press conference, the company also used differentiation to distinguish its expert testimony and scientific evidence from NBC's, creating doubt regarding the latter. It used minimization to demonstrate that the risk of explosion was not nearly as likely as the news program had implied (Hearit, 1996; Smudde, 2011). In the case of the Mercedes A-class situation in 1997, the company at first denied that design flaws could be responsible for a vehicle overturning during its own tests of the vehicle (Ihlen, 2002). When trade publications and other publics did not believe Mercedes Benz, it adopted changing strategies over time—and used different combinations of them within particular discourse conventions (e.g., a news conference). Due to the wide variation in crises that occur, the specifics of the accusation against organizations, and the purposes that they have in alleviating the crisis, corporate *apologia* does not fit a definition of discourse genre. It is a rhetorical genre that can make use of multiple discourse genres when it requires a particular combination of style, strategies, and tactics for a given situation.

The combination of situation, audience expectations, organizational purposes, and rhetorical choices thus suggests some important assumptions that we can make about genres—and a few remaining important questions. Genres somehow become agreed on between message sources and receivers, but why do some genres stabilize through repeated use (e.g., eulogies, public service announcements) and yet invite variation (e.g., news releases, corporate apologia)? Certainly the key aspects we must recognize when using a generic perspective for message planning include attention to the constraints imposed on strategic choices by the situation, the audience, and the organization's purpose in communicating. But how do these genres come into being, and what influences their persistence, evolution, and perhaps demise?

According to Campbell and Jamieson (n.d.), genres indeed have a life cycle: Figuratively, they are born, mature, perhaps change, and sometimes go dormant through lack of use. The news release had its origins in journalism. Although the basic form remained the same, when journalists left the profession to do public relations on behalf of business, efforts to build up clients and organizations were added to an objective-sounding style and the inverted pyramid. This, of course, has persisted, with variations, even with the migration of news releases to electronic formats. Although some have hailed its demise in recent years, the news release continues to play a central role in corporate communication. Some genres maintain their basic, strategic integrity across media (e.g., public service announcements). Other types of discourse (e.g., annual reports, employee newsletters, press kits) have been adapted to new technologies, changing audience expectations, and the explosion of information available through multiple channels.

Corporate discourse conventions therefore are more than just recipes for organizing ideas. The principles behind genre theory require communicators to have intimate knowledge of the organization and its goals, values, and purposes. Research of the situation that a campaign and its messages are designed to address takes on even greater significance when we realize that information drawn from research directly informs the substance of what should be said. The same is true for audience research. Moreover, good writing skills and experience become even more important because an understanding of style and message strategies is central to the better use of genre conventions. These imperatives require sensitivity to the relative stability and flexibility of specific genres. (After all, some of the best jazz artists are classically trained: They know the rules and when they can bend them.)

Genre as a Method for Strategic Message Planning

Broad understanding of the underlying assumptions of genre theory thus guides our appreciation and use of specific writing conventions. Let's reconsider each component of the genre theory we covered earlier. In this section, we recap the basic assumptions regarding corporate discourse conventions and then illustrate and extend them.

1. *Why genres?* Discourse genres exist because of the recurring confluence of types of situations that suggest appropriate symbolic responses to them.

One of the key controversies in late 20th-century rhetorical study has been the chicken-or-the-egg question: Which comes first, the message or the situation? A good deal of the time, discourse conventions are employed to respond to situations: a product introduction, an increased need for organ donors, and so on. This does not mean, however, that such messages might not be employed to *shape* perceptions of a situation. In the early 1990s, Ketchum Public Relations worked on behalf of Sunsweet Growers to change the image of the lowly prune, "the Rodney Dangerfield of fruit," as a feature story placed in the magazine *Eating Well* put it. Certainly the use of the feature as a discourse convention was a response to the prune's image as a laxative and something people ate in their old age, but the story also capitalized on the development of new uses for the product (e.g., prune puree as a shortening substitute) that would appeal to health-conscious publics. Although growers eventually changed the marketing label to "dried plums," such publicity items helped to change audience perceptions of why and when prunes could be used.

Messages also may be employed in advance of a situation. Much of corporate strategic planning includes anticipating what might happen. This effort includes public relations professionals thinking about the future and what may lie down the road so the organization avoids obstacles or, at least, is better braced for impact. Proactive situations, such as the introduction of a wholly new and innovative product or special events, rely on sound future-oriented thinking about, in the case of innovations, the great value that can be obtained and, in the case of events, the exceptional community development that can be shared. Other instances, such as emergencies, require advanced, contingency planning as well because corporate officials have good reason to be prepared "when things get ugly." Although contingency plans provide much of the material needed to manage and communicate about an emergency situation, contingency plans include places for the exact specifics of a situation to be filled in.

Discourse genres, then, work both ways: as reactive and proactive means for organizations to communicate with their publics (and vice versa). The communication is conducted in ways that invite degrees of literal participation with an organization's work (e.g., understanding more about causes and effects, agreeing with a policy, or buying a product or service). Publics and organizations co-construct meaning about what is going on and the influence and effects it has.

2. *Form follows function.* The purposes that drive the use of a particular genre are governed by sound rhetorical strategies, not simply an adherence to a familiar pattern of organization.

Perhaps one of the oddest news conferences on record has to be the October 4, 2005, announcement of a partnership between Sun Microsystems and Google (Sun Microsystems, 2005). The respective principal speakers, Scott McNealy, Sun's CEO, and Eric Schmidt, Google's CEO, talked about Schmidt's credentials and commented on how he had worked for Sun at one time. After a long discussion of the ups and downs of Sun's history, McNealy introduced Andy Bechtolsheim, saying that Bechtolsheim had invested money in both companies at their beginnings, not mentioning that he was a cofounder of Sun—but trade publications found no real news: "The announcement left many bloggers less than thrilled, and blog entries with titles such as 'Big whoop,' 'That's it?,' and 'Google and Sun announce yawn' abound on blog search site Technorati" (Guevin, 2005). The two CEOs also were vague during the question-and-answer period that followed. WebProNews reported, "A few attempts to gain some deeper meaning to the press conference, besides seeing Messrs. McNealy and Schmidt trade a Sun server and software for a Google-branded lava lamp, were brushed aside by the duo" (Utter, 2005). Reporters and technorati in the blogosphere were left to speculate about what degree the two companies were taking on Microsoft and what products would result from the partnership. By failing to follow discourse conventions, the only news gained from what the *Los Angeles Times* called "an often confusing Silicon Valley news conference" (Gaither, 2005) was that the news conference occurred and that great things could be expected from Sun and Google.

Those organizations that use genre conventions properly can build on them to create messages with visual and discursive impact. Honda, in addition to its full-color annual report in a PDF file, provides a similar report on corporate social responsibility. Two of these sections are expanded into separate annual reports on environmental efforts and, in Japanese only, its Driving Safety Program (Honda Worldwide, 2008a, 2008b). General Electric Company (2009) has made its "Our Company" heading on its website easy to follow so that investors, consumers, and other interested publics can link to a separate page for investor relations and individual sites dedicated to General Electric's Ecomagination environmental campaign and to its efforts at corporate citizenship.

3. *Two-way communication.* Genres are not simply responses that the organization employs to respond to situations. Audience perceptions of the situation—and expectations of what the organization should say and how it should say it—are as much a part of what shapes the strategic, organized response as the organization's interpretation of what needs to be said and done.

The ideal of ethical public relations as "symmetrical communication" can be recast as dialogue that is a co-creation of meaning. Shared meaning is negotiated meaning. The genre conventions associated with employee relations serve as cases in point. Willihnganz, Hart, and Leichty (2004) tell of difficult changes in a small manufacturing company. A married couple, owners of Auto Tech, decided to retire and move out of state. A CEO change resulted in organizational decisions no longer being made through informal communication, but rather via memos and formal meetings. The change in genre conventions created a crisis situation that was finally resolved with the return of the original owners. In contrast, when Dow Chemical and Union Carbide merged in 2001, Ketchum Public Relations assisted Dow, among other things, in implementing a "merger mailbox" to answer employee questions and having Dow leaders give in-person presentations on the first day of the merger at all 90 company sites (Public Relations Society of America, 2002). This Silver Anvil award-winning campaign achieved 85% employee satisfaction with communication on Day 15 of the merger and less than 1% resignations during the first month.

Organizations and audiences need to be on the same page regarding what genre conventions are appropriate. This is not only true when organizations communicate, but also when publics address them as receivers. People for the Ethical Treatment of Animals (PETA) rarely are given a hearing by organizations because of its penchant for outrageous behavior reminiscent of the protest genre, the diatribe, employed by the Greek Cynics, and, more recently, the Yippies in the 1960s (see Windt, 1972). Consumers can be more effective when they use reasonably stated letters, e-mails, and telephone calls to convey their concerns. This is what happened when New Englanders learned that Nabisco was stopping production of Crown Pilot Crackers, a product associated with growing up with the weekly evening meal of chowder. Sustained consumer communication and resulting media coverage changed the company's mind (Escrock, Hart, D'Silva, & Werking, 2002).

4. *Stability and Flexibility.* Public relations practitioners not only should know the characteristics of a given discourse convention, but they should recognize how much latitude they have in using them. Some genres allow for great creativity. Others, especially those prescribed by government agencies, restrict the strategic choices the communicator may make.

The beauty of discourse genres is that they are rule-governed, which means people can use any discourse exactly as prescribed by the rules or bend or even break the rules to fit specific rhetorical purposes. The stability of discourse genres for public relations is especially needed when time is of the essence. Emergency situations (i.e., organizational crises, issues, and disasters) leave practitioners little time to consider other artful ways to handle communications. Hurricane Katrina is an example of all three types of emergency communication. It naturally was a disaster because of the havoc it wreaked on the city of New Orleans and the surrounding area, including southern Mississippi. It precipitated organizational crises for the city of New Orleans, the state of Louisiana, and the Federal Emergency Management Agency (FEMA). Indeed, FEMA was the "poster child" for ineffectiveness because of, in part, the top administrator's misuse of internal communiqués via e-mail, as reported by journalists. It also stood as an issue of public safety that was poorly addressed over the years because, as news reports revealed, civil engineers and government officials knew well about the limitations and weaknesses of New Orleans' levee system and what should have been done to better protect the city (Littlefield & Quenette, 2007). The art of effective public relations in emergency situations is more concerned with content than its innovative presentation. Traditional conventions for press releases, news conferences, interviews, and so on work like recipes for what to say about what happened, why, and how it can be avoided in the future.

The conventions for public relations discourse also are flexible so they can accommodate situational needs for both an organization and its publics. The requirements for publicly traded companies to report on their annual performance are an example of genre flexibility in the face of stability. Regulations such as the U.S. Securities and Exchange Act of 1934 (and its subsequent regulations that fall under the purview of the U.S. Securities and Exchange Commission) specify particular kinds of information and their presentation that must be shared with investors. Corporations are obligated to annually publish a simple, text- and table-heavy, black-and-white Form 10-K. But many companies also choose to publish a "flashy," four-color report that shows more about the organization's story for the previous year in addition to the required information. For example, Indian Oil's 2007–2008 annual report provides readers with its document totally online through dedicated links to it and its sections, which seems at first blush innovative and appropriate. The document, however, is simply divided up into excerpts in separate PDF files of black-and-white pages for each section, and each simply presents fundamental messages about the business area or topic required without innovation highlights. In contrast, Samsung's 2007 annual report provides a full-color report that, along with the detailed financial data and analysis, features artistic photography of personnel and products, but beneath these "flashy" images are straightforward messages about company performance on required subjects.

5. *Generic Adaptability.* Because genres have a life cycle, we extend that metaphor to recognize that discourse conventions do not merely change over time in response to audience expectations and organizational needs. Some readily transfer to new media channels, whereas others require adjustment to be more, we might say, user-friendly.

Today's variety of media choices make possible what business now calls "repurposing"—using items in ways different from the original intent behind them. To some degree, public relations professionals have done this with genre conventions for the past century. Some press kit material is made specifically for it; whereas, other items have been used in previous campaigns. Biographical statements and backgrounders are frequently repurposed. Yet our point is more profound: Today's corporate communications environment invites novel use of genre conventions in ways that might, at first blush, seem to invite questionable choices.

Consider the case of Steve Irwin, the Crocodile Hunter, who in 2004 twice had to defend his reputation. The first situation, in which a visitor to Australia Zoo videoed Irwin feeding Murray the Crocodile while holding his 1-month-old son in his arms, created an ethics stir that polarized even his most loyal fans. Despite a rather disjointed apologia on NBC's *Today Show* (Lauer, 2004), the media firestorm that January died down, with only the Australian state of Queensland considering some regulation to cover such incidents of alleged child endangerment (Callinan, 2004). That summer, however, another reputational crisis occurred when scientists accused Irwin of swimming far too close to animals while filming a documentary, *Ice Breaker*, in the Antarctic (Middleton, 2004). This time Irwin's crew created a well-framed apologia, a program episode called "Confessions of the Crocodile Hunter" (Dowling & Stainton, 2004). Aired on the Discovery Channel in the United States, the program presented Irwin's life story with an emphasis on his philosophy regarding and practices in the wild. So much more effective than his earlier apologia, this program was repurposed and continuously run in tandem with "Steve's Story" (Dowling & Stainton, 1999) on the Discovery Channel for at least the first 24 hours after Irwin's accidental death on September 4, 2006. The apologia became part of a fitting eulogy.

Not all repurposes are successful. During the second author's former life in radio broadcasting, he saw many times when companies and nonprofit organizations would send print news releases without any adaptation to the needs of audio presentation. Indeed, often print releases were sent for use on the radio station's community calendar without being converted into what today would be called a media alert. This one-size-fits-all mentality even can occur in Top 100 media markets. When the second author was working in public radio, the city's arts foundation created its theme for its annual fundraising event, replete with preproduced public service announcements. At the time, the station aired both classical music and jazz. However, the agency hired to produce the public service announcement had used a country music bed for the recording. At the request of the station's manager, a script was provided for use by its announcers, although the foundation representatives would have preferred to have the recorded announcer's voice used for the entire campaign.

Clearly, attention to genre conventions in corporate communication can make public relations efforts more coherent and appealing. Although they can be used reactively, the best use of genres is proactive. With awareness of their characteristics, degree of flexibility, and adaptability to different uses, professional communicators can use these genre conventions more effectively and, most important, strategically. These genres for public relations (see Figure 2.2) are specific types that fall into Aristotle's (1954/1984) broader, tripartite system. It is our contention that most of what public relations does falls under one of those categories, *epideictic* (i.e., celebratory rhetoric).

Public Relations Genres as Celebrations of the Organization

Public relations involves the measured and ethical use of language and symbols to inspire cooperation between an organization and its publics. This work subsumes various purposes, such as persuasion, education, celebration, and so on. Of these purposes, much of the literature about public relations puts the greatest emphasis on persuasion (e.g., Fawkes, 2007; Miller, 1989; Read, 2007). Indeed, public relations and persuasion are often equated with one another (and sometimes with manipulation) (see Grunig, 1989). This is not surprising because public relations' most noticeable efforts are usually when organizations face Aristotle's (1954/1984) forensic situation (i.e., the courtroom), actually, the court of public opinion. Our earlier examples certainly include efforts to persuade (e.g., General Motors' defense against *Dateline NBC*'s accusations of making trucks with gas tanks that could potentially explode, the Crocodile Hunter's *apologia* of being more concerned for showmanship than the safety of his child or of the natural world that he so loved). Similarly, Aristotle's deliberative genre is not confined to the legislature but can apply to any occasion in which people are being asked to change how they will do things in the future. The *Eating Well* feature article was an attempt to get consumers to use prunes (hopefully Sunsweet prunes) in new ways, and the failures of FEMA in the wake of

Figure 2.2. Public relations discourse genres.

Press releases	White papers	Avertorials
Video news releases	Case studies	Public Service Announcements (PSAs)
Audio news releases	Articles	Press conferences
Photo news releases	Interviews	Satellite media tours (SMTs)
Media advisories	Pitch calls	Press kits
Prepared statements	Meetings	Newsletters
Fact sheets	Speeches	Magazines
Tip sheets	Podcasts	Video news programs
Frequently Asked Questions (FAQs)	Pitch letters	Annual reports
Biographical statements	Written correspondence	Issue reports
Matte releases	Wikis	Brochures/pamphlets
Backgrounders	Weblogs (blogs)	Websites
Fliers	Posters	Advertisements

Source: Extended from Smudde (2000, 2004, 2011).

Hurricane Katrina stemmed from a lack of proper timing and persuasion to tell storm survivors what to do next.

We believe that the focus on persuasion is limited and overprivileged, although this perspective has been well defended. Public relations books and scholarship have used myriad pages to examine campaign mistakes ("I can't believe they did . . .") or celebrate Silver Anvil Award winners. Case studies have their place, but public relations is not just focused on audience behavior, purchasing patterns, and the bottom line (although we must not forget those important goals). The quest for cooperation between an organization and its publics truly seems more appropriately encompassing because professional communicators are purpose-driven, whether that purpose is to persuade, inform, refute, or celebrate. In short, the essence of public relations is to establish identification between publics and organizations such that they see themselves in each other's positions no matter what their respective stances on matters are (see Smudde, 2011). For this reason, we maintain that the bulk of what public relations people do on a day-to-day basis is epideictic.

The Epideictic Nature of Public Relations Discourse

There is no exact translation of the Greek word, but its origins are found in the games and festivals of ancient Athens, when part of the event's program included public speaking and written composition (Perelman & Olbrechts-Tyteca, 1969). Confined to such situations, scholars typically explain to students that epideictic messages are ceremonial in character, focused on "praise" and "blame" (i.e., extolling the virtues that the community holds dear, and sometimes vilifying what it does not stand for, at times even casting aspersions on enemies). Thus, funerals are epideictic situations that invite eulogies of praise for the deceased. Today, all sorts of celebrations provide opportunities for epideictic discourse: a ribbon cutting, a retirement dinner, and all sorts of organizational events. Its utility for organizations, however, is far greater and untapped (pragmatically and academically).

As Perelman and Olbrechts-Tyteca (1969) assert, the epideictic genre of discourse conventions form "a central part of the art of persuasion, and the lack of understanding shown toward it results from a false conception of the effects of argumentation" (p. 49). As such, we argue that much of what public relations does stems from its celebratory nature (see also Crable & Vibbert, 1983). Scholarship has moved well beyond viewing epideictic messages as opportunities for speakers to display rhetorical skill and audiences to appreciate it. From this scholarship, we have determined epideictic's four core functions: celebratory, performative, epistemic, and preservative.

These functions are not simplistic, unidimensional terms: Each has specific components that make public relations key not only to organizational success, but also to a more enlightened view of publics as audiences and how organizations seek to inspire cooperation with them.

Celebratory Function

The celebratory function of epideictic discourse concerns the effective presentation of ideas, and it includes ritualistic and axiological dimensions. Ritualistic dimensions concern how a special occasion is particularly memorialized. This means that speakers make a special point to follow established, accepted patterns of language and behaviors for exalting or decrying something. Public relations discourse in this case need not be as dramatic as that sounds. In public relations, the ritualistic dimension is obvious in new-product unveilings, statements of self-defense, and news conferences, but it also is subtle in news genres, in which the writer should temper word choices so that the message conforms to the journalistic standard of objectivity. The other dimension of the celebratory function is axiological, which focuses on values-oriented statements that address something in terms of praise and blame. Public relations' axiological function is seen at its best when organizations explicitly or implicitly communicate values that the organization stands for or opposes, values that its products or services represent or do not represent, or, through issue advocacy, values associated with the corporate position regarding an issue at hand. The axiological function explains why opposing sides on some matter can use the same or other forms of discourse to address it. Simultaneously, the values expressed through the discourse also should reflect those held by target publics. Public relations influences society through invocation of organizational core values, but it must be a reflection of the environment in which clients operate as well. Values appeals, therefore, work best when they are shared by the organization and its publics.

Performative Function

The performative function of epideictic discourse is chiefly concerned with *ethos*, and, in the case of public relations, performative epideictic discourse establishes who the organization is and how it develops a relationship with the audience (Black, 1970; McMillan, 1987). There are three components to the performative function. First, the political component sees the speaker as a leader who is acting as a member of a community. In this social role, the speaker has a "bardic" (i.e., grand promoter or evangelist) and/or prophetic voice (Lessl, 1989), both of which mean the speaker "sings the praises" of the organization and the past, present, and future value the community derives from it, although the prophet also might cast aspersions on enemies or chastise a community for not living up to its values. By the same token, audiences have the role of observer, judge, and participant (Oravec, 1976) as they experience the speaker and the message, evaluate what is said, and choose whether to take action. In public relations, the political component of its discourse is evident in feature articles and annual reports, for example. Second, the identity management component concerns reputation building through ethos (see Sullivan, 1993) so that audiences acknowledge and embrace a speaker's credibility and authority. In public relations, fact sheets and corporate social responsibility reports, for example, fulfill this need to manage an organization's identity. Third, the rhetorical (or symbolic) component of performative epideictic discourse involves the creation of consubstantiality between an audience and the speaker. The discourse in this vein is designed to influence audiences immediately and over the long term, defining their roles and relationship to each other. In public relations, Lindemann's (2006) view of outputs, outtakes, outcomes, and outgrowths are dimensions of the range of results sought to inspire cooperation between an organization and its publics.

Epistemic Function

The epistemic function of epideictic discourse focuses on the knowledge-building capacity it has for speakers and, especially, audiences. This function covers two dimensions: educational and explanatory. The educational dimension features messages that inculcate values and encourage the imitation and buy-in to certain virtues that are established through socialization (Oravec, 1976). Public relations practitioners exercise this dimension when they publish advertorials or public service announcements. The second epistemic dimension is explanatory, which involves defining or otherwise facilitating audience understanding of something. This dimension can be realized when discourse addresses what the audience already knows as the basis for connecting it with something new they do not know and should embrace, and that new knowledge balances audience and organizational needs. It also can be realized as discourse, which

> refers to the power of epideictic to explain the social world. Audiences actively seek and invite speech that performs this epideictic function when some event, person, group, or object is troubling. The speaker will explain the troubling issue in terms of the audience's key values and beliefs. (Condit, 1985, p. 288)

Thus, the epistemic and celebratory functions work in tandem. The celebratory function reflects the worldview that the organization and its publics share, and the epistemic function attempts to influence how audiences think about the world and what they believe to be true.

Preservative Function

The preservative function of epideictic discourse conserves and reinforces the community values that may be celebrated or vilified through messages (see Cherwitz & Hikins, 1982; Perelman & Olbrechts-Tyteca, 1969). There are three important components to this function. The first is coherence, which concerns how the language and the very structure of the discourse helps everything work together within the text and, especially, among all other epideictic functions. Public relations discourse must always cohere with other corporate discourse on many levels, at the least to "stay on message." The second preservative component is reflexive: Rhetoric functions as a means of self-persuasion (Burks, 1970) in two ways: for the organization and for its publics. For the organization, discourse becomes part of the public record and, therefore, influences how the organization and its members perceive themselves in relationship to their surroundings. Rhetoric thus becomes a historical record of what the organization says and does—a repository of organizational memory from which anyone may draw ideas for new discourse. For publics, however, persuasion of the self occurs when the message invites the audience to "fill in the gaps" with what they already know or hold true. Audience members mentally may supply values, decision-making premises, beliefs, and other cognitions held in memory, thereby becoming part of their own persuasion. Finally, epideictic preserves messages for future usage. The most obvious way this occurs is repurposing, in which practitioners create premises for future communication to inspire cooperation (even forensic or deliberative discourse) (see Cheney & Vibbert, 1987) and for other epideictic situations. In the practice of public relations, organizations regularly reuse discourse for multiple purposes, and that can include the reapplication of text from one document or occasion to another, like information from a fact sheet to a news release to a speech. However, the public availability of organizational discourse allows others—publics, opinion leaders, the news media, activists—to quote, paraphrase, or recast ideas as they see fit. This futuristic dimension can be quite far-reaching because public discourse may be invoked long after its original moment of communication (see Courtright, 1991). For example, what an organization's founder said or wrote becomes fodder for press kits, speeches, annual reports, and advocacy advertising. Also, what an organization says in its financial discourse about its past performance has implications for people's perceptions of its potential future performance (e.g., whether investments in a publicly traded company may be prudent).

A Holistic View of Epideictic Public Relations

Taken together, the four functions of epideictic discourse provide us with a usable and useful view of public relations that can be used at the tactical level, but they are especially potent at the *strategic* business level. This view represents an untouched and powerful way to plan, act, and evaluate public relations. Because celebratory rhetoric showcases community (or societal) values, much of what passes for newsworthy information is focused on those values that organizations and their publics share—and these are shared through the conventions of the discourse genres in Figure 2.2. Corporate officials must take into consideration their constituents', stakeholders', customers', markets', and other audiences' viewpoints, needs, and expectations when making *epideictic* arguments about what is going on. (This approach is no different than it would be with forensic or deliberative discourse.) Epideictic arguments are not only about the news or other matters, although that is important. The arguments are invitations to participate, even if it is only momentary or intellectually if not ultimately behaviorally, in the dramatic celebration of what is going on within, for and about an organization that also concerns its publics. The invitations also include claims, backed by evidence and reasoning (see Toulmin, 1958), that participation would be good. When the news is good, bad, or neither, the invitation to the celebration is relevant.

During his years in the industry, the first author felt this kind of dynamic was the root cause for communications (but could not put his finger on it), not just merely releasing news or information. Indeed, the use of information in the service of persuasion, education, celebration, and so on was always the means to the end of inspiring cooperation between an organization and its publics. Some audiences are friendlier than others. Communicating with particular audiences should be helpful in some ways while targeting others not so much: Detractors will almost never change their minds against something and should be targeted cautiously, advocates can help evangelize about something and should be targeted as ambassadors, and those in the middle are more numerous and most prone to moving toward one extreme or the other depending on the forcefulness and effectiveness of the discourse directed to them. Publics are not mere observers, although admiration of the organization-as-speaker's abilities certainly contributes to positive impressions. Indeed, Oravec (1976) maintains that Aristotle (1954/1984) linked such discourse to practical wisdom, commonsense understandings of the world. Such discourse contributes to audience learning and asks them to make judgments that may serve as the basis for later persuasion. (This is exactly what Crable and Vibbert [1983] argued that Mobil Oil did with its "Observations" series of advertisements in Sunday supplement magazines.) Values-based arguments reinforce or change beliefs (what publics accept as true), which in turn prime specific attitudes that lead to somewhat predictable behaviors. As Edward Bernays observed, "People want to go where they want to be led" (cited in Blumer, Moyers, & Grubin, 1983).

These connections are vital to practicing professional communicators also. Public relations efforts that extol the innovativeness of a product or service, for example, are engaging in *epideictic* discourse. The purpose is to celebrate the launch of a new product or service, and that celebration is worthy, virtuous, important, and so on because of specific persuasive arguments about its value, benefits, and so on. Public relations efforts to thwart attacks on an organization, for example, also are *epideictic* discourse. The purpose in such cases is to persuade people that the attacks are baseless, inappropriate, ill-informed, and so on while people should join the organization in the celebration of itself and what good it stands for. Public relations efforts to support a public policy measure, for example, also are *epideictic*. The purpose in this case is to promote the soundness, efficacy, value, and so on to society and invite participation and support from publics as the organization leads the charge. (Note that the first example of these three would be a purely *epideictic* form, the second could follow a forensic form, and the third example could follow a deliberative form.)

The conventions for the discourse in Figure 2.2 (and discussed further in this book) not only can prepare audiences for action, but they also are reputation-building opportunities for organizations (see Beale, 1978). The formal *epideictic* dimensions of public relations discourse generally involve what is fine/crude, honorable/abhorrent, noble/base, virtuous/shameful, and so on. The discourse forms that are chosen and the messages designed must be those that best meet with the target audiences' needs and expectations while balancing the organization's position. The nature of *epideictic* discourse, then, necessarily involves ethics, and Aristotle (1951/1971, 1954/1984) makes clear the connections between them. Not only must organizations try to identify with and live up to societal values, but they also must use the discourse forms that audiences use to gain information—and they must do so without insulting the audiences' intelligence or affronting their sensitivity to what they consider proper, ethical communication. Related to our world ethics, however, is one of Aristotle's (1954/1984) principal means of argument, ethos—the character of the speaker as implied within messages.

Persuasive aspects of public relations may indeed be the most noticeable and, therefore, most public. However, as a graduate student of ours once observed, the best public relations is obviously subtle. With appropriate attention to situations as opportunities to present corporate values, address audience values, and invite cooperation as a result, public relations messages at heart are *epideictic*. The true test of any campaign is not only its immediate goal, but also how the organization's use of discourse conventions within it serves the organization and its publics over the long term. Public relations genres build and sustain relationships with publics and, simultaneously, strengthen corporate reputation. Every message is an opportunity to inspire cooperation. Of all the purposes that public relations seems to fulfill in its quest to inspire cooperation, celebration is key.

We use the category epideictic as an overarching orientation to these discourse conventions because it really is a broader category than genre. *Genus* is a nice word for it, but we won't pursue the biological analogy to its discourse parallels; readers may do so if they like. Indeed, the 39 specific types of public relations discourse that public relations and other organizational members must deal with, many on a daily basis, are the focus in this book. The next seven chapters examine the genres of public relations discourse in particular groups or families that emphasize certain similarities (see Appendix 1). Within the broad category of epideictic, we treat public relations discourse conventions as genres that have specific characteristics with implications for message design. Our generic approach to public relations recognizes the important role that rules play in effective public relations discourse. Our approach also recognizes how important competence in those discourse genres is to effectively planning, executing, and evaluating communications.

Note

1. Deeper exploration into rhetorical genres and their reliance on discourse genres is beyond the scope of this project, and research on rhetorical genres is available to begin the quest (e.g., Benoit, 1995; Brummett, 1984; Cali, 1996; Campbell & Jamieson, n.d.; Johannesen, 1985; Ryan, 1988; Simons & Aghazarian, 1986).

References

Aristotle. (1971). *The ethics of Aristotle: The Nichomachean ethics translated* (J. A. K. Thomson, Trans.). London: Penguin Books. (Original translation published 1951)

Aristotle. (1984). *The rhetoric and the poetics of Aristotle* (W. R. Roberts, Trans.). New York: Modern Library. (Original translation published 1954)

Beale, W. H. (1978). Rhetorical performative discourse: A new theory of epideictic. *Philosophy & Rhetoric, 11*, 221–246.

Benoit, W. L. (1995). *Accounts, excuses, and apologies: A theory of image restoration strategies.* Albany, NY: SUNY Press.

Black, E. (1970). The second persona. *Quarterly Journal of Speech, 56*, 109–119.

Blumer, R., Moyers, B. (Writers), & Grubin, D. (Producer/Director). (1983). The image makers [Television series episode]. In M. Koplin (Senior Executive Producer), *A walk through the 20th century with Bill Moyers.* New York: Corporation for Entertainment Learning.

Brummett, B. (1984). Premillennial apocalyptic as a rhetorical genre. *Central States Speech Journal, 35*, 84–93.

Burks, D. M. (1970). Persuasion, self-persuasion and rhetorical discourse. *Philosophy & Rhetoric, 3*, 109–119.

Cali, D. D. (Ed.). (1995). *Generic criticism of American public address.* Dubuque, IA: Kendall-Hunt.

Callinan, R. (2004, January 22). Crocodile ban looms for Irwin children. (Queensland) *Courier Mail*, p. 1. Retrieved July 26, 2004, from Lexis Nexis (Academic Universe).

Campbell, K. K., & Jamieson, K. H. (n.d.). Form and genre in rhetorical criticism: An introduction. In K. K. Campbell & K. H. Jamieson (Eds.), *Form and genre: Shaping rhetorical action* (pp. 9–32). Falls Church, VA: Speech Communication Association.

Cheney, G., & Vibbert, S. L. (1987). Corporate discourse: Public relations and issue management. In F. M. Jablin, L. L. Putnam, K. H. Roberts, & L. W. Porter (Eds.), *Handbook of organizational communication* (pp. 165–194). Newbury Park, CA: Sage.

Cherwitz, R. A., & Hikins, J. W. (1982). Toward a rhetorical epistemology. *Southern Speech Communication Journal, 47*, 135–162.

Condit, C. M. (1985). The functions of epideictic: The Boston Massacre orations as exemplar. *Communication Quarterly, 33*, 284–298.

Courtright, J. L. (1991). "Tactics" and "trajectories": The argumentative resources of Supreme Court dissenting opinions. Doctoral dissertation, Purdue University, West Lafayette, IN. Retrieved January 15, 2009, from Dissertations & Theses: Full Text database. (Publication No. AAT 9215536)

Crable, R. E., & Vibbert, S. L. (1983). Mobil's epideictic advocacy: "Observations" of Prometheus-bound. *Communication Monographs, 50*, 380–394.

Dowling, G. (Writer), & Stainton, J. (Director). (1999). Steve's story. In J. Stainton (Producer). *The Crocodile Hunter.* Silver Spring, MD: Discovery Communications.

Dowling, G. (Writer), & Stainton, J. (Director). (2004, June 17). Confessions of the Crocodile Hunter. In J. Stainton (Producer), *The Crocodile Hunter.* Silver Spring, MD: Discovery Communications.

Esrock, S. L., Hart, J. L., D'Silva, M. U., & Werking, K. J. (2002). The saga of the Crown Pilot: Framing, reframing, and reconsideration. *Public Relations Review, 28*, 209–227.

Fawkes, J. (2007). Public relations models and persuasion ethics: A new approach. *Journal of Communication Management, 11*, 313–331.

Gaither, C. (2005, October 6). *Microsoft challenged (sort of)*. Available at http://www.redorbit.com/news/technology/262307/microsoft_challenged_sort_of/index.html

General Electric Company. (2009). *Our company: Leadership, history, culture, advertising*. Retrieved January 17, 2009, from http://www.ge.com/company/index.html

Grunig, J. E. (1989). Symmetrical presuppositions as a framework for public relations theory. In C. Botan & V. Hazelton, Jr. (Eds.), *Public relations theory* (pp. 17–44). Hillsdale, NJ: Erlbaum.

Guevin, (2005, October 4). *Google and Sun deal: That's it?* Retrieved November 12, 2008, from http://news.cnet.com/Google-and-Sun-deal-Thats-it/2100-1012_3-5888798.html

Hearit, K. M. (1996). The use of counter-attack in apologetic public relations crises: The case of General Motors vs. NBC. *Public Relations Review, 22*, 233–248.

Honda Worldwide. (2008a). *Honda annual environmental report 2008*. Retrieved November 11, 2008, from http://world.honda.com/environment/ecology/2008report/pdf/2008_report_English_full.pdf

Honda Worldwide. (2008b). *Honda philanthropy 2008*. Retrieved November 11, 2008, from http://world.honda.com/community/report/doc/2008report_EN.pdf

Ihlen, Ø. (2002). Defending the Mercedes A-class: Combining and changing crisis-response strategies. *Journal of Public Relations Research, 14*, 185–206.

Indian Oil Corporation Ltd. (2007–2008). *Financial performance*. Retrieved October 2, 2008, from http://www.iocl.com/Aboutus/FinancialPerformance.aspx

Johannesen, R. L. (1985). The Jeremiad and Jenkin Lloyd Jones. *Communication Monographs, 52*, 156–172.

Kunkel, A. D., & Dennis, M. R. (2003). Grief consolation in eulogy rhetoric: An integrative framework. *Death Studies, 27*, 1–38.

Lauer, M. (Writer). (2004, January 5). Steve Irwin, the Crocodile Hunter, responds to outrage over a crocodile stunt while holding his baby [interview with Matt Lauer]. In T. Touchet (Producer), *The Today Show*. New York: NBC.

Lessl, T. M. (1989). The priestly voice. *Quarterly Journal of Speech, 75*, 183–197.

Lindemann, W. K. (2006). *Public relations research for planning and evaluation*. Gainesville, FL: Institute for Public Relations Research. Retrieved June 15, 2007, from http://www.instituteforpr.org/research_single/relations_research_planning/

Littlefield, R. S., & Quenette, A. M. (2007). Crisis leadership and Hurricane Katrina: The portrayal of authority by the media in natural disasters. *Journal of Applied Communication Research, 35*, 26–47.

McMillan, J. J. (1987). In search of the organizational persona: A rationale for studying organizations rhetorically. In L. Thayer (Ed.), *Organization↔communication: Emerging perspectives II* (pp. 21–45). Norwood, NJ: Ablex.

Middleton, K. (2004, June 14). Crocodile Hunter's frolic with whales gets frosty reception. *The West Australian*. Retrieved June 21, 2004, from Lexis Nexis (Academic Universe).

Miller, G. R. (1989). Persuasion and public relations: Two "Ps" in a pod. In C. H. Botan & V. Hazelton, Jr. (Eds.), *Public relations theory* (pp. 45–66). Hillsdale, NJ: Erlbaum.

Murphy, J. J., Katula, R. A., Hill, F. I., & Ochs, D. (2003). *A synoptic history of classical rhetoric.* Mahwah, NJ: Erlbaum.

Oravec, C. (1976). "Observation" in Aristotle's theory of epideictic. *Philosophy & Rhetoric, 9,* 162–174.

Perelman, C., & Olbrechts-Tyteca, L. (1969). *The new rhetoric: A treatise on argumentation* (J. Wilkinson & P. Weaver, Trans.). Notre Dame, IN: Notre Dame University Press.

Public Relations Society of America. (2002). *An ideal marriage: Dow + Union Carbide* [Silver-Anvil Award of Excellence Winner]. Product Code 6BE-0212B03. Retrieved November 7, 2008, from http://auth.iweb.prsa.org/xmembernet/main/pdfpull.cfm?prcfile=6BE-0212B03.pdf

Raaflaub, K. A., Ober, J., & Wallace, R. W. (2007). *Origins of democracy in ancient Greece.* Berkeley: University of California Press.

Read, K. (2007). "Corporate pathos": New approaches to quell hostile publics. *Journal of Communication Management, 11,* 332–347.

Ryan, H. R. (Ed.). (1988). *Oratorical encounters: Selected studies of twentieth-century political accusations and apologies.* Westport, CT: Greenwood Press.

Samsung. (2007). *Samsung electronics annual report.* Retrieved October 2, 2008, from http://www.samsung.com/us/aboutsamsung/ir/financialinformation/annualreport/downloads/2007/00_SEC_07AR_E_Full.pdf

Simons, H. W., & Aghazarian, A. A. (Eds.). (1986). *Form, genre, and the study of political discourse.* Columbia: University of South Carolina Press.

Smudde, P. M. (2000). The rhetorical and organizational nature of public relations: The case of General Motors' C/K pickups. *Dissertation Abstracts International, 61*(10A), 3982.

Smudde, P. M. (2004). Implications on the practice and study of Kenneth Burke's idea of a "public relations counsel with a heart." *Communication Quarterly, 52,* 420–432.

Smudde, P. M. (2011). *Public relations as dramatistic organizing: A case study bridging theory and practice.* Cresskill, NJ: Hampton Press.

Sullivan, D. L. (1993). The ethos of epideictic encounter. *Philosophy and Rhetoric, 26,* 113–133.

Sun Microsystems, Inc. (2005, October 4). *Sun and Google news conference* [Webcast]. Retrieved November 11, 2008, from http://wcdata.sun.com/webcast/archives/VIP-2166/

Toulmin, S. E. (1958). *The uses of argument.* New York: Cambridge University Press.

Utter, D. (2005, October 10). *Gartner slams Sun/Google "non-announcement."* Retrieved November 12, 2008, from http://archive.webpronews.com/topnews/topnews/wpn-60-20051010GartnerSlamsSunGoogleNonannouncement.html

Willihnganz, S., Hart, J. L. & Leichty, G. B. (2004). Telling the story of organizational change. In D. P. Millar & R. L. Heath (Eds.), *Responding to crisis: A rhetorical approach to crisis communication* (pp. 213–231). Mahwah, NJ: Erlbaum.

Windt, T. O., Jr. (1972). The diatribe: Last resort for protest. *Quarterly Journal of Speech, 58,* 1–14.

3

News

All the News That's Fit to Print and Broadcast

Much public relations work is done in writing. Perhaps the biggest reason is that public relations must follow so many things internally and externally to an organization that it has to write stuff down to keep track of them and maintain records of them. It also helps that the first people who became public relations professionals also came from the journalism field (see Cutlip, 1994). The idea was that if an organization needed news coverage, the best way to get it was to have people who knew the business on staff. Much of public relations discourse practices, then, have their roots in journalism and the news business.

With the advent of market-journalism, press releases and their progeny assist news media at increasingly short-staffed newspapers, for radio and television news, some of which is 24/7, and with the Web. Indeed, they are an information subsidy (Gandy, 1982): "controlled access to information at little cost or effort to the person receiving the information" (Curtin, 1999, p. 54).

Public relations is a writing-intensive profession, and the demands for written discourse, or "literate" genres (see Chapter 6), dominate practitioners' work. That work naturally includes the discourse that is needed to publicize what is going on in and around an organization for internal and external audiences. This chapter focuses on the news-oriented genres of press releases, video news releases, audio news releases, photo news releases, media advisories, and prepared statements.

Genres and Their Conventions

So many things occur daily that matter to an organization and its publics, and public relations professionals have the privilege of facilitating the process for sharing the news about what is going on internally and externally. Not all things are suited for public disclosure because some things must be kept confidential to protect an organization's plans, strategic advantage, assets, and other factors. But for all the news that is fit to print and broadcast, public relations professionals have a collection of discourse genres that are especially helpful and impactful. The conventions for each of those genres are specific and foundational to the profession, and they make up the substance of our first family of public relations genres—news genres—that we consider for message design and strategic potency.

Press Releases

Although Ivy Lee is often credited with using the first "modern" press release (e.g., Breakenridge, 2008; Wilcox & Cameron, 2008), he was far from the first to employ one. Indeed, the first corporate press offices were in place decades earlier on both sides of Atlantic. In Germany in 1870, Alfred Krupp hired a "literate" to write articles, brochures, and correspondence on his steel company's behalf. According to Bates (2002/2006), in the late 19th century, General Electric and Westinghouse fought the battle between alternating current (AC) and direct current (DC) with former newspapermen as their publicists. Bates notes, however, that press releases, of course, also were used to attract reporters to press briefings or to entice them to contact the public relations official to arrange interviews.

If you had complete control over the story or drama that any news organization would tell, what you write in a press release would be it. But to even hope for anything from a press release to be used, it must fulfill the expectations of its chief audience—journalists. Press releases (also called "news releases" or "announcements") must meet a journalist's idea of news that meets with her or his "beat" and her or his news organization's focus. Application of the rules from the Associated Press (AP) style guide or the style of specific media (e.g., a magazine's own style guide, such as the *Economist*) is absolutely essential because it contains the rules of the game if communicators want to play on journalists' terms. Plus writing in proper, effective English is expected, and anything less risks losing the interest of these important decision makers about what news gets told. After all, public relations people are dealing with professional writers too, so it's vital—like with any audience—to know and meet their expectations and make their job of telling the news easier.

Press releases are written to announce breaking news in sufficient detail, such as a significant event, issue, achievement, situation, or major action taken by an organization or specific members of it. They apply journalistic writing conventions based on the inverted pyramid, which puts the most important information first and adds increasing levels of detail as the text goes on. At a minimum, press releases must cover the five Ws and the H—who, what, where, when, why, and how. Press releases present narratives about something specific going on in or for organizations, and those narratives must reflect certain messages that an organization wants to emphasize to its publics and stakeholders. A "key message platform," which consists of a thesis, theme, or slogan and copy points to back up the thesis, theme, or slogan should be constructed separately and used as a guide in writing any press release. A compelling quote from an organizational authority on the news should be included in a separate paragraph early in a press release's text.

Press releases are produced on organizational letterhead that can be used in hardcopy or electronic form (e.g., PDF or webpage) to show the organization's logo and make the announcement official-looking.[1] At the top of the page, the press release must say "for immediate release" or "embargoed" in all capital letters, and the date must be clearly given in either case. Also at the top of the page, opposite from the release date, there must be information about whom to contact about the announcement. (Alternatively, the contact information could be placed at the end of the press release.) Next there must be a concise, descriptive, and attention-getting headline that immediately asserts the announcement's newsworthiness. A "kicker," or secondary headline, can be used to add additional detail. The first line of the lead paragraph begins with a dateline, which shows the city and state (according to AP style) from where the news originates. The date for the announcement (whether released immediately or embargoed) can be put in the dateline after the city and state. The dateline is separated from the opening sentence of the lead paragraph by a long dash. The lead paragraph begins the inverted pyramid approach and is written so that it summarizes all the news in just a few sentences and pays off on the headline.

The text of a press release should be double spaced or, at least, set at a line and a half spacing so journalists can read, edit, and otherwise use the text easily. If a press release is longer than one page, all subsequent pages must be numbered, ideally including the date and the organization to make sure that, if the pages get separated, they can be reassembled correctly and easily. Plus, for multiple-page press releases, the bottom of all pages before the last page must have a footer that says "-more-" to indicate that more text follows. After the final paragraph of the text about the news, a boilerplate paragraph must be added that restates the organization's name, chief location, "claim to fame," any awards or recognitions earned, website address, general telephone number, and e-mail address. After the boilerplate paragraph, three hash marks (i.e., ###), asterisks, or some other nontext-based marking (e.g., "-0-" or "-30-") are used to signal that no more text follows and the press release's text has ended. Press releases are issued over third-party "wire services" (e.g., PR Newswire, BusinessWire, etc.) that include online access. With the advent of the Internet, press releases are read by everyone outside the journalism community as well because organizations know this genre, when posted on their websites, is a potent way to share the news with the world that is fit to print or broadcast.

Video News Releases

Paper news releases don't work well for television, so an alternative approach is needed. Video news releases (VNRs) do both the showing and telling of the news. They are short, complete videotaped productions of an organization's news that mimic television news segments, including voiceover commentary, B-roll of pertinent scenes for the story, and on-screen interviews with a corporate spokesperson, recognized public figures, or other people as appropriate. Times are announced with media advisories (discussed below) for television news organizations to record a VNR from a satellite broadcast or to download a VNR from an Internet website using specialized software (e.g., RealVideo or QuickTime). A script for the VNR is usually made available for news outlets' use in the event that they want to have their own journalists do the voiceover.

VNRs work best when they have a local "hook" to catch news directors' attention. The actual video content should present a coherent, concise, and complete story in less than 2 minutes. No on-screen graphics should be used over the video so that news directors can have their stations' own supers and other graphics on screen. An off-camera narrator is best, but an on-camera reporter can be used instead. The drawback to an on-camera reporter is that the person will not be recognized by local audiences. A final VNR package includes four parts: (a) on-screen information identifying the organization responsible for the VNR, a summary statement about the VNR's content, the list of people who appear on screen in the order of their appearance by name and title, and a list of the contents of the whole VNR package with running times indicated; (b) the completed VNR that public relations officials would like to have aired, which includes the narrator/reporter and sound on tape; (c) the completed VNR with only the sound on tape and no narrator/reporter, so local stations can use their own news talent's voice instead of the narrator; and (d) B-roll of additional interviews and scenes in case a news organization would like to lengthen or otherwise edit the original VNR. The package must be accompanied by a script of all four parts that shows the video and audio content that news directors can use as they prepare the piece for broadcast and contact information for follow-up.

Audio News Releases

Like television, radio needs an alternative approach to paper news releases. Audio new releases (ANRs) tell the news but with the "color" of ambient sound. ANRs are specific, recorded announcements on audiotape about newsworthy subjects produced for radio broadcast. Content is usually focused on a particular issue (e.g., rising prescription drug prices and pro-posed government cutbacks on Medicare coverage) and targeted at one segment of the population (e.g., retired and elderly Americans), including those who are not demographically part of that segment but are sympathetic toward it. Tapes or CD-ROMs are typically sent to radio stations in target markets for specified air times or an ANR is made available for download from a secure website as an electronic audio file.

Also like VNRs, ANRs are produced to mimic radio news segments. So ANRs should be short and complete news stories. They should feature actual sounds from or pertaining to the news (as background and context) and sound bites from interviews with organizational officials who are authori-tatively involved in the news. ANRs should include information about the organization providing it, who to contact for follow-up, and, if possible, a script so producers can use it to help them prepare the segment in case any editing is desired.

Photo News Releases

Photo news releases (PNRs) are focused primarily on showing the news and secondarily on telling something about what's shown. PNRs consist mainly of a photograph of a specific, unique, and newsworthy subject that visually captures journalists' interests and "tells the story" by itself. In some ways, PNRs resemble press releases because of the way they use organizational letterhead to present the image with a concise, descriptive, and compel-ling caption; the statement that it's "for immediate release," the date, and contact information. PNRs are published in hardcopy or electronically (i.e., CD-ROM, Internet download, or e-mail).

The caption is critical because it directs the viewer's attention to what is important in the photo. Like a press release, addressing the five Ws and the H is key—and do so in around 50 words or less. A caption should be centered beneath a photo and include a relevant and pithy headline in all capital letters that precedes the caption's text. People should be identified in any photo where the people are part of the news, and they should be identified from the left to the right. Editors tend to focus on what is going on in the photo, which must grab their attention, then lean on the caption to bolster the story behind the photo.

No writing should be done on a photo if it is produced in hardcopy on photopaper. Any labeling needed for a hardcopy photo should be done with a label that is prepared separately and adhered to the back of the photo, in case the photo is separate from the letterhead and adhered to it. Only high-resolution photos should be used when printed directly on letterhead that is meant for photo reproduction. Lower resolution, electronic images should be made available over the Internet or other channels that meet journalists' needs. It is best to have a professional photographer to shoot the photos you want so that you have the best quality images to choose from and make available to others.

Media Advisories

Media advisories (sometimes called "media alerts") are sent to the news media to announce an event that is scheduled in the near future and inspire editors and journalists to attend it. The notice is usually less than a page long and outlines details in concise statements about who is involved or hosting the event, what the big news is that will come out of it, why the event and the news from it is important, where the event will be held, when it is scheduled, how people can get more information about the event and any other aspect related to it, what is slated for the event's program, what the general attendance policy (if any) is, and any historical background that may apply about the people, hosting organization(s), or event.

Prepared Statements

Prepared statements are the simplest genre of the lot in this chapter. They provide journalists with an authoritative comment on a specific, perhaps contentious subject emerging or that has already emerged on the public stage. Prepared statements amount to a lengthy quote from which only part of it would be used in a press release, but the forcefulness of a document that is a single, long, and reasonably detailed quote from an organizational authority is the point of this genre. A prepared statement is dated and can be on blank paper or organizational letterhead, include a prefatory remark about the statement being attributed to a named corporate spokesperson or official or to the organization itself, and then show the public relations contact at the bottom. Prepared statements are especially potent when a press release is too much and all that is needed is a quote about a well-publicized situation that can be documented and shared with journalists to use in any medium.

Message Design

Even to students taking their first course in public relations writing, a poorly written press release is obvious. Hallmarks are bad grammar and spelling, poor or no application of Associated Press (AP) style, inaccurate statements of facts, use of hyperbole ("hype") to sell rather than inform, broken discourse conventions for no apparent reason, and so on. The epideictic markers of good news writing also are obvious. Releases, advisories, and statements are epistemic in that they explain a particular situation.

Well-written news stories are a cohesive statement of the organization's perspective on a situation, thus preserving in print, audio, or visual form that particular perspective (i.e., it becomes part of the historical record). The preservative function of news genres has been extended through the retention of press releases and other material in online press rooms. The perspective on the situation also is axiological. The values held by the organization are presented through a press release, media advisory, or prepared statement in a way that celebrates those values and shares those values with key publics. Indeed, in a previous study, we recognized the epideictic quality of public relations discourse when analyzing the press releases of innovative companies (Courtright & Smudde, 2009).

Yet the primary epideictic function of news genres lies below the surface. News in public relations functions chiefly as performative. News genres provide unique rhetorical opportunities that their framing and organizational patterns provide. In contrast to their journalistic roots, news genres invite strategic opportunities for identity management. In addition, by defining the organization—and, at least implicitly, the audience—through its discourse, news allows organizations to articulate relationships between themselves and their publics in the sense that the persona and values they present invite publics to identify with the organizations and those values. In this section, we examine the four epideictic functions in order of their priority in news writing for public relations purposes: performative, epistemic, preservative, and celebratory.

1. Performative Function

As noted in Chapter 2, there are three dimensions within epideictic's performative function: rhetorical, identity management, and political. In this and subsequent chapters, we present these dimensions in their order of importance to each chapter's family of discourse genres, in the same fashion in which we prioritize the importance of each of the four epideictic functions here. In the case of news genres, the performative function is most important to understanding the genre, and its rhetorical dimension is the main concern, closely followed by the related dimension of identity management and then the political dimension.

Rhetorical dimension. News, above all, must assist in the development, maintenance, and improvement of relationships between an organization and those publics the news items are designed to target. Grounded within the inverted pyramid pattern, the structural basis for all news genres, their rhetorical appeal lies to some extent in the organizational pattern. As noted in Chapter 1, Kenneth Burke (1931/1968) writes that "form is the creation of an appetite in the mind of the auditor [or reader], and the adequate satisfying of that appetite" (p. 31). Perhaps a better word for *appetite* is *expectation*, but the fulfillment of the appetite, the desire to see the familiar form being followed, is part of what makes genres compelling to audiences. Although true of all news genres, the principle of Burke's appeal to form is best demonstrated with the press release.

The "creation of an appetite" in the audience occurs with the lead paragraph of a story (and with a good headline, but our focus for the moment is the principal text in the body of the document). According to Ryan (1995)—and many practitioners in both journalism and public relations—the first phrase of the first paragraph should include the most important information determined by which of the five Ws and the H is/are the most important aspect(s) of the story. Not only does this make intuitive sense in terms of primacy (i.e., readers tend to remember the first thing they read), but it also prepares the audience for what is to come as the story develops. This approach establishes expectations for the audience and then fulfills them with the details of the story.

For example, in late 2008, General Mills announced, "Three important findings based on a decade of dietary data tracking reveal that children and adolescents who eat cereal for breakfast may have an advantage when it comes to getting both the essential daily nutrients their bodies need and physical activity" (para. 1). The story then proceeds to tell how the results of the company's Bell Institute of Health and Nutrition study would appear in the November 21 issue of *Nutrition Research*. Similarly, 3M began its March 24, 2008, release this way: "One of Brazil's largest electric utilities, Companhia de Transmissao de Energia Eletrica Paulista (CTEEP), will install the 3M Aluminum Conductor Composite Reinforced (ACCR) to upgrade the capacity of a key transmission line crossing an environmentally sensitive river bed" (Business Wire, 2008, para. 1). In each case, the most important ideas are placed first to get the reader's interest.

Similarly, many top companies target news editors as the audience to reach with the lead. For example, "Sara Lee opens its new Douwe Egberts

Cafitesse Academy today in Joure, the Netherlands" (Sara Lee Corporation, 2008, para. 1). But before the editor reads the lead, the headline grabs attention: "SARA LEE BOOSTS OUT-OF-HOME STRATEGY WITH CAFITESSE ACADEMY: Fully Equipped Training and Education Center Immerses Sales Force in World of Liquid Coffee." Likewise, Kodak (2008) privileges its name in the headline, although it puts the company featured in its latter half in the first position of the lead paragraph: "KODAK NEXPRESS M700 Digital Color Press Helps Full House Press Deliver Value to Consumers and Corporate Clients." It works as a sort of rhetorical namedropping, putting the company's well-known name first. Although this practice might make for a "boring lead" (Ryan, 1995, p. 26), there are rhetorically sound reasons for cashing in on a recognizable name in the headline because not only will it appeal to media gatekeepers, but it attracts audiences' attention as well.

Identity management dimension. Even celebrities and well-known organizations should not rely on prior reputation alone to gain media attention with news genres. One thing we have found among the news efforts of innovative companies (Courtright & Smudde, 2009) and our look at various companies for this chapter is that businesses pay attention to the image-building potential of well-placed news. The discursive display of the organization's character (Aristotle's concept of ethos) is not merely a function of a good headline and/or lead. Any spokesperson, business partner, product, or service functions as a representative of the organization and therefore can be part of a good identity management strategy. This dimension need not be confined to the opening lines of a press release, VNR, or prepared statement.

It has long been understood that news placement carries the implicit endorsement of the medium that carries it. However, the choice of specific media channels is a tactical one, and successful placement cannot be controlled by the public relations strategist or the client. What *can* be controlled is the quality of how the organization appears in the particular news genre and any quotations used in support of the story. Within the confines of a press release, for example, a good quote from a key organizational leader or a subject-matter expert is helpful and, based on our observation and experience, belongs within the early details of the release, unless what was said *is* the news (which, of course, would move it to the lead paragraph). Quotations, particularly from third parties with high ethos, may be the strongest strategic choice regardless of which news genre is used.

Consider the following examples and evaluate the impression that these genres might leave with a media contact. When the U.S. Postal Service issued its 30th stamp in the Black Heritage commemorative series in 2007, its ANR featured the son of the honoree, Ella Fitzgerald:

Ray Brown Junior is Ella Fitzgerald's son.

"There was a true love and elegance that my mother expressed every time she sang. A flawless voice, really like a gift from God, extremely well disciplined. I appreciated how she was able to capture both love and heartache with the same grace and nuance and that's part of what I'll miss most about her." (United States Postal Service, 2007, para. 2)

Prepared statements, of course, depend completely on quotations as an important indication of newsworthiness and credibility. For example, when General Motors defended itself against allegations that C/K pickups' fuel delivery systems were defective, single pages of quotable responses were made available to refute claims made by opponents (i.e., consumers and plaintiff attorneys) and erroneous information conveyed through the media (Smudde, 2011). News in its various forms allows for different ways of managing identity.

The press release's aural and visual progeny, ANRs, PNRs, and VNRs, for example, rely on nonverbal and visual cues that accentuate the meaning of the verbal. In 2004, the U.S. Department of Health and Human Services, Centers for Disease Control and Prevention (2004) issued ANRs regarding the need for residents in areas where West Nile virus had been reported to take particular steps to prevent mosquito bites that could contain the virus. Dr. Julie Gerberding, the Centers for Disease Control and Prevention's (CDC's) director and spokesperson featured in the details of the stories, augments her professional credibility with a voice that is clear and authoritative. The announcer used to introduce and close the ANR is similar in tone. Similarly, through VNRs and PNRs, visuals create associations in audience minds. Editing of visuals and sound, in fact, may vary from one culture's newsrooms to another's (Silcock, 2007), so it is important to have not just compelling sound bites delivered with credible tone, pitch, and inflection, but consistency in their use throughout the entire message is also vital.

Such attention to detail can make for compelling use of news genres. For example, a PNR prepared Americans for the 2004 debut of the redesigned $50 bill (U.S. Department of the Treasury, 2004b). The U.S. Treasury Department set the stage with a larger-than-life poster-board display of the new currency. The PNR frames the photo with a headline at the top and a three-sentence caption underneath. Also, photographs can evoke emotions that may in turn influence audiences' storage of the visual in long-term memory (Fahmy, Cho, Wanta, & Song, 2006). Such might be the case of the patriotism evoked by a U.S. Department of the Treasury (2006) PNR featuring two pictures of soldiers in Iraq using EagleCash kiosks in order to obtain money just as civilians do at home at ATMs. The first picture possibly could stir emotions with its caption: "A soldier uses an EagleCash kiosk in Al Faw Palace, formerly owned by Sadaam Hussein, near Baghdad, Iraq" (para. 1).

Political dimension. Note, however, with the previous example, that it is unlikely that providing an easier way to obtain cash would be perceived as supporting the Bush administration's policies in Iraq. Thus, the PNR supports U.S. troops without being explicitly political. News, by its very definition, should have as little bias as possible. Although today we may question just how objective some U.S. news media outlets are, a public relations professional is wise to respect "objectivity" as a core value that journalists are trained to uphold. Maintaining this stance has become most difficult among the various news genres with the increasing acceptance and prevalence of VNRs as a ready means of today's news—broadcast 24/7—to provide audiences with interesting, informative stories.

VNRs have become controversial because, although news organizations know VNRs' sources and have a history of using them (see "The increasing use of VNR's," 1992), news producers have tended to not disclose the sources (an ethical problem for journalism), and doing so would appear to overstep the boundaries of objectivity and into the role of advocacy. This problem is most apparent in the criticism directed at the Bush administration and 20 of its agencies for using news videos to promote the war in Iraq (Buncombe, 2006). According to a spokesperson for the watchdog Center for Media and Democracy, "[Corporations] have got [sic] very good at mimicking what a real, independently produced television report would look like" (para. 5), which makes VNRs a potent genre to combine with marketing objectives. For example, the second author, when living north of the Cincinnati media market, every morning at 6:30 a.m. could watch a syndicated news segment, on the local NBC affiliate, devoted to travel that clearly was produced not simply to report on travel destinations but to feature particular hotels, transportation, and other businesses. It does not take too much imagination to guess what companies had been involved in producing the news segment, even if it was monetary consideration for the media mentions.

In contrast, those concerned most with the ethics of VNRs have advocated source identification and avoidance of blending news with advocacy or advertising. A VNR showing America's Dairyland Cycling Team, sponsored by the Wisconsin Milk Marketing Board (2008) and other organizations (both for-profit and nonprofit), on tour in schools across the state, clearly promotes healthy eating through healthy food choices and implicitly identifies the primary sponsor. A University of California at Berkeley VNR explains how mechanical engineering professor, Boris Rubinsky, applied cell-phone technology to advance the process of medical imaging (UC

Regents, 2008). Such VNRs maintain concerns for the public interest and the public's right to be informed.

2. Epistemic Function

News genres feature both dimensions of epideictic's epistemic function—explanation and education. These genres always should be used to develop and fulfill the explanatory dimension of knowledge production. The previous VNR examples illustrate the types of information that become news that people can use or at least reinforces that knowledge for some publics (e.g., many school students may already be convinced of the need for milk in the diet and healthy habits in general because of existing school programs, parents/guardians, etc.).

Unfortunately, corporate news bureaus and some agencies seem to forget that, when it comes to press releases, less is more. If a release does not facilitate understanding of ideas that are in some way relevant to a specific public, then it is not newsworthy and should not be issued. That principle may seem obvious, but the first author's experience in industry has included the education of management that monthly press release quotas are not necessary and, indeed, risk the trust of media contacts who see an organization suffering from a kind of "Chicken Little syndrome": Issuing announcements only makes it look like something big is going on, but there is little or no real news, so journalists stop paying attention. This may be less of a problem with easily searchable, online pressrooms on corporate websites (media contacts can treat these much like a library, looking for specific news among multiple releases) (see e.g., Fujitsu, 2000–2009; Toyota Motor Corporation, 1995–2009). Still, there is a major difference between a news release that announces a memorandum of understanding between two or more companies but explains only what it does for the country and not publics (Indian Oil Corporation, 2008) and explaining how an advanced communication system will support "improvements for security, safety and operational reliability" (General Electric, 2009) for California's Golden Gate District and its bridge, ferry, and transit systems. Consider this excerpt from a detailed press release regarding Disney World's "American Idol" attraction (Walt Disney Company, 2008):

> The attraction, slated to debut in late 2008, will be located at Disney's Hollywood Studios theme park and will follow the model of the high-energy show. Disney guests will be able to experience the challenge of auditioning, the rush of performing on stage in competition, or the thrill of judging the performances in a live interactive entertainment setting with all the glitz and glamour of the distinctive "American Idol" set. (para. 2)

The level of explanation is sufficient here to interest publics who are fans of the TV show.

Although news genres always include an explanatory dimension, they sometimes serve to educate audiences. In the case of some messages, this can be done indirectly. In the following excerpt from a prepared statement regarding Nebraska defensive tackle Ndamukong Suh's return to the Huskers in 2009, Suh's comments might serve as an example to others:

> School is a huge thing with me and my family. I definitely want to graduate from the University of Nebraska. Also, although the seniors had a great start in pushing this program the right way, I think I can help push it even more into the right direction this upcoming season. (Nebraska Athletics, 2009, para. 7)

New York State Attorney General Andrew Cuomo's November 17, 2008, prepared statement contains a moral lesson:

> Citigroup's announcement today that it will cut an additional 50,000 jobs is a sad and disturbing development for the company. As Citigroup suffers, so too do investors, employees, and taxpayers. . . . After four consecutive quarterly losses, it seems only fair that top executives should shoulder their fair share of these difficult economic times. . . . Citigroup is, of course, not the only company in this situation. Other companies like AIG, who have received billions in rescue financing from taxpayers, also need to take a hard look in the mirror when determining the right thing to do on executive bonuses during these very difficult economic times. (New York Office of the Attorney General, 2008, paras. 1–2)

PNRs also may be educational. Research shows that photographs labeled as "real" may cause viewers to react more emotionally to them, although those labeled "fictional" (e.g., staged) may appeal more to visual learners and evoke more ideas (Mendelson & Papacharissi, 2007). Photos from the real world are taken as a matter of fact, but they can vividly substitute for details of a story.

3. Preservative Function

Regarding the retention of messages for other uses, news genres are quite pliable. Practitioners may avail themselves of all three dimensions of the preservative function: repurposing, self-persuasion, and cohesion, particularly the first. It is clear from our earlier discussion that news releases may be transformed into video, audio, and photographic versions or media advisories. Likewise, quotations suitable for identity management in a news release may be grouped together to form the primary messages for a prepared statement. For news genres, repurposing is as natural as breathing because one discourse pragmatically begets another (e.g., earnings announcements help in annual report writing, press releases about customer successes become case studies, speeches lend themselves to white papers' content, etc.). For example, Wal-Mart (2008a, 2008b), as part of its activities during a sustainability summit in China, simultaneously produced a news release and a video news release to introduce its Global Responsible Sourcing Initiative. In addition, public relations professionals would be remiss not to return to the news files when later events recall earlier stories. For example, Courtright and Slaughter (2007) argue that messages issued during crisis communication may become useful resources when preparing news contacts' queries when the crisis' anniversary rolls around (e.g., the Gulf Coast a year after Hurricane Katrina, the 10-year anniversary of a plane crash).

Cohesion across campaign messages naturally follows repurposing and often goes hand in hand with it. The U.S. Coast Guard (2004a, 2004b) issued a photo media advisory 4 days after it made a news release available regarding capture of suspected smugglers in the Caribbean and the seizure of the drugs they allegedly were trafficking in. BP has been particularly deft at staying on message with its environmental commitment (although many of its news releases and other news material are devoted to the bottom line and expansion of its access to natural gas and petroleum). News releases range from a focus on BP Solar's completion of a solar system for a FedEx Freight distribution center (BP, 2008d), a partnership to "accelerate the commercialization of cellulose ethanol" (2008c), and cooperation with Abu Dhabi's initiative for renewable and alternative energy and clean technology, BP Alternative Energy, and Rio Tinto (2008a). The same year, BP's new chief executive, Tony Hayward, delivered a speech on current trends in renewable energy to the International Renewables Energy Conference in Washington, DC (2008b).

News genres also may be self-persuasive to some extent. As Burks (1970) argues, human beings often intensify their own commitment to positions when they communicate with others (and perhaps even convince themselves if they are not completely sure). With organizations, this depends on the purposes behind the message: Is it directed at both employees and other publics? Is it both a commitment to a position (and therefore related to the performative function's identity-management dimension discussed earlier) and an attempt to influence other audiences? The answer to the first question depends on the ordering of presentation: Some news is announced to employees before generally announced to the world; at other times, employees are treated as members of other publics who receive the news from uncontrolled media outlets. Regarding the second question, consider an example from HSBC. Regarding results of a study released by the bank's Climate Partnership, HSBC's news release (2008) included the following quote:

> Lord Nicholas Stern, adviser to HSBC on economic development and climate change, said: "This research demonstrates the need for decisive action on climate change. The urgent challenge is to build a framework for a global deal so that consensus can be reached in Copenhagen next year and the discussions in Poznan are a critical stepping stone to achieving this. Now is the time to lay the foundations of a new form of growth that can transform our economies and societies." (para. 5)

Considering the bank's effort is a 5-year partnership from 2007 to 2012 with the Climate Group, Earthwatch Institute, Smithsonian Tropical Research Institute, and World Wildlife Fund, it is plausible that reinforcement of environmental values within the company could result from this news. In this way, the news release is an example of Kenneth Burke's (1937/1984) observation that symbols are the "coaching of an attitude" (p. 322); for example, the Air Transport Association of America (2008) about its anticipation of working with Secretary of Transportation designate Ray LaHood "on critical issues affecting airlines, their customers and the nation" (para. 2).

4. Celebratory Function

Of the news genres discussed earlier, only the axiological dimension of the celebratory function of epideictic seems to be at work. These genres have no particularly ritualistic dimension because, as we have seen through the examples, their uses and purposes vary widely. Our study (Courtright & Smudde, 2009) of press releases and other genres used by innovative companies gives evidence for the conclusion that news genres are values-driven. Although we consider the celebratory function last in importance for these genres, by no means do we intend to say that this function is minor. Indeed, in earlier examples of the other three functions, a wide array of values— among them, nutrition, environmentalism, music appreciation, health and safety, and patriotism—may be found in press releases, VNRs, ANRs, PNRs, and prepared statements. Because discourse inherently must include values in order to produce cooperation between organizations and their publics, it should come as no surprise that even the most minimalist of news genres, the media advisory, contains them.

Given their description earlier in this chapter, however, media advisories would not seem to fit the celebratory demands of news genres at all. After all, they are the bare bones of a story and would not seem to do much to imply organizational and audience roles or foster identification between sender and receiver. Still, news advisories may look like summaries (see Chapter 4), but their primary purpose is to gain newsworthy attention and invite identification between an organization and the media through shared values.

These values, however, need not be stated. For example, on March 30, 2004, the U.S. National Aeronautic and Space Administration (NASA) provided bulleted information regarding its Great Moonbuggy Race to be held at the U.S. Space & Rocket Center in Huntsville, Alabama. The advisory provided the essentials of where and when the event would occur, what high school student teams would be doing, and how they would compete (U.S. NASA, 2004, paras. 1–4). However, the roles of NASA and its media targets, along with the values that might unite them, are clear within the minimal amount of information. The headline actually begins the local angle that defines the media's role: "Student teams from your area race. . . ." NASA's role—and the values that should create identification with the media con-tacts (and, by extension, their audiences) are clear from the Why: The race was inspired by the successful lunar rover, developed at the Center in the 1960s (para. 5); also, "the 2004 race comes on the heels of the President's new goals for the space program to return to the Moon and explore beyond." Additionally, these hometown students could be "among those who return humans to the Moon, or whose designs are adapted for future vehicles" (para. 6).

Such values, however, need not be stated explicitly in an advisory. The Gardenia Restaurant and Lounge (n.d.) in West Hollywood alerted local media to the fact that cabaret singer/actress Mary Jo Mundy would return to its stage in a show called "Half-Off," in which her obesity surgeon also would appear. The fact that Mundy and her doctor would be telling her story via the show implies the rhetorical battle between them and the enemy—obesity. Local media can identify with the values of health and victory over personal struggle without being explicitly told that the story provides newsworthy angles of a current issue, proximity, and human inter-est. The principles at work here are Aristotle's example (Mundy herself) and *enthymeme*—a premise that the audience already accepts and recognizes as part of the argument being made.

It is clear that the main audience for news genres is the media contact or editor (even when press releases in their various forms are made gen-erally available on the Web). The coordination of epideictic's celebratory and performative functions becomes critical, especially through strategic planning efforts. As to the former, the values that the organization displays through its use of news genres must resonate with values that the media perceive their audiences to hold and perhaps they themselves regard as important: "Many large organizations (1) make use of the unquestioned pervasiveness of certain cultural premises and (2) foster their 'own' premises linked to the broader ones" (Cheney & Vibbert, 1987, p. 185). Values thus become the grounding for identification between organizations and their publics. The priority of the rhetorical identity management aspects of epideictic performance are thus central to inducing cooperation, celebrating the organization, and celebrating values that the media and their audiences hold dear.

Strategic Planning Implications

Form follows function. Don't put the cart before the horse. Have all your ducks in a row. Get your act together. Think before you speak.

The common theme across these familiar colloquialisms is planning ahead. This is essential to ensure that the right thing is done in the right way for the right people at the right time for the right reasons. In this section of this chapter, we do two things: (a) set the framework for divining strategic implications that are behind the enactment of public relations tactics that will be covered in this and the following seven chapters, and (b) apply that framework for this chapter's genres. In business and, indeed, public relations, strategy is key, and the word *strategy* is often paired with *planning*. Peter Drucker (1967/2006) pointed out that Napoleon, who was a meticulous planner before every battle, recognized that he needed a detailed plan every time, even knowing it was highly likely the plans would not play out exactly the way he wanted (Waterloo notwithstanding). The reason: He had to know precisely what he wanted his military to do and accomplish and not just go in with guns blazing and hope for the best. The same must be the case for public relations.

Far too many conversations among corporate officials—with and without public relations professionals present—recommend going into situations with rhetorical guns blazing with little or no thought about why and for what big-picture results—we need a press release, let's do a news conference, get an interview with *BusinessWeek*, we must be at the next trade show. This approach is what project-management experts call "jumping to solution." For public relations we call it "jumping to tactics," and it is endemic in the profession (Woodall, 2006; Woodall & Smith, 2003). It is a knee-jerk reaction symptomatic of an attitude about public relations as a corporate mouth and its professionals the vocal chords, saying what the management brain wants them to say. Worse is when public relations professionals jump to tactics with or without sufficient experience in the field—doing something mainly because it is cool, trendy, worked for someone else, management commands it, or whatever. In some ways jumping to tactics is understandable, but it is ill-informed and ill-advised.

A bias toward tactics has as its primary motive the gaining of attention, as if attention is an end in and of itself. Indeed, as Davenport and Beck (2001) argue, attention for any organization has such a high value as an economic commodity—a raw material necessary for conducting business—that public relations tactics (and other communication tactics) seem natural means to that end. Fueling the desire for getting attention is instant gratification, because attention for an organization can be easily gained and crudely measured (e.g., news clips, advertising value equivalency), but attitude change and action, which are ultimate outcomes that must be sought, take time to develop and assess after mere awareness is established. Note that instant gratification is just one of four levels of gratification, the others being short-term, long-term, and eternal, and they will be explained shortly (see Figure 3.1). In general, gratification, at least in a business context, is simply the quenching of the thirst for data about results from communications work done. Or in other words, corporate officials seek proof of the fulfillment of particular communication goals with target audiences through public relations or other selected means.

When instant gratification from attention is wanted for an organization, like a child in a room with other people, there are ways to get it. Social media, like Twitter and Facebook, fit that bill, but other tactics, like reports and even books, will not. Figure 3.1 shows a scheme to analyze how tactics achive different levels of gratification along the continua of attention, media type, permanence, and return on investment (ROI).

Beyond attention in Figure 3.1, three other continua for gratification are essential to understanding the bias for or the jumping to tactics among corporate officials. Media type concerns what Marshall McLuhan (1964)

Results Sought	Attention	Media Type	Permanance	ROI
Instant Gratification	Easiest	Hottest	Lowest	Fastest
Short-term Gratification	↕	↕	↕	↕
Long-term Gratification				
Lasting Gratification	Hardest	Coolest	Highest	Slowest

Figure 3.1. Analysis scheme for tactical gratification.

referred to "hot" and "cool" media. For example, television is a cool medium because it does not require high involvement and people do not always pay attention to its substance. In contrast, the Internet would be a hot medium because it requires significant involvement and creativity on the part of the user. Permanence concerns the relative amount of time that a form of communication lasts. Twitter tweets, for example, are very fleeting 140-character strings and, thus, have the lowest level of permanence (notwithstanding the saving of messages), while social values and mores have the highest degree of permanence. And ROI concerns how much value (financial or nonfinancial) will return to an organization for the communication in which it invested. A book would require a longer period of time to measure its ROI than a Facebook page or a printed advertisement because the sales cycle of books is far longer than that which would result from Facebook exposure or a print ad.

Given these continua, it becomes apparent why some tactics have greater appeal than others to corporate officials, including public relations professionals. That appeal must be purposeful and founded on strategic planning, which will be covered shortly. But when jumping to tactics rules the day, instant gratification of results through attention gained in the hottest media with the lowest permanence and fastest ROI will likely be chosen. Fortunately, there is more to this scheme to analyze tactical bias in terms of gratification and even strategic planning.

Gratification through attention, media type, permanence, and ROI can occur on at least four levels, as Figure 3.1 shows, and those levels conform to the epideictic nature of public relations. For example, those reporters seeking instant gratification might turn to news genres of brevity, such as media advisories and prepared statements. News releases may serve short-term or long-term gratification, depending on how long an organization keeps it available in online newsroom archives. News releases, in whole or in part, can provide lasting gratification when they become picked up as news stories and thus part of the public record, serving the ideal preservative function of epideictic rhetoric.[2]

Granted, those with much more experience have more data in their minds to help them process information very quickly about a situation and arrive at a sound *recommendation*. Even then it is just that: a suggestion that begs the questions, "Given everything that I know and everything I just learned about the situation, is this recommendation still the best option among others? Why?" This is where strategic thinking and planning are vital to making sure tactics carry their weight and fulfill the big-picture purpose. As Sun Tzu said in his *Art of War*, "Strategy without tactics is the slowest route to victory. Tactics without strategy is the noise before defeat."[3] The two must go together and be in balance: Being overly strategic risks making real progress on getting things done, and being too tactical risks understanding why and how success can be achieved and sustained.

Public relations pioneer and "father" of the field, Edward L. Bernays, is known for his social-scientific approach to his work (see Grunig & Hunt, 1984). Key to his approach is strategic planning within the context of a big picture. As Tye (1998) explains in his biography of Bernays, "his philosophy in each case was the same. Hired to sell a product or service, he instead sold whole new ways of behaving, which appeared obscure but over time reaped huge rewards for his clients and redefined the very texture of American life" (p. 52). Bernays knew well what had to be done, regardless of whether his clients understood or embraced it, and he did it well (see Bernays, 1965). Bernays recognized the problems with jumping to tactics. He said in his book, *Public Relations* (1952), "Do not think of tactics in terms of segmental approaches. The problem is not to get articles into a newspaper or obtain radio time or arrange for a motion-picture newsreel; it is, rather, to set in motion a broad activity, the success of which depends on interlocking all phases and elements of the proposed strategy, implemented by tactics that are timed to the moment of maximum effectiveness" (p. 167).

Bernays understood more than most then—and stands as a prime example now—that the outputs of public relations must have a larger yield than the gratification gained immediately upon their release. Bernays has much to teach us: There is always much more at stake in the bigger picture for both an organization and its publics, and public relations can and must complete the work systematically to realize that bigger picture. So the work of public relations counselors is "to create circumstances which will modify [group habits for the better]" (Bernays, 1928/2005, p. 77). Bernays presents a basic planning process in *Propaganda* (1928/2005)[4] that must be teased out from the text. It is quite simple and consistent with his later treatment of planning in his book, *Public Relations* (1952), and especially with contemporary thinking (e.g., Botan, 2006; Ferguson, 1999; Heath & Palenchar, 2009; Moffitt, 1999; Oliver, 2007; Smudde, 2011): study the present situation and audience behaviors and disposition within it, identify the big idea that is truly at stake for the audience an organization can genuinely help, identify what could be done (from objectives to resource allocations to key messages to tactics) to inspire cooperation between audiences and the organization on that big idea, put that plan into action, and observe how well target audiences change their habits to discern whether all was successful.

Bernays (1928/2005) asserts how important planning is when he says, "At whatever point a business enterprise impinges on the public consciousness, it must seek to give its public relations the particular character which will conform to the objectives which it is pursuing" (p. 86). Moreover, public relations counselors who put their plans into action successfully also further promote "the socially constructive cause" and "by doing so he [sic] is actually fulfilling a social purpose in the broadest sense" (Bernays, 1928/2005, p. 93). The true art of developing relations with publics, then, is when organizations' and their publics' interests and needs truly mesh for mutual benefits (see E. Burke, 1999).

Divining Strategy Behind Genres

The strategy behind public relations tactics is more profound than what is typically thought. Our analysis of public relations discourse genres in this book reveals that the conventions for each genre drive how and why they can be used and used effectively. This is the stuff of strategy. Indeed, Smudde (2007) lays out a template for planning public relations that accounts for the ways that discourse drives practitioners in their work, not the other way around. Effective public relations—the measured and ethical use of language and symbols to inspire cooperation between an organization and its publics—comes through an astute combination of discourse competence and strategic thinking. This combination is essential among the best practitioners. But public relations professionals (students also) too often jump to tactics: What was used in the past worked well or is the hot, new trend, so it must be the right thing to do in the present. (All the hype around the use of social media in public relations is a good example.) More important on this point is this: Public relations professionals who jump to tactics probably only understand discourse conventions at a surface level, and deeper understanding of discourse conventions within the context of the "big picture," as we cover in this book, would better inform their thinking to be more strategic and, presumably, more successful. Form must, indeed, follow function. Alternatively, tactics must follow from a sound strategy.

Strategy can be as simple or complex as an opportunity requires, but the approach is fundamentally the same, as the example from Bernays showed. Smudde's (2007) discourse-centered approach to public relations strategy serves as the basis for a formal strategic plan and, more for our purposes in this book, grounds the thinking about what the strategic implications for public relations genres are so they may be applied well in any formal plan. (Chronologically speaking, Smudde's [2007, 2011] planning approach was created before the matter of tactics was addressed in this book, just like it should for "real-world" opportunities.) The resulting program we use to account for the strategic implications of public relations genres is simple and will be applied in each chapter. The program actually began with our analysis in the preceding section. We showed in the previous section and similarly show in the following chapters that the epideictic nature of public relations includes four functions. Those functions are prioritized differently for the various discourse genres because of what they allow practitioners to do to design effective messages within the frameworks of their discourse conventions. Next, the challenge is to look at each lot of discourse genres and answer the question, "Now what?"

The answer to this pragmatic question concerns how public relations discourse can be made to work within the day-to-day world of public relations business. The answer in each chapter varies a bit from the others, and that is understandable because the ways that discourse conventions direct practitioners in using discourse effectively varies depending on many factors (e.g., business vision, mission, objectives, model, and plan; opportunity; resources; environment). But the variance is not so pronounced that it is unwieldy. Indeed, our groupings of discourse genres in each chapter enable us to divine strategic implications that are rather like tools in a toolbox: We introduce and apply certain approaches that would work better for the genres catalogued in each chapter, and they may or may not be as useful for other categories covered in the other chapters. That is okay because, just like fixing a car, you need many tools to make sure you can do the job right the first time, and it is good to have those tools in your toolbox for when you need them.

Strategy Implications for News Genres

Part of public relations is not just defining who the organization is in relationship to the news story, but it is also a matter of suggesting to publics, particularly media contacts, the role(s) that they might adopt in relationship to the story. Organizations are often seen as similar to people, having the capacity to speak on their own behalves, being subject to particular laws and practices, and participating in commerce with each other and in society in general. What is important to recognize here is that the performative aspects of news, as epideictic rhetoric, rely heavily on identity management in public relations. The identity dimension subsumes the impact of the news on who and what the organization is and stands for. The identity dimension also includes the publics' view of an organization in light of the news. This identity is akin to ethos. Organizations, like individuals, possess and project an ethos—a first persona—that they and their publics perceive and evaluate through communication. Just as there is an organizational ethos or "persona" (McMillan, 1987) implied in news genre discourses, there is an audience implied in the message—a "second persona" (Black, 1970)—which is the audience's role as it is invited to participate in an organization's messages. Even in the simplest of forms, the two *personae* together—the desired image the organization wants to communicate *and* the role that the message invites the media contact to adopt—must not be treated lightly. In terms of the strategic implications for news genres, *personae* are the keys to strategically managing the drama of news and the epideictic qualities they obtain.

The messages reflecting the *personae* must be handled expertly and strategically to ensure that news genres add the value expected of them. The other two performative dimensions of news genres—rhetorical and political—are also at play and have strategic implications that also depend on *personae*. As we saw, the rhetorical dimension concerns the content and presentation of organizations' messages about the news, its role in it, and, most important, adaptation to the audience. The political dimension addresses matters about how the news affects the relationship between an organization and its publics (without being perceived as trying to influence public policy in some way). To address these dimensions with identity, professional communicators consider how news relies on and affects first and second *personae*. The key is to address the matters of first and second *personae* in tune with the five Ws and the H discussed earlier in this chapter, but to do so in such a way that the real *drama* of the news comes to the fore and can be handled strategically.

Kenneth Burke (1945/1969) gives us the necessary tools to use news genres effectively through his dramatistic pentad, which are the five essential aspects for any human action: the scene (where and when), act (what), agent (who), agency (how), and purpose (why). The pentad can be used prospectively for strategic planning of public relations, as Smudde (2004, 2011) has shown. Although *personae* ultimately affect all five of these dramatistic dimensions, they are featured most prominently in agent, agency, and purpose. The scene concerns the literal news and when and where it happened. The act is the actual organizational thing that is the news. The agents in the communication naturally involve the organization (e.g., corporate spokespeople) and include the audiences it targets (plus audiences it does not target but obtain the communication anyway). The agency covers the means by which the agents are involved in making the news, including the discourse genres used to announce it to audiences. The purpose concerns the reasons an organization chooses to share the news with its audiences. All five of these elements support the matters of strategy that are important in effective planning, as covered earlier (for complete discussions, see Smudde, 2007, 2011).

If practitioners are not careful, they can fall into the trap of neglecting big-picture matters at the expense of fulfilling the demands of any given tactic. If there is anything that we emphasize the most in this book, it is the idea that tactics serve larger purposes in systematic ways. Every word an organization uses is important as it bridges the separateness between an organization and its publics. With the growing usefulness of the Internet for all kinds of communication, there is now a risk of message design degeneration. Search engine optimization (SEO) has quickly become a guiding approach for writing news. SEO involves the identification and application of key words that will easily tie a text to results that come up in an Internet search engine. As Faulhaber (2009) describes the process:

> Before writing a news release for online publication [presumably includ-ing all other means of public dissemination], and once the direction of the release is established [presumably the key message platform], you should determine the keywords that apply to the release and use them strategically throughout the copy. (p. 19)

The key words must be genuinely relevant to the announcement, not any-thing used to merely increase "hits" in search engine results.

On the surface, the SEO approach has some practical merit, primarily for helping an organization's news rise to the top, but it suffers from one major problem: The channel guides the tactics, not the message or strategic plan. That is, although a practitioner has a basic idea about the content of a news genre, what must be said can be subservient to a mere list of words whose sole or, at least, primary purpose is to make a text more prominent in an Internet search rather than to ensure effective communication of ideas. Key words should come from the message, which is in tune with the strat-egy, not the other way around. If not, strategy and message design, then, are relegated to mere matters of statistical probability rather than the outgrowth of thorough planning and communication savvy. If SEO is an indication of things to come, the inordinate stress on tactics over all else will continue to undermine the profession's value and solidify it as merely mouths for corpo-rate-speak. An understanding of the discourse conventions, message design matters, and strategy implications of news genres present practitioners with a much more complete approach to managing news and *personae* for the mutual benefit of organizations and their publics.

Other genres important in public relations serve other purposes, as the following chapters elucidate. The next chapter addresses a group of genres we call "summaries," and they adhere to epideictic functions in particularly different ways from news genres that make them especially useful for mul-tiple opportunities.

Notes

1. "Social media news releases," at first glance, may seem a separate genre, but they are not. Upon close examination, these documents follow the discourse conventions of news releases as we discuss them here. The only difference is that social media news releases, or "social media releases" for short, are press releases designed to cater to technology's parameters; whereas, the purpose and content of the document is tailored to fit the categories of information structures called for in

specific social media, including categories of links to related online content (text, audio, video, photo, blogs, etc.). We address this matter elsewhere in this book, especially Chapter 10. In fact, social news releases rely on the news release genre. The additional links in a social media release serve to augment message cohesion and, especially, aid information gathering for users. See Shift Communications' (2006, 2008) templates for a social media release.

2. Blumler and Katz (1974) and researchers who have used their Uses and Gratifications Theory provide deeper insights into how audience members (i.e., *media users*) seek out particular media channels (i.e., *uses)* and what gratifications (e.g., news gathering, entertainment) they receive from their media choices. This theory has great utility for public relations professionals because audiences play an active role in the selection and consumption of message genres and their contents. In light of this theory, Figure 3.1 suggests future research could possibly be used to correlate media use and attention with the type of gratification, the duration of gratification, and the organization's return on investment.

3. This quote is very profound and relevant, which makes its use ubiquitous by many in their works understandable, but interestingly the quote has not been cited from a particular translation of *Art of War*. Indeed, Kaplan and Norton (2008) found "a careful reading of several translations does not identify the actual use of this quote" (p. 32). The quote that we use here (as others have used it), then, appears to be an aphoristic reduction of the ideas in Chapter 3 in *Art of War* in any translation.

4. Bernays correctly argued that the word *propaganda* had been bastardized by negative associations with evil communicative purposes during and since World War I. Propaganda, in its proper meaning, refers to actions to "propagate the faith," which is neither ethical nor unethical. Public relations, therefore, is synonymous with propaganda in its original, proper sense and reference.

References

Air Transport Association of America. (2008, December 18). *ATA statement on reports that Congressman Ray LaHood will be named Department of Transportation secretary.* [Online prepared statement]. Retrieved December 20, 2008, from http://www.airlines.org/news/releases/2008/news_12-18-08.htm

Bates, D. (2002/2006). *"Mini-me" history: Public relations from the dawn of civilization.* Retrieved November 22, 2008, from http://www.instituteforpr.org/files/uploads/MiniMe_HistoryOfPR.pdf

Bernays, E. L. (1952). *Public relations.* Norman, OK: University of Oklahoma Press.

Bernays, E. L. (1965). *Biography of an idea: Memoirs of public relations counsel Edward L. Bernays.* New York: Simon & Schuster.

Bernays, E. L. (2005). *Propaganda.* New York: IG. (Original work published 1928)

Black, E. (1970). The second persona. *Quarterly Journal of Speech, 56,* 109–119.

Blumler, J. G., & Katz, E. (1974). *The uses of mass communications: Current perspectives on gratifications research.* Beverly Hills, CA: Sage.

Botan, C. (2006). Grand strategy, strategy, and tactics in public relations. In C. H. Botan & V. Hazleton (Eds.), *Public relations theory II* (pp. 223-247). Mahwah, NJ: Lawrence Erlbaum Associates.

BP p.l.c. (2008a, January 21). *Masdar and Hydrogen Energy plan clean energy plant in Abu Dhabi.* [Online news release]. Retrieved February 15, 2009, from http://www.bp.com/genericarticle.do?categoryId=2012968&contentId=7040789

BP p.l.c. (2008b, March 4). *Current trends and issues: Renewable energy.* [Online speech transcript]. Retrieved February 15, 2009, from http://www.bp.com/genericarticle.do?categoryId=98&contentId=7042010

BP p.l.c. (2008c, August 6). *BP and Verenium announce significant partnership to accelerate the commercialization of cellulosic ethanol.* [Online news release]. Retrieved February 15, 2009, from http://www.bp.com/genericarticle.do?categoryId=2012968&contentId=7046627

BP p.l.c. (2008d, September 4). *FedEx Freight and BP Solar complete second solar power installation.* [Online news release]. Retrieved February 15, 2009, from http://www.bp.com/genericarticle.do?categoryId=2012968&contentId=7047713

Breakenridge, D. (2008). *PR 2.0: New media, new tools, new audiences.* Upper Saddle River, NJ: Pearson Education.

Buncombe, A. (2006, May 29). American TV stations in "fake news" inquiry. *The Independent*, p. 19. Retrieved November 3, 2010, from LexisNexis Academic database.

Burke, E. K. (1999). *Corporate community relations: The principle of the neighbor of choice.* Westport, CT: Praeger.

Burke, K. (1968). *Counter-statement.* Berkeley: University of California Press. (Original work published 1931)

Burke, K. (1969). *A grammar of motives.* Berkeley: University of California Press. (Original work published 1945)

Burke, K. (1984). *Attitudes toward history* (3rd ed.). Berkeley: University of California Press. (Original work published 1937)

Burks, D. M. (1970). Persuasion, self-persuasion and rhetorical discourse. *Philosophy & Rhetoric, 3*, 109–119.

Business Wire. (2008, March 24). *Brazil's Companhia de Transmissao de Energia Eletrica Paulista chooses 3M ACCR for upgrade of line over Parana River in Sao Paulo State.* [Press release]. Retrieved December 15, 2008, from http://www.businesswire.com/portal/site/3m/template.NDM/menuitem.b8d35 848927f3fd47da60710e6908a0c/?javax.portlet.tpst=90eae28b915b3189760 6fe57a519b602_ws_MX&javax.portlet.prp_90eae28b915b31897606fe57a51 9b602_viewID=news_view_popup&javax.portlet.prp_90eae28b915b3189760 6fe57a519b602_newsLang=en&javax.portlet.prp_90eae28b915b31897606fe57 a519b602_ndmHsc=v2*A1199192400000*B1207102893000*C4102491599000* DgroupByDate*J2*N1000940&javax.portlet.prp_90eae28b915b31897606fe57a 519b602_newsId=20080324005126&beanID=75290669&viewID=news_view_ popup&javax.portlet.begCacheTok=com.vignette.cachetoken&javax.portlet. endCacheTok=com.vignette.cachetoken

Cheney, G., & Vibbert, S. L. (1987). Corporate discourse: Public relations and issue management. In F. M. Jablin, L. L. Putnam, K. H. Roberts, & L. W. Porter (Eds.), *Handbook of organizational communications: An interdisciplinary perspective* (pp. 165–194). Newbury Park, CA: Sage.

Courtright, J. L., & Slaughter, G. Z. (2007). Remembering disaster: Since the media do, so must public relations. *Public Relations Review, 33*, 313-318.

Courtright, J. L., & Smudde, P. M. (2009). Leveraging organizational innovation for strategic reputation management. *Corporate Reputation Review, 12*, 245-269.

Curtin, P. A. (1999). Reevaluating public relations information subsidies: Market-driven journalism and agenda-building theory and practice. *Journal of Public Relations Research, 11*, 53-90.

Cutlip, S. M. (1994). *The unseen power: Public relations, a history.* Hillsdale, NJ: Erlbaum.

Davenport, T. H., & Beck, J. C. (2001). *The attention economy: Understanding the new currency of business.* Boston: Harvard Business School Press.

Drucker, P. F. (2006). *The effective executive: The definitive guide to getting the right things done.* New York: HarperCollins. (Original work published 1967)

Fahmy, S., Cho, S., Wanta, W., & Song, Y. (2006). Visual agenda-setting after 9/11: Individuals' emotions, image recall, and concern with terrorism. *Visual Communication Quarterly, 13*, 4-15.

Faulhaber, P. (2009, February). Working words: SEO style for search-engine optimization. *Public Relations Tactics*, p. 19.

Ferguson, S. D. (1999). *Communication planning: An integrated approach.* Thousand Oaks, CA: Sage.

Fujitsu. (2000-2009). *Recent press releases: All topics (Fujitsu United States).* Retrieved January 29, 2009, from http://www.fujitsu.com/us/news/pr/recent/

Gandy, O. (1982). *Beyond agenda setting: Information subsidies and public policies.* Norwood, NJ: Ablex.

Gardenia Restaurant and Lounge. (n.d.). *On a lighter note . . . local cabaret performer singing a different tune thanks to obesity surgery: Obesity surgeon to watch former patient, Mary Jo Mundy, perform in "Half-Off."* [Interview advisory]. Retrieved December 16, 2008, from http://www.centinelamed.com/News/default/HalfOffCabaretSinger.doc

General Electric Company. (2009, January 28). *GE transportation to serve Golden Gate Bridge District on new advanced communications system.* [Press release]. Retrieved January 29, 2009, from http://www.genewscenter.com/Content/Detail.asp?ReleaseID=5627&NewsAreaID=2&MenuSearchCategoryID=

General Mills, Inc. (2008, October 14). *Warm, hearty family style meal; no family required: New Stove Top Quick Cups delivers the taste of a home-cooked family meal even when dining alone or on the go.* [Press release]. Retrieved December 15, 2008, from http://www.generalmills.com/corporate/media_center/news_release_detail.aspx?itemID=35188&catID=227

Grunig, J. E., & Hunt, T. (1984). *Managing public relations.* Fort Worth, TX: Harcourt Brace Jovanovich.

Heath, R. L., & Palenchar, M. J. (2009). *Strategic issues management: Organizations and public policy challenges* (2nd ed.). Thousand Oaks, CA: Sage.

HSBC, Inc. (2008, November 26). *International consensus: Time to stop haggling and agree on carbon "fair share."* [Online news release]. Retrieved December 20, 2008, from http://www.hsbc.com/1/2/newsroom/news/news-archive-2008/

international-consensus-time-to-stop-haggling-and-agree-on-carbon-fair-share-

The increasing use of VNR's reflects a growing interdependency between television news and. . . . (1992). *Broadcasting, 122*(35), 17–18.

Indian Oil Corporation Ltd. (2008, December 8). *Indian Oil and Adani Energy Limited (AEnL) sign MoU on city gas distribution.* [Press release]. Retrieved January 29, 2009, from http://www.iocl.com/MediaCenter/News.aspx?NewsTypeID=8&NewsID=3919

Kaplan, R. S., & Norton, D. P. (2008). *The execution premium: Linking strategy to operations for competitive advantage.* Boston, MA: Harvard Business School Press.

Kodak. (2008, November 24). *KODAK NEXPRESS M700 Digital Color Press helps Full House Press deliver value to consumers and corporate clients.* [Press release]. Retrieved December 15, 2008, from http://www.kodak.com/eknec/PageQuerier.jhtml?pq-path=2709&pq-locale=en_US&gpcid=0900688a809fed75

McLuhan, M. (1964). *Understanding media: The extensions of man* (2nd ed.). New York: Mentor.

McMillan, J. J. (1987). In search of the organizational persona: A rationale for studying organizations rhetorically. In L. Thayer (Ed.), *Organization↔communication: Emerging perspectives II* (pp. 21–45). Norwood, NJ: Ablex.

Moffitt, M. A. (1999). *Campaign strategies and message design: A practitioner's guide from start to finish.* Westport, CT: Praeger.

Nebraska Athletics. (2009, January 12). *Suh to return to Nebraska for senior season.* [Online prepared statement]. Retrieved January 13, 2009, from http://www.huskers.com/ViewArticle.dbml?ATCLID=3644078&db_oem_id=100

New York Office of the Attorney General. (2008, November 17). *Statement from Attorney General Andrew Cuomo concerning bonuses to top executives at Citigroup.* [Online prepared statement]. Retrieved January 13, 2009, from http://www.oag.state.ny.us/media_center/2008/nov/nov17b_08.html

Oliver, S. (2007). *Public relations strategy* (2nd ed.). London: Kogan Page.

Mendelson, A. L., & Papacharissi, Z. (2007). Reality vs. fiction: How defined realness affects cognitive & emotional responses to photographs. *Visual Communication Quarterly, 14,* 231–243.

Ryan, M. (1999). Models help writers produce publishable releases. *Public Relations Quarterly, 40*(2), 25–27.

Sara Lee Corporation. (2008, December 11). *Sara Lee boosts out-of-home strategy with Cafitesse Academy: Fully equipped training and education center immerses sales force in world of liquid coffee.* [Press release]. Available at http://www.saralee.com/~/media/D3AB24EB124D459B87A8480659B53919.ashx

Silcock, B. W. (2007). Every edit tells a story: Sound and the visual frame: A comparative analysis of videotape editor routines in global newsrooms. *Visual Communication Quarterly, 14,* 3–15.

Smudde, P. M. (2004). Implications on the practice and study of Kenneth Burke's idea of a "public relations counsel with a heart." *Communication Quarterly, 52,* 420–432.

Smudde, P. M. (2007). Public relations' power as based on knowledge, discourse, and ethics. In J. L. Courtright & P. M. Smudde (Eds.), *Power and public relations* (pp. 207–238). Cresskill, NJ: Hampton Press.

Smudde, P. M. (2011). *Public relations as dramatistic organizing: A case study bridging theory and practice.* Cresskill, NJ: Hampton Press.

Toyota Motor Corporation. (1995–2009). *Toyota: Company news.* Retrieved January 29, 2009, from http://www.toyota.co.jp/en/news/08/index.html

Tye, L. (1998). *The father of spin: Edward L. Bernays & the birth of public relations.* New York: Holt.

UC Regents. (2008, April 29). *Engineers harness cell phone technology for use in medical imaging.* [Video news release]. Retrieved January 29, 2009, from http://berkeley.edu/news/media/releases/2008/04/29_cellphone.shtml

U.S. Coast Guard. (2004a, Janurary 24). *Virginia cutters busting up Caribbean smugglers.* [Online news release]. Retrieved January 12, 2009, from https://www.piersystem.com/external/index.cfm?cid=586&fuseaction=EXTERNAL.docview&pressid=28697

U.S. Coast Guard. (2004b, Janurary 28). *Interdicted drugs, suspected smugglers arriving at Coast Guard Air Station Clearwater this afternoon.* [Online photo media advisory]. Retrieved January 12, 2009, from http://www.piersystem.com/go/doc/586/28715/

U.S. Department of Health and Human Services, Centers for Disease Control and Prevention. (2004, August). *CDC: West Nile virus—audio news releases, August 2004.* Retrieved January 26, 2009, from http://www.cdc.gov/ncidod/dvbid/westnile/misc/anr082604/

U.S. Department of the Treasury. (2004b, April 26). *Treasury Secretary John W. Snow applauds the unveiling of the new $50 bill.* [Photo news release]. Retrieved January 29, 2009, from http://www.treas.gov/press/releases/js1478.htm

U.S. Department of the Treasury. (2006, August 23). *Photo: Treasury pitches in to improve deployment life for US soldiers.* [Photo news release]. Retrieved January 29, 2009, from http://www.treas.gov/press/releases/hp68.htm

U.S. National Aeronautic and Space Administration. (2004, March 4). *Student teams from your area race for the Moon to compete in NASA's 11th annual "Great Moonbuggy Race!"* [Radio interview release #04-083]. Retrieved December 16, 2008, from http://www.nasa.gov/centers/marshall/news/news/releases/2004/04-083.html

U.S. Postal Service. (2007, January 9). *Ella Fitzgerald stamp—Black Heritage series.* [Audio news release]. Retrieved December 13, 2008, from http://www.usps.com/communications/news/press/2007/audio/usps_anr_010907.htm

Wal-Mart Stores, Inc. (2008a, February 11). *Wal-Mart Foundation donates $250,000 to Museum of African American History.* [Online news release]. Retrieved February 15, 2009, from http://walmartstores.com/FactsNews/NewsRoom/7928.aspx

Wal-Mart Stores, Inc. (2008b, February 11). PHOTO ADVISORY—*Wal-Mart Foundation donates $250,000 to Museum of African American. . . .* [Online media

advisory]. Retrieved February 15, 2009, from http://www.reuters.com/article/
pressRelease/idUS188113+11-Feb-2008+PRN20080211

The Walt Disney Company. (2008, February 7). *American Idol attraction coming to
Disney's Hollywood studios.* [News release]. Retrieved November 3, 2010, from
http://www.wdwmagic.com/Attractions/The-American-Idol-Experience/
News/07Feb2008-American-Idol-attraction-coming-to-Disneys-Hollywood-
Studios.htm

Wilcox, D. L., & Cameron, G. T. (2008). *Public relations: Strategies and tactics* (9th
ed.). Boston: Allyn & Bacon.

Wisconsin Milk Marketing Board. (2008, March 17). *Dairy news: Nutrition program.*
[Video news release]. Retrieved January 29, 2009, from http://www.wisdairy.
com/AdvertisingAndNews/moredairynews.aspx?currentpage=5

Woodall, K. (2006). The future of business communication. In T. L. Gillis (Ed.), *The
IABC handbook of organizational communication: A guide to internal com-
munication, public relations, marketing, and leadership* (pp. 514–529). San
Francisco, CA: Jossey-Bass.

Woodall, K., & Smith, S. (2003). What will the future hold? *Communication World,
20*(2), 18–21.

4

Summaries

Just the Facts, Please

Today's most pressing problem, according to Davenport and Beck (2001), is that there is "not enough attention to meet the information demands of business and society" (p. 2). This "attention economy" is the result of the Information Age becoming an age of information overload. How can anyone wade through the "wealth" of information available on the Internet alone? Which sources are credible and reliable? Just how much do you have to sift through in order to find what you were looking for? We recognize that these questions are nothing new (see Wurman, 2001). With each new medium, the availability of news, facts (or factoids), and opinion has grown exponentially in quantity—expedited by search engines and techniques for optimizing texts' appearances in searches—although, some might argue, the quality of communication has withered.

In the age of business doing more (responsibilities, tasks, results) with less (resources, time, attention span), public relations practitioners have met the challenges of the attention economy with streamlined material for media gatekeepers and publics alike. It is clear from the previous chapter that the "bare bones" of news releases may be transformed ("repurposed") into new discourse conventions based on raw information alone (e.g., the media alert, the prepared statement). This tendency befits our times: a fast-food mentality toward information and its accessibility, which is unprecedented in history.

However, public relations people need to treat information as newsworthy, not data assembled in a particular organizational pattern. In this chapter, we focus on four discourse genres that, on a surface level, would seem to rely on the transmission of mere facts and potential sound bites. There is more here than meets the eye. Fact sheets, frequently asked questions (FAQs), fliers and posters, tip sheets, and biographical statements are a set of related discourse genres predicated on the assumption that a distillation of core information can accomplish more than simply gaining the attention of media contacts. As with the humble news release and its generic offspring (in the previous chapter), they present information in the service of persuasion—and in the service of the four epideictic functions outlined in Chapter 2. After a naturally brief description of the "summaries" genres for public relations, we discuss strategies that underlie the framing of information in readily accessible forms. We then conclude the chapter with key concerns that practitioners should have in decisions to use such genres.

Genres and Their Conventions

Summary discourse genres present core information about subjects and news in the service of cooperation and its relative purposes of persuasion, education, celebration, and so on. Across these genres is the common thread of "visual and intellectual digestibility." People want these genres, and organizations provide them with these genres because they work well as fast and direct ways to verbally and visually present sufficient details about something that can involve much more text than that for which someone has time to consume. When time is of the essence, fact sheets, fliers and posters, tip sheets, FAQs, and bios give audiences just the facts they need for the reasons they need them.

Fact Sheets

Fact sheets succinctly present only important facts (i.e., who, what, where, when, why, how, how much, etc.) in context about a complex subject that an organization faces. Indeed, fact sheets are simple and direct ways to cover a single topic. Fact sheets are typically pleasing and, most important, useful in their design so that verbal and visual content are easily identified and read. In this regard, a key character of fact sheets is the "chunking" of content, which involves the use of headings and subheadings, images and other graphic elements, and short paragraphs and bullet lists to condense complex notions into easily digestible bites of information that build on and complement one another. A descriptive title is often used and includes the words "fact sheet" to make it plain what the document is and what its function is. The responsible organization's logo, background information, and contact information should also be part of the content to ensure that readers know who has provided them with the discourse.

Fliers and Posters

From windshields and lamp posts to bulletin boards and direct mailings, fliers are, perhaps, the most ubiquitous genre of all because they can be made by anyone, and you do not need a computer to make them, but a mass-duplication method helps. Also referred to as "leaflets," fliers can be thought of as a minimalist version of a fact sheet. In the space of one side of a single sheet of paper (A-11 or 8.5" × 11", although other sizes may be used, such as 5.5" × 8.5" or 11" × 17"), a flier presents only the plainest facts about its subject—the five Ws and the H (i.e., what, who, where, when, why, and how). Plus, the verbal content should be presented within a utilitarian visual design and with visual elements that are enough to attract attention and present the very basics of the flier's subject. Some fliers include tear-off features so people can take contact or other information with them. On a larger scale, a more aesthetically developed version of fliers is posters. Because posters have a history of being treated as art, their content is much more highly visual, with verbal content being integrated within the overall design. If we think of posters as fliers on steroids, the visual muscle that posters exercise because of their aesthetics is key. However, like fliers, the five Ws and the H are essential to ensuring that audiences understand the essence of the poster's subject. Interestingly, because of their artistic nature, posters may not present all of the five Ws and the H because a poster may be focused on as few as one of them, such as a brand, event, or a single product (e.g., cars, the U.S. Postal Service's promotion of commemorative stamps, art museum exhibits) and doing so chiefly through visual content. Both posters and fliers promote something to people, and they know (either explicitly through the discourse or implicitly through personal experience or both) what it is, why it is important, who is responsible for it, when and where it can be experienced, and how it will benefit audiences. Both posters and fliers carry the weight of their promotional power in similar ways but in different sizes and degrees of visual design.

Tip Sheets

Tip sheets are simplified fact sheets but with a difference: They are meant to present the barest-bones recipe about what something is so that, in a kind of verbal "thumbnail sketch," the most basic of background data are given. Tip sheets serve simply to remind people about the basics of what they already know, whereas other summary discourse adds more detail beyond the basics. The metaphor of recipe is useful because tip sheets offer, in effect, a stepwise progression of ideas that build into the individual topics they address. Tips sheets are often the starting point for orienting someone or one's self on a subject in such a way that more detailed information in other discourse can be found more easily (see Stewart, 2000). Like other summary documents, an organization's identity, contact information, and, possibly, brief background should be given on tip sheets to show who is responsible for it and where to go for help.

Frequently Asked Questions

Frequently asked questions (FAQs) are indispensible documents for the preparation of other public relations discourse because of the intense process of viewing a subject from many viewpoints, especially publics and stakeholders. FAQs are lists of anticipated questions that target audiences might have and appropriate answers prepared in advance, usually to supplement an announcement or other PR discourse, to elucidate interrelated issues of some subject. Public relations practitioners brainstorm possible questions that publics may ask and work with subject-matter experts to augment those questions and, most important, devise answers to the questions. FAQs, then, serve the primary purpose of keeping an organization's officials "on message" about the news or other subject it is addressing. A secondary purpose of FAQs is to function as a reference document to which publics can turn for information presented in a question-and-answer (Q&A) format that gives them what they need. FAQs are typically formatted in a narrative form that follows a Q&A pattern. The title "Frequently Asked Questions" is used, and it may be accompanied by a statement about the precise subject, such as "Frequently Asked Questions about Product Safety." Organizational contact information may be given, and the organization's logo/brand identity should be present. Electronic versions of FAQs are available on websites that fulfill the same purpose and take advantage of the Internet's flexible technology for design and usability.

Biographical Statements

Biographical statements describe relevant experience and background of selected people who are cited experts or spokespeople on an issue. "Bios," as they are often called, are typically presented in narrative form, describing the subject person's career, areas of expertise, credentials, and personal background in reverse chronological order, starting with the current position and going backward in time. For example, a bio should address a person's present and past jobs by title and areas of responsibility for each; assert special areas of special experience and expertise; and show educational degrees, awards, and other achievements that support her or his credibility and suggest certain character traits. Sometimes additional information about someone's home town, family, hobbies, and so on may be added—usually as the last paragraph—to "humanize" the person. Bios can be produced in full color with the organization's brand identity, a professional photo of the person, and factual, personal, and formal information about the person. Web-based bios offer the most flexibility because of the variations of formatting and information linkages that the Internet allows, but the purpose of the genre remains the same. The style of writing for bios in hardcopy or electronic media can range from thorough and formal to cursory and casual. Either way and in between, bios must reflect the truth about someone's background in ways that most suit the occasion and the audience which will receive it.

Message Design

Information may be intrinsically interesting for individual people (e.g., sports trivia), but summaries of information should be relevant for both an organization and its audience(s). According to Gronbeck (1997), "News is never comprised of random or isolated data but always put into forms that give it social relevance and justify its publicness" (p. 363). In the previous chapter, we discussed Burke's concept of formal appeal. The principles of form and organization of ideas are central to summaries as genre because they (a) frame ways of understanding pieces of information, (b) draw on audience thought processes, (c) engage publics by getting them to read "between the lines," and (d) thereby unite organizations and publics through the assumption of shared values. These effects are achieved through the four epideictic functions in the following order of importance: epistemic, performative, preservative, and celebratory. Because these genres rely on audiences making connections, the latter two functions depend on the same rhetorical processes as the first two. Therefore, the bulk of this section is devoted to epideictic's epistemic and performative functions of summaries.

1. Epistemic Function

Summary genres are first explanatory and then sometimes educational. As such, the genres featured in this chapter not only function at the level of familiar, usable patterns, but audiences also may process the information based on what they already believe and what they have accepted through previous corporate messages and/or is relevant to their particular interests. The framing of ideas and the organization of information there is based on how human beings naturally perceive the world around them and how they learn new information to assimilate it with what they already know as "facts" about a given subject. Authors have a responsibility to audiences for making connections between new information and old, known information. This approach is called the "given-new contract," and it is instrumental for achieving cohesion—understanding and retaining new information an audience does not know by connecting it effectively with old information that an audience already knows and accepts as true (Clark & Haviland, 1977; Kent, 1984; Vande Kopple, 1984).

Regardless of genre, human beings generally process information in a fairly efficient manner. We cannot possibly handle all of the stimuli in the world around us. This is particularly true in societies where the explosion of the Information Age has resulted in more bits of information than any of us could perceive in a lifetime. At a fundamental level, the given-new contract is at play as we choose what "bits" to pay attention to, organize them in some meaningful way based on a variety of factors, and determine which sets of information to retain as part of our experience from moment to moment. In terms of information processing, we engage in selective exposure, perception, and attention (Ferguson, 1999). *Selective exposure* entails the choice of what we pay attention to, *selective perception* the organization of it, and *selective attention* "what we want to see and what we expect to see" (p. 149). This all happens very quickly. Indeed, Weick (1979) argues that the process of retaining experience is actually retrospective: We may do these three steps in reverse order so that we can manage our experiences and organize them in memory for later retrieval. The process of perception is, therefore, critical to understanding how to influence audiences with the way public relations professionals strategically present information so that message retention is encouraged, fulfilling the given-new contract in effective ways. The process of presenting and organizing ideas in this way is called *framing*.

Framing is a way of presenting information so that it "provides context and promotes a certain understanding of a phenomenon" (Ihlen & Nitz, 2008). FAQs utilize this function at two levels of form: the minor form of a particular question leading to a specific answer, and the larger pattern of organization, the ordering of the questions themselves. General Motors (2008), for example, applies this approach by providing answers to questions about its Mobility Reimbursement Program, which deals with the extras necessary for persons with disabilities to be able to drive or ride in a General Motors vehicle. Although the FAQ is on the Web, it still utilizes the minor form of a question that the consumer logically would ask (e.g., "What adaptive equipment qualifies for reimbursement?"), which is followed by a concise five-sentence paragraph with a hotlink to a list of eligible equipment. The development of the questions and answers presumes that the audience would ask these same questions and be looking for the types of information found in the answers. These questions may be organized in a variety of ways. Yahoo! (2009) organizes questions concerning its Flickr® photo and video editing program according to topics such as, "Content Filters," "Photos," "Sharing," and "Using Flickr Tools." The overall pattern of organization may follow any recognizable pattern familiar from other discourse genres human beings have encountered: inductive, deductive, chronological, problem-solution, and so on—at the very least, topically.

Similarly, fact sheets and tip sheets orient the reader to the desired understanding of the bulleted points of information through framing opening paragraph(s):

> Should I disconnect the cell phone? Boycott voice mail? Throw the PDA out the window? As a chaotic 2008 comes to a close and workers resolve to regain sanity in 2009, where do they go for answers to questions about how to cope with information overload? For more than 30 years, Xerox Corporation (NYSE: XRX) social scientists have been studying how workers communicate, organize and generally get things done. In fact, they pioneered the science of ethnography, where researchers track the habits of workers as they go about their day.
>
> Inspired by their Future of Work study, here are nine tips to help you save time and manage information overload. (Xerox Corporation, 2008, paras. 1–3)

Xerox's nine tips that follow the paragraphs are labeled quite simply: "Breathe," "Simplify Your Schedule," and so on. Media advisories (discussed in Chapter 3) share this characteristic with summaries, incidentally, of an opening paragraph or so to frame the bulleted points, but their other characteristics and functions place them within the category of news genres. It is important to note in this example that Xerox labeled this document a "news release" when, in actuality, it is a tip sheet because it fulfills the conventions for it. It is apparent that the choice to call this document something other than what it is was driven more by a motive to gain media attention for its content that is not, strictly speaking, truly news as much as it is "evergreen" information that applies at all times.

Summaries as genres thus are governed in part by how audiences process information both visually and verbally, and framing is key to gaining attention and shaping audience usage of information found within fact sheets, FAQs, and so on. Organizational patterns common to how human beings organize ideas, often drawn from other discourse conventions for other contexts (see Bernhardt, 1986; Keyes, 1987; Kostelnick & Hassett, 2003), suggest to the public relations practitioner how to best present information that gains the audience's attention by selecting information and perceiving it in a way that the audience might have done had they gathered the information on their own. In this way, public relations practitioners must pay close attention to the development of messages in their verbal content and visual presentation *simultaneously*. This intersection of the visual and verbal is the realm of document design, and ample resources are available that address it more credibly than can be done here (see Jacobson, 1999; Mortimer, 2003; Romano & Riordan, 2007; Schriver, 1997; Tufte, 1990; Wurman, 1989/1990, 1992).

The educational dimension of the epistemic function occurs when summaries introduce new information that audiences must incorporate into existing memory structures with old information. Without getting into too much detail about theories of cognitive psychology, schema theory helps explain how this works. According to schema theory, human beings store information in meaningful, organized patterns based on experience. (This is a natural extension of our discussion of the perception process.) When the brain processes new information, that information is compared to the patterns in memory or schemata. A schema, then, is a set of thoughts that are organized to form assumptions about our world (Axelrod, 1973). If the new information fits current assumptions, it reinforces the existing schema. If the new information does not fit existing schemata, the receiver may do one of several things: (a) combine the new information with the old; (b) reject either old or new information by comparing the credibility of their sources; (c) fit the information to the schema that most closely accommodates it; or (d) modify and extend a schema by filling in gaps suggested by the new information, assign higher credibility to its source, and thereby bolster confidence in the new interpretation of things expressed within the schema.

The key at this point is schema theory's utility to practitioners as they design messages. Kent (1987) explains that schema theory can drive the writing process for technical documentation because authors understand the audience's schemata and, therefore, prepare information in ways that help people better connect the dots between what they know and what they are coming to know. For example, a World Wildlife Fund (n.d.) fact sheet links global warming to its impact on poverty around the world. If a person has doubts about global warming's effects, the following information might evoke one of the choices just described:

> Climate change has started to affect weather patterns, sea levels, seasons, and both glacial and polar ice. The global weather system is threatening to spin out of control. For people this means that seasons become unpredictable, farming becomes riskier, freshwater supplies become unreliable, storms and rising sea levels threaten to take away whole islands and coastal areas. Survival under such conditions becomes ever

more difficult—in the last few years, there have been more environmental refugees then at any other time. (p. 1)

People who doubt global warming's predicted catastrophic effects would not necessarily buy into the final conclusion because their schemata disagree with the premises expressed in the previous sentences. However, those publics whose schemata dovetail with the premises would be more likely to accept the link to world poverty.[1] The epistemic function therefore leads to the performative function and its considerations of audience adaptation because "formalized information is structured and unitized in some socially understandable way" (Gronbeck, 1997, p. 362; italics deleted).

2. Performative Function

Summary genres fulfill all three of this epideictic function's dimensions (in order of importance): rhetorical, identity management, and political. The political dimension, which allows organizations and other sources of public relations activities to avoid the appearance of advocating positions on public issues, even when they are informing people of ideas associated with those issues, typically is handled through the framing of the message (see previous section). In this section, then, we focus on the rhetorical and identity management dimensions.

Summary genres are first and foremost rhetorical because they require public relations practitioners to research audiences and adapt what information is explicitly communicated to the audience's beliefs, attitudes, and values. This may sound quite similar to our discussion of schema theory because such adaptation requires the integration of information with the audience's mindset, but there is more to audience appeal than this. Information presented for information's sake, quite obviously, has no place in public relations message design. At the very least, however, it is important for public relations practitioners to appreciate *why* summaries appeal to audiences. To reduce ideas to mere data runs the risk of what Kenneth Burke (1931/1968) called the psychology of information, which, he argued, leads to "an atrophy of form" (p. 33) when writers rely on information alone to convey ideas. Not taking the audience into account reduces facts to sterile information presented for its own sake and without purpose or consideration of its utility.

Consider how important it is for communication professionals to put themselves in the place of the audience when crafting a FAQ. The Internal Revenue Service (United States, 2010) organized its online FAQ into two groups of questions: those most frequently asked and all questions previously asked, grouped by category. By basing the webpage on what taxpayers already have asked, answers are tailored to that public's information needs and the ways people think of tax issues. This alignment of an organization's interests with those of a particular public is what some readers may recognize as public relations' use of Burke's (1950/1969) concept of *identification*: "A is not identical with his colleague, B. But insofar as their interests are joined, A is *identified* with B" (p. 19). Bios, FAQs, and the like rely on Burke's most basic form of identification: identification through similarity. For example, fact sheets about the organization present information of wide interest to various publics, particularly investors. Such fact sheets vary widely in design and length. Some companies rely on text alone, while others employ color and graphics. For investors, Kraft's (2008) fact sheet is six pages long and uses pie charts and other features to convey ideas.

How fact sheets, FAQs, and bios are framed, therefore, has implications for how audiences process information and assimilate it, as pointed out in our discussion of these genres' epistemic function:

> *Relevant* information has . . . been constructed and structured so as to be linked to the lives of the people to whom it is presented. Unless some datum can be linked to my country, region, government, bank, church, family, health and well-being, or livelihood, I will probably care little about it. (Gronbeck, 1997, p. 362)

Rhetorically, then, summaries require audience adaptation. We suggest, however, that audiences also make inferences about the source of the information's intent behind the message based on its content. Summaries therefore serve the identity management dimension of the performative function.

As noted in Chapter 3, messages imply the character of its source. The first persona and the identity management dimension of summaries often are less apparent than in news genres. Similar to the ways in which these genres fulfill their epistemic function, summaries rely on audiences connecting ideas in ways favorable to the source's image (and, by extension, reputation). Some messages, of course, must be more explicit about the character of the organization behind the message (e.g., bios). Sirius Satellite Radio's (n.d.) bios of its management team begin with a paragraph that identifies each person's role and function within the company. What follows the opening, however, are paragraphs that easily could be converted into bulleted chunks of facts of each person's credentials that would fit a fact sheet. Their current responsibilities, the various broadcasting industry positions each has held, and the length of time in business together invite publics to ascribe high credibility to the management team. In such cases, the person writing the message should recognize what inferences publics will make based on prior knowledge (i.e., the intersection of the given-new contract and schema theory). In traditional argument, these are called "warrant-using" arguments (Toulmin, 1958) because they connect a general conclusion (in this case, the inference that Sirius has highly qualified broadcast professionals) to the evidence (the credentials). The warrant would be that the amount of credentials, the high-profile media company names found within them, the years of experience, and so on are what people look for when we assess the professionalism of a company. The various criteria publics have for judging what constitutes good management therefore are schema that publics use as warrants to fill in the information left out of summaries.

In the case of product recalls, organizations may use tip sheets, fact sheets, or FAQs to convey the most important information to consumers. When Peanut Corporation of America was forced to recall various product lines because of a salmonella outbreak, PetSmart (2009) was among the many companies alerting consumers to possible dangers: ". . . we are working closely with all of our vendors to verify whether there are any implications for our customers and their pets through the products sold in our stores. Although we're not aware of any confirmed illness related to products we offer, we voluntarily removed the below products as a precaution" (paras. 1-2). The online fact sheet included a table of the products recalled and also a section of FAQs most pertinent to salmonella and what to do if their pets should become ill. The links also led to other facts that followed the question-and-answer format used in the sheet.

This final example provides good evidence of how audience warrants may provide links to identification between inferences made about PetSmart (2009) and the schemata in publics' minds. For example, the worries that consumers have about their pets may be summarized in the resulting warrant, "I care about my pet's health." The questions, answers, and reassurance that PetSmart presents through its fact sheet provide audiences with evidence that the company cares about pets as much as consumers; indeed, PetSmart is "deeply concerned," and its "first thoughts are for the well-being of you and your pets" (para. 13). Like the Xerox example, PetSmart also mislabeled the document as a "news release" when it truly fulfills the conventions for a fact sheet. PetSmart's fact sheet touches on many points that could make up schemata of what makes for responsible pet owners and responsible pet stores. The likely result when the company handles a recall carefully and courteously: an identification, a meeting of minds between company and consumer.

3. Preservative Function

The PetSmart example and others in this chapter help explain why cohesion, self-persuasion, and repurposing (in that order) are important dimensions of the preservative function of summaries. By simply paying attention to how particular publics organize information, incorporate it into existing thoughts, and how they perceive organizations (i.e., image) and connect those activities, practitioners can create more cohesive messages. This is particularly true in the case of information about a company's reputation that has been sustained through summaries and news genres (among others), for example. The key points in the following bio should be well established in most readers' minds:

> Martha's creative vision is the blueprint for Martha Stewart Living Omnimedia and the expansive multimedia and merchandising portfolio that includes award-winning magazines such as Martha Stewart Living and Martha Stewart Weddings; the nationally syndicated, Emmy Award-winning television series "The Martha Stewart Show"; Martha Stewart Living Radio on Sirius XM; the marthastewart.com website; best-selling books. . . . (Martha Stewart Living Omnimedia, 2009)

Not only has the information we know about Martha Stewart been preserved, it has provided cohesion across countless messages—to the point that the words "Martha Stewart" serve as a schema packed with a variety of stored cognitions.

Such schemata depend on audiences receiving, organizing, and storing information in ways that create a relationship, a sense of identification, with an organization (even for publics who don't care for Martha, in which case a public that identifies in its common distaste for her). For those who find the information bios and other summary genres of interest, the degree to which the audience brings its experiences, schemata, and thoughts to bear on filling in details is the essence of self-persuasion when applied to publics. Publics cooperate in the communication through such mental "work" that they participate in their own persuasion (at the very least, persuaded to accept new information as important to retain). Even the recognition of familiar information may serve to reinforce its importance.

The point may be obvious, but summaries invite repurposing. They are repositories of facts and information on which good relationships with publics depend. Bios, FAQs, and fact and tip sheets, if anything, only require updating. Their preservative function is an "evergreen" quality that makes them ideal components for press kits, as any good practitioner knows. Our earlier discussion of their epistemic and performative functions demonstrate how much an important repository of potentially potent material they actually can be—as we have argued, a less obvious point because our focus on public relations genres as epideictic has uncovered summaries' deeper strategic importance.

4. Celebratory Function

Of course, because summaries are somewhat minimalist in form, the celebratory function of epideictic would not appear to be present. Once again, look below the tactical surface to discover the strategic axiological and ritualistic dimensions that summaries may perform as genres. As Gronbeck (1997) observes, "*Public* information is made up of data that are worthy of communal sharing" (p. 362). Summaries are value-laden because their contents imply certain core principles that an organization wants to represent and an audience may identify with. The Sirius Satellite Radio bios mentioned earlier probably would not appeal to many consumers; the values embodied in the job descriptions and credentials, however, would appeal to broadcast media junkies and industry trade media contacts.

It might be a bit of a stretch, but there is some ritual involved in today's society's penchant for facts: trivia, factoids, and so on. The information age requires genres that are quickly scanned, easily processed, and readily connected to all the other schemata of information that people amazingly keep organized in their heads. The fact that these summary genres have become standard practice in providing media and publics with the information they want suggests that these genres will retain stable forms and functions for decades to come.

Therefore, although summaries may seem to be mere collections of facts, their functions as epideictic discourse make them far richer than we might suspect. Bios, FAQs, and fact and tip sheets are primarily epistemic because they use framing to explain and shape ideas in ways that are conducive to audiences' mental frameworks. In some cases, they provide new information and therefore educate. Adaptation to audience schemata become part of the important performative function that these genres share because they rhetorically invite audiences to rely more on what they already have organized through learned patterns and those they create through perception (i.e., schemata). In turn, the performative function's rhetorical dimension works in tandem with the rhetorical to build organizational image in ways that encourage audiences to identify with it. After all, the audience has to "connect the dots" by filling in the gaps that summary genres leave open for them to relate to how they already perceive the world to be. The lesser functions, preservative and celebratory, naturally arise out of summary genres' prevailing epistemic and performative functions.

Strategic Planning Implications

What makes summary genres so useful is their succinctness. They quench the thirst for instant gratification of information in ways that other genres cannot. Summary genres possess and project in their verbal content and visual design enough information about topics of any degree of complexity so that audiences can both build and extend on their foundation of knowledge related to the subject. These basic traits stem from the two epideictic functions that summary genres fulfill simultaneously—epistemic and performative—and benefit from the subsequent support of the preservative and celebratory functions. Crable (1982) argues that all information can be contested, and in terms of strategic implications, summary genres stand as quintessential examples of information used in the support of communicative purposes.

Summary genres present facts, evidence, and other information in a controlled way. That is, the organization that publishes any summary genre publishes and disseminates it exactly as it wants to target audiences without intervening parties. This controlled nature of summary genres gives organizations an advantage in producing documents that focus on subjects in the ways they want to and, most important, frame the information in ways that most effectively work for target audiences and how they use information. Merely naming a document a genre other than what it truly is (e.g., labeling a fact sheet or a tip sheet a news release) does not that genre make, but such a misnomer reveals motives for obtaining attention from a particular audience, such as journalists. Strategically speaking, then, summary genres can be used alone or especially in conjunction with other genres; both uses befit communication plans. Summary genres must be able to stand on their own and can act as supporting documents that present core data, facts, evidence, and so on that are essential and important to highlight in particular communications situations requiring the building of knowledge in tune with audience's schemata. In short, summary genres essentially serve as documents of argumentative support to organizational claims about a subject and any public debate about it.

Interestingly, there is a bigger, more strategic role that summary genres play. The key to effective strategy for summary genres is a highly integrated use of ways to direct perceptions, attention, and retention with schema theory, all of which are essential to the epistemic function, which is primary to this family of epideictic discourse. As Crable (1982) explains, once debate has settled, information becomes facts that we assume. Based on audience analysis, these facts, and how they are organized into schemata of interconnected information that enable people to manage their perceptions, attention, and retention of them, are the building blocks of warrants that audiences can invoke when framing their own ideas. The schemata are reinforced by the document design, which helps lead audiences through the text and gives them cues to use content as they wish. Summary genres, therefore, become warrant-using arguments because they rely on cognitive structures that people have retained in order to make sense of the world. These structures and the inferences made with them when faced with missing information are the stuff from which identifications are achieved. At times the ambiguity of connections can thwart an organization's intent to be perceived in a certain way and connect with a key public in a certain way. But that is why it is so important to decide which of these genres provides enough structure for effective message content for audiences to fill in the gaps in preferred ways.

What becomes most important, then, in the design of messages for summary genres is the interrelationship between the epistemic and performative functions and their relationship to the cultural values held by target publics. Certainly, practitioners must take into account such values in all message design, but the limited amount of information presented through summary genres requires audiences to read into the text, filtered through their own experience, secondhand information, and the sociocultural context (see Moffitt, 1999; Williams & Moffitt, 1997). To a large degree, the genre families represented in other chapters embody choices made to produce what McGee (1990) calls "finished discourse" (p. 280). Audiences may pay attention to a text (its verbal content and visual presentation) to determine the value of the ideas presented to them. In contrast, summary genres present messages that are made up of the "fragments" that constitute copy or talking points found in genres that require more complete messages. We must recognize that, for audiences, "the discourse derives its rhetorical power more from the *silence* of the cultural imperative than from the imperative itself" (McGee, 1990, p. 281). In other words, the impact of culture and discourse conventions on audiences' interpretations of messages is greatest when there is the least but most salient amount of information. In comparison with other genres, summaries most strikingly demonstrate how public relations not only influences culture, but also how public relations must serve as a reflection of it.

In this chapter, we presented more strategic ways to think about and design summaries of information. These genres need not function as mere collections of data and sound bites. Indeed, such a view would be a type of *informationism*: "a 'faith' in the collection and dissemination of information as a route to social progress and personal happiness" (Schultze, 2002, p. 21). Summary genres are much more argumentatively important as both supplemental documents of evidential support and stand-alone "primers" to subjects that audiences use to build and extend their knowledge. At a minimum, summaries provide answers to the essential questions of life (the five Ws and the H), which were presented as parallel to the five members of Burke's pentad in Chapter 3. Whether supplementary or stand-alone documents, summary genres for public relations beg the question, "What else is going on?" A natural response to such a question is to tell something of a story, and the next set of genres allows practitioners to do just that and to do so in more narratively dynamic and effective ways, which summary and news genres cannot do.

Note

1. Acceptance of the connection between climate change and increasing world poverty also can be explained through Social Judgment Theory (Griffin, 2008). If the audience can organize the information into patterns consistent with existing beliefs and attitudes, the more likely they are to accept new information presented within the message. This process is called *assimilation.*

References

Axelrod, R. (1973). Schema theory: An information processing model of perception and cognition. *American Political Science Review, 67,* 1248–1266.

Bernhardt, S. A. (1986). Seeing the text. *College Composition & Communication, 37,* 66–78.

Burke, K. (1968). *Counter-statement.* Berkeley, CA: University of California Press. (Original work published 1931)

Burke, K. (1969). *A rhetoric of motives.* Berkeley, CA: University of California Press. (Original work published 1950)

Clark, H. H., & Haviland, S. E. (1977). Comprehension and the given-new contract. In R. O. Freedle (Ed.), *Discourse production and comprehension* (pp. 1–40). Norwood, NJ: Ablex.

Crable, R. E. (1982). Knowledge as status: On argument and epistemology. *Communication Monographs, 49,* 249–262.

Davenport, T. H., & Beck, J. C. (2001). *The attention economy: Understanding the new currency of business.* Boston: Harvard Business School Press.

Ferguson, S. D. (1999). *Communication planning: An integrated approach.* Thousand Oaks, CA: Sage.

General Motors Corporation. (2008). *GM mobility reimbursement program FAQ.* Retrieved January 28, 2009, from http://www.gm.com/vehicles/services/gm_mobility/faq/

Griffin, E. (2008). *A first look at communication theories* (7th ed.). New York: McGraw-Hill.

Gronbeck, B. E. (1997). Tradition and technology in local newscasts: The social psychology of form. *Sociological Quarterly, 38,* 361–374.

Ihlen, Ø., & Nitz, M. (2008). Framing contests in environmental disputes: Paying attention to media and cultural master frames. *International Journal of Strategic Communication, 2,* 1–18.

Jacobson, R. (Ed.). (1999). *Information design.* Cambridge, MA: MIT Press.

Kent, T. (1987). Schema theory and technical communication. *Journal of Technical Writing & Communication, 17*, 243–252.

Kent, T. L. (1984). Paragraph production and the given-new contract. *Journal of Business Communication, 21*(4), 45–66.

Keyes, E. (1987). Information design: Maximizing the power and potential of electronic publishing equipment. *IEEE Transactions on Professional Communication, 30*(1), 32–37.

Kolstelnick, C., & Hassett, M. (2003). *Shaping information: The rhetoric of visual conventions.* Carbondale, IL: Southern Illinois University Press.

Kraft. (2008). *Kraft at a glance—2007 consumer sector data.* Retrieved February 16, 2009, from http://www.kraft.com/assets/pdf/2008_Kraft_Fact_Sheet.pdf

Martha Stewart Living Omnimedia, Inc. (2009). *About Martha Stewart.* Retrieved February 17, 2009, from http://www.marthastewart.com/martha-stewart

McGee, M. C. (1990). Text, context, and the fragmentation of contemporary culture. *Western Journal of Speech Communication, 54*, 274–289.

Moffitt, M. A. (1999). *Campaign strategies and message design.* Westport, CT: Greenwood Press.

Mortimer, P. (2003). *Document design primer.* Alexandria, VA: Graphic Arts Technical Foundation.

PetSmart Store Support Group. (2009, January 20). *PetSmart voluntarily recalls Grreat Choice° Dog Biscuits.* [Fact sheet]. Retrieved February 17, 2009, from http://phx.corporate-ir.net/phoenix.zhtml?c=196265&p =irol-newsArticle&ID =1246514&highlight

Romano, F., & Riordan, M. (Eds.). (2007). *Pocket pal: The handy book of graphic arts production* (20th ed.). Memphis, TN: International Paper.

Schriver, K. A. (1997). *Dynamics in document design: Creating texts for readers.* New York: Wiley.

Schultze, Q. J. (2002). *Habits of the high-tech heart: Living virtuously in the information age.* Grand Rapids, MI: Baker Academic.

Sirius Satellite Radio. (n.d.). *Management bios.* Retrieved February 16, 2009, from http://www.sirius.com/aboutus/bios

Stewart, J. (2000). *The basics of tip sheets: Get publicity by providing publications with useful information.* Retrieved December 2, 2008, from http://entrepreneur.com/marketing/publicrelations/gettingpress/article35216.html

Toulmin, S. E. (1958). *The uses of argument.* New York: Cambridge University Press.

Tufte, E. R. (1990). *Envisioning information.* Cheshire, CT: Graphics Press.

Vande Kopple, W. J. (1984). Something old, something new: Functional sentence perspective. In R. L. Graves (Ed.), *Rhetoric and composition: A sourcebook for teachers and writers.* Upper Montclair, NJ: Boynton/Cook. (Reprinted from *Research in the Teaching of English, 17*, 85–99.)

U.S. Department of the Treasury, Internal Revenue Service. (2010, March 15). *Frequently asked tax questions and answers.* Retrieved October 28, 2010, from http://www.irs.gov/faqs/index.html

Weick, K. E. (1979). *The social psychology of organizing* (2nd ed.). New York: McGraw-Hill.

Williams, S. L., & Moffitt, M. A. (1997). Corporate image as an impression formation process: Prioritizing personal, organizational, and environmental audience factors. *Journal of Public Relations Research, 9,* 237–258.

World Wildlife Fund. (n.d.). *Global warming and poverty.* [Fact sheet]. Retrieved January 27, 2009, from http://assets.panda.org/downloads/factsheet_on_poverty.pdf

Wurman, R. S. (1990). *Information anxiety: What to do when information doesn't tell you what you need to know.* New York: Bantam Books. (Original work published 1989)

Wurman, R. S. (1992). *Follow the yellow brick road: Learning to give, take, & use instructions.* New York: Bantam Books.

Wurman, R. S. (2001). *Information anxiety 2.* Indianapolis, IN: Que.

Xerox Corporation. (2008, December 2). *Overloaded with information? Get back to business in 2009.* [Online tip sheet]. Retrieved December 19, 2008, from http://www.xerox.com/go/xrx/template/inv_rel_newsroom.jsp?app=Newsroom&ed_name=NR_2008Dec2_Xerox_Information_Overload_Tips&format=article&view=newsrelease&Xcntry=USA&Xlang=en_US

Yahoo! Inc. (2009). *Flickr help/FAQ.* Retrieved January 28, 2009, from http://www.flickr.com/help/faq/

5

Features

The Stories Behind the Story

There is always more going on than what is announced in various public relations discourse. "Features" genres give organizations opportunities to present the stories behind the news they share with their publics and stakeholders. Features function as focused forms of communication that reveal the inner workings, thinking, people, and genius of an organization and its offerings. This kind of "pulling back the curtain" of a corporate context expands the content and context of what external (and sometimes internal) publics know about an organization. The revelations, then, are potentially potent or even profound as the stories are provided, picked up, published, and pondered by people throughout the process.

Genres and Their Conventions

Features genres are chiefly informative in nature, and they can be easily adapted to persuasive and other purposes. These genres include matte releases, backgrounders, white papers, case studies, and articles. Among all these genres, the basic corporate desire to inspire cooperation between an organization and its publics is realized through detailed accounts of what has been going on in and for that organization. This approach feeds the hunger of publics and stakeholders for information that reduces uncertainty, fills in gaps, presents new ideas and insights, and suggests greater opportunities for an organization and its audiences alike.

Matte Releases

Matte releases (also spelled "mat" or "MAT" releases) are complete and concise print-news stories written by public relations professionals then laid out by an organization such as North American Precis Syndicate (NAPS), PR Newswire, NewsUSA, and others, which distribute these stories free (similar to news releases) to news organizations according to the client's target audiences. (Matte release companies can also offer to write the stories.) Written in a journalistic style, usually following a problem/need-solution-benefit formula (including expert quotes and where to get more information), the content of these "prefabricated" stories generally concerns consumer-oriented matters that are not anchored in time (i.e., they are "evergreen") and feature an organization and its product or service as part of the story. The finished stories are camera-ready, including any art or sidebars, which allows editors to drop in these stories on a page "as is" or add to them with little editing, if an advertiser pulled its ad or space somehow opens at the last minute. Common users of matte releases are community and suburban newspapers, but larger ones in the top 100 national papers have been known to use them as well.

Backgrounders

Backgrounders specifically define an issue and then comprehensively and concisely present it without editorializing. The main purpose for backgrounders is to fill in the gaps in other public relations discourse, such as press releases or statements. Backgrounders provide readers with basic foundational knowledge about a subject so that it can be understood in context and more consideration of options and alternative views can be made and applied. Backgrounders are like fact sheets on steroids because they add important reasoning and contextual and, perhaps, historical dimensions while providing readers with background information and source material on a subject and possible next steps. At the same time, backgrounders often reflect an organization's particular views of subjects along with other views, and the discourse serves as a way to document and share the principles of and supporting data for those views. In this way, backgrounders focus on a thesis about a subject and develop all sides of an argument that is more informative or educational than persuasive. Organizations use backgrounders as foundational documents on which other discourse can be developed. Backgrounders, then, are concerned more about the state of things now and, potentially, the state of things to come. The content of backgrounders can be both verbal and visual, and it is laid out effectively in a format that allows for easy reading. Backgrounders are usually published in a manner similar to traditional essays and include abstract/executive summary, bibliography, appendices, and so on. Cover pages are typically used to give the title, authors, date, and contact and other information along with the organization's logo.

White Papers

White papers are heavily researched and treat a subject "objectively" by presenting a favorable balance of the issues upheld by an organization, opponents, and target publics. The piece reflects a level of and relies on research and analysis like that applied in scholarly work. White papers (also known as "position papers") focus on subjects that emphasize an organization's perspective to an extent that does not cross the line into a veiled sales pitch. In this way, white papers resemble backgrounders but with an important twist: They advance a position and argue for it and requisite action within the larger context of available options and alternative thinking. IBM is credited with inventing this genre in the late 1970s, and organizations that feel they have something profound to add to specialized knowledge about a subject vital to them, such as industry analysis firms, choose to produce and publish these academic analyses so that the organization can influence others' thinking about the subject on a more public level than just within its small circle of business partners and sympathizers. The best white papers tend to be those that soundly advocate for particular matters while also treating alternative views and options reasonably well with proper evidence and effective reasoning—ultimately affirming the paper's central thesis through a combination of persuasive and informative arguments and proposing next steps. White papers, like backgrounders, are usually published as traditional essays (including abstract/executive summary, bibliography, appendices, etc.) with basic cover pages that give the title, authors, date, and contact and other information along with the organization's logo.

Case Studies

Case studies sufficiently and concisely describe individual customers' applications and benefits of an organization's product or service. These short stories work as documented testimonials of an organization's clients and how well served they were by what the organization provided them. Case studies, sometimes called "case histories," follow a predictable and simple pattern of problem-solution-results-value. An organization may have a happy client who agrees to be featured in a case study, and the case study begins with a summary of the problem the client needed to be solved—and only the organization's product or service was the answer. The solution is described in sufficient detail and named specifically because a given product or service was used. Next the results the client received are documented and explained. The case study ends with clear statements about the added value the solution provided for the client, which can be on financial and nonfinancial levels. This story includes statements of the client's personal experiences and positive support about an organization and what it offered for the featured customer. Case studies also usually include a brief summary outline of the problem, solution, results, and added value before the detailed story begins. Visually speaking, case studies are usually not more than two pages long and can be laid out in various ways, but the key is usability. Headings, color, graphics, layout, and other facets of effective document design are all critical to help readers follow the story and find what they want.

Articles

Articles are written by or ghostwritten for organizational leaders or authored by third-party "experts" or journalists to advance specific and detailed messages on an issue to readers of selected publications. Such articles can be published as bylined pieces to develop a particular thesis (e.g., feature stories; organizational, product/service, or personal profiles; histories; how-to or Q&A pieces) or to advance an opinion in response to a specific issue raised in a periodical or by the public at large (e.g., letters to editors or "op-ed" essays). In general, articles help raise the subject organization's visibility and tout its expertise on the subject to target audiences. Articles follow traditional journalistic practices and, especially, the stylistic and news orientations of target publications. An appropriate "angle" (e.g., timeliness, prominence, proximity/localness, significance/relevance, unusualness/rarity, human interest, conflict, first-to-market/first achiever) must be clear and developed effectively to make the story attractive to editors and their publications' readers. Illustrative material, such as photos, graphics, and so on, can make a story more attractive and potent, and rhetorical devices, such as anecdotes, examples, statistics, quotations, and so on, help enliven the content for readers.

More so than other public relations discourse, features genres stress two of the most important assumptions referred to in Chapter 2: Discourse genres exist because of the recurring confluence of types of situations that suggest appropriate symbolic responses to them, and the purposes that drive the use of a particular genre are governed by sound rhetorical strategies, not simply an adherence to a familiar pattern of organization. Backgrounders, white papers, case studies, and articles are means to particular ends because they are targeted to specific media channels (e.g., a trade publication, a particular newspaper or magazine) and typically specialized audiences. The purposes to which these genres may be put to use vary widely, but the approach used is narrative in form.

Message Design

People are natural storytellers (Fisher, 1987) and respond naturally well to stories. Stories and their narrative structures are grounded in the appeal to form mentioned earlier in our discussion of news genres (Chapter 3). Part of the appeal of features genres is based on our familiarity with their patterns, which can be understood as literary genres. Gronbeck (1997) argues that news (and, by extension, other public relations genres that present news-worthy information) follows this basic principle:

> *Formalized* information has been structured and unitized in some socially understandable way. Most news is structured narratively, as stories about people doing something to some effect, that is, as a coher-ent series of events with beginnings, middles, and endings enacted by particular people with specific purposes. News also, however, can be structured as an announcement (a recitation of coherent facts about some present or future event), or an anecdote (a humorous, heart-warming, or angering story about someone's trials or triumphs in life). (p. 362)

In this chapter, however, we are less concerned with the particular forms of features genres and the stories they contain than we are their epideictic functions. Along the way, we certainly will refer to minor forms, such as a story's "characters" used within any narrative, but only when they are related to the functions we have employed in other chapters. In the case of features genres, epideictic's performative function predominates. In order of importance, narrative's remaining functions are celebratory, epistemic, and preservative. Within each, we address how these stories work pragmati-cally—how features genres serve not only to accomplish particular organi-zational objectives, but also as a narrative means to fulfill these functions.

1. Performative

For any story, the bond created between writer and reader is an important concern, just as it is in literary theory (see Booth, 1983; Eagleton, 2008; Tompkins, 1980). For public relations message design, the parallel relation-ship between an organization and its target audience makes epideictic's performative function of paramount concern. Accordingly, the rhetorical appeal to the audience is its most important dimension. Second, although the identity-management dimension might be thought to come next for nar-rative genres, because narratives are filled with heroes, villains, and other such characters, the political dimension follows instead. In order to increase the credibility of the organization, the political dimension, therefore, precedes identity management.

Rhetorical dimension. The importance of a feature genre's appeal to an audience's interests and needs cannot be underestimated. Narrative specialists in English and communication studies agree on this point. For example, Frye (1982) and Fisher (1987) both argue that stories must be understood not only in terms of their narrative structure, but also in terms of their potential effects on audiences. In other words, "Does the story make sense to the target public?" "Does it evoke the meanings that were intended by the public relations practitioner?" These questions are just as important as, "Does the story 'constitute a coherent story'?" (Fisher, 1987, p. 64). By using features genres' epideictic functions well, an answer of "yes" to all three questions should be possible.

How a story makes sense, what Fisher (1987) calls "narrative probability," is judged by its "truthfulness and reliability" (p. 47)—its internal consistency. One of the criteria to determine whether a story hangs together is useful in determining potential audience effect: Fisher's concept of material coherence, which is judged "by comparing and contrasting stories told in other discourses" (p. 47). This point is especially important in public relations and the nearly 40 discourse genres in which practitioners must be competent. For example, regardless of the type, features genres hang together with similar appeals to audience interests. To target a well-defined audience that is a hallmark of good features genre writing, context is key:

> It has been almost 25 years since antenna-free TV was introduced in Germany. In July 1982, television and radio programs were received in German living rooms via cable for the first time. Within ten years, 34 percent of households had bid farewell to terrestrial TV reception. Today, more than half of all households are connected to a cable network, with the vast majority, in excess of nine million, as customers of Kabel Deutschland (KDG)—Germany's largest cable operator. (Cisco Systems, 1992–2008a, para. 2)

Therefore, in addition to having a title and lead that should arrest the audience's attention, laying the scene for the reader provides a realistic context for the story, whether a features genre is an article about the fight against diabetes around the world (e.g., Novartis, 2008), a case study of a process or product in action (e.g., The Alliance to Save Energy, 2008a; Hewlett-Packard, 2003), a backgrounder for public policy advocacy (e.g., National Paint & Coatings Assocation, 2004, 2007), or a white paper on cancer treatment (Optivus, 2006).

The movement of the text in the development of the narrative "plot" for a public relations story is essential for audience adaptation. The practitioner's use of the genre, therefore, must ring true with the audience's prior knowledge, experience (both first- and secondhand), and within the particular situation (i.e., the sociocultural context in which the target audience lives). For example, Safe Tables Our Priority (S.T.O.P.), a consumer-activist organization focused on eliminating food-borne illness, situates its report on food-borne diseases with reference to the 1993 Jack-in-the-Box *E.coli* O157:H7 crisis (Eskin, Donley, Rosenbaum, & Mitchell, 2002). The backgrounder then proceeds to paint the federal government as one of the villains, an appeal likely to resonate with readers:

> Federal government efforts to control microbial contamination on farms and in feedlots are largely nonexistent. . . . Both FDA and FSIS have acknowledged that existing statutory authority is sufficient to issue federal regulations governing the safe transportation of food, but the agencies have not moved toward finalizing such regulations. (pp. 6, 7)

Plot lines, therefore, also may have victims, as is the case in the Commission of the European Communities' (2008) white paper on violations of antitrust rules. In that case, the "victims" are unspecified. They simply are anyone who has been harmed by unfair business practices. The white paper then turns them into beneficiaries of what the paper recommends in cracking down on unnamed villains.

The plots in features genres generally end by offering a moral to the story. In S.T.O.P.'s backgrounder (Eskin et al., 2002), the answer is downsizing government: The "multiplicity and complexity of the current system" needs to be replaced with consolidation of "federal food safety responsibilities in one agency" (p. 59). Jarzinski's (2001) article in *Strategic Finance* ends with a moral in the form of a promise: "MPC software systems herald a new milestone in the financial systems marketplace. Such systems can truly help business leaders increase levels of certainty about the business and be more effective so their organizations can thrive" (p. 63). The inclusion of a moral consistent with the story's evidence is indicative of Fisher's second criterion for narrative probability: argumentative coherence. The story hangs together because it offers good reasons for its conclusion.

In terms of message design, the narrator's voice must be considered prior to placing the hero within the context. Common elements of features genres, therefore, offer three key plot elements. First, the writer sets the story in a context familiar to an audience, often a particular discourse community (see Chapter 1) such as retail business owners (e.g., Czubkowski, 2008), companies that have to coordinate operations of multiple site locations (e.g., Messaging Architects, 2008a, 2008b), students (News USA, 2005a), and education systems (e.g., De Grow, 2009; Poulson, 2008). Second, the characters within that situation include villains to overcome, victims to be remembered or saved, and those who benefit from what the organization does or advocates. Finally, the narrative ends with a moral, a recommendation that is supported by the plotline that precedes it. In many ways, then, features genres are well suited to adapt messages to the ways publics respond to narrative patterns, think about the world around them, and judge whether a message makes sense (Fisher, 1987; see also Moffitt, 1994).

Political dimension. The public relations practitioner must straddle the line between objectivity and bias in order to address audience familiarity with the situation through features genres. Although the credibility of the organization certainly is a concern in establishing, maintaining, or improving relationships with publics through features genres, management of a story's political dimension is strongly related to the identity management. According to Hauser (1999), the storyteller in epideictic genres is both hero and narrator. The organization's position regarding the subject matter of a story and the narrative voice that presents that story has implications for how publics might perceive the organization. Therefore, considerations of advocacy and bias must come before presenting or implying the organization's lead role in the story.

Ideally, the narrator should be an unbiased third party. In narrative terms, the "voice" of the story is third-person omniscient. Special Olympics' (2009) webpage of brief case studies offers testimonies of how corporate sponsors such as Proctor & Gamble, Bank of America, Cingular Wireless, and the Bank of Ireland benefitted its cause. Excellent, more extended examples can be found among The Alliance to Save Energy's (e.g., 2008a, 2008b, 2008c, 2008d, 2008e) case studies. Each story reports a corporate hero who has decreased energy consumption:

> Mercury Marine has a solid foundation for corporate-wide energy management. . . . The centerpiece of these efforts in 2004 was the installation of a new, centralized compressed air system that saves roughly half a million dollars in annual electricity costs. (The Alliance to Save Energy, 2008e, p. 1)

In articles, most often the organization is treated in the third person, with the hope that the media contact will use the story, which implicitly gives that media channel's endorsement. In such cases, articles quote credible sources with the same effect. When CISCO Systems and 14 other companies formed the E-Skills Industry Leadership Board to bring consistency to technology education and standards to Europe, Cisco Systems (2002–2009) noted several favorable responses from officials, including European Union (EU) Commissioner Günter Verheugen, vice-president of the European commission responsible for enterprise and industry:

> Your initiative is addressing an issue at the heart of the policy challenges faced by the European Union. . . . A highly skilled and adaptable workforce will be the foundation for Europe's competitiveness and prosperity in the 21st century. (paras. 4–5)

White papers appear to be even more subtle. As noted earlier, this genre presents a fairly balanced view of an issue, but the information is likely to be supportive of an organization's own position. Therefore, the voice is as objective as possible, with most of the white papers we looked at mentioning the company's name only a handful of times and then within the context of facts.

If anything, from a narrative standpoint, the author could be said to have a third-person omniscient voice in features genres. Articles may be a bit more forward in promoting the organization but not overly so as compared with white papers. For example, the University of Wisconsin's (Mitchell, 2008) feature story could be perceived as having an environmental agenda, but its article on making golf courses more environmentally friendly is grounded in knowledge of what golfers want and how the sport has become more "green." In contrast, many case histories clearly present the voice behind the story as proud of its achievements, of what its products, services, or issue positions have done for key publics.

With our understanding of the organizational narrative voice within features genres well established, we are now ready to also recognize that voice as that of the hero, which fulfills the final performative dimension, identity management.

Identity management dimension. If the voice presenting a story is both its hero and the narrator, it behooves practitioners when using features genres to recognize how the "characters" in the story seem to relate to one another. Heroes, villains, and people in need of help all must be realistic if the narrative is to succeed as a credible story. Our standard for the organizational narrator/hero is Fisher's (1987) concept of characterological coherence: "Determinations of one's character is made by interpretations of the person's decisions and actions that reflect values" (p. 47). The hero presented must act predictably, consistent with the situation, the rest of the story's plot elements, and its moral *and* with the audience's previous perceptions of the organization (i.e., the hero's corporate identity must fit with the organization's reputation).

A good case in point would be technology companies. Cisco Systems' products assist in building Internet capabilities in Eastern Europe (1992–2008b); enhancing control of mobile, wireline, and cable networks (2006) and dealing with problems caused by competing technology sources (2007); and helping companies provide technology customers "experiences," not merely access (2008). In each white paper or case study, Cisco takes on the role of problem solver. For health care providers, Symantec (2007) becomes the hero who has come to the rescue:

> Ensuring fast access to stored data in a hospital can be a matter of life and death. . . . The hospital [Children's Healthcare of Atlanta] . . . was supporting three separate clustered server environments, and the lack of standardization required separate IT management of each of the software solutions. . . . [The] solution allowed the IT team to increase the utilization of existing storage so the hospital would not have to purchase additional hardware. Children's realized an immediate savings of $2.3 million and a four-year total savings of $4.7 million. (pp. 10–11)

Symantec also takes on the role of adviser at the end of its white papers with specific solutions (2002) and tips (2007) for its readers. Good message design in features genres should assist in building a positive image with publics—and, with characterological coherence across messages, reputation—as a good corporate citizen acting on behalf of key publics.

2. Celebratory Function

Although there is a ritualistic dimension to the use of features genres (e.g., tailoring and pitching an idea to a specific media contact and using words in ways suitable to storytelling), features genres' celebratory function is primarily axiological. Fisher (1987) argues that stories offer audiences good reasons for their acceptance. Such reasons are explicit or implied values within the message. For our purposes, Fisher's view is caught up in the celebratory function's axiological dimension of features genres. As such, practitioner use of these genres must address values that the target public will judge as relevant, prudent, consistent with human experience, and an ideal basis for public conduct. These same five standards may be used in crafting a story and using it within a backgrounder, article, white paper, or case study. Let's apply Fisher's five standards to an example to illustrate how such messages may properly fulfill them.

In November 2008, Novartis (2008) held a lighting ceremony as part of the International Diabetes Federation's (IDF) Monument Challenge. In the analysis of this article, we first identify "the *implicit and explicit values* embedded in the message" (Fisher, 1987, p. 109; italics added). Novartis' "commitment . . . in providing innovative therapies for the treatment of diabetes" (para. 1) is explicit at the outset. The company also appears "serious" about the issue because it is fighting a disease that has a "very serious nature" (para. 5). Novartis' compassion for diabetics can be inferred from its stated purpose "to raise awareness of diabetes among those who are at risk and their families" (para. 5) and its other initiatives with partners such as IDF. Therefore, Novartis' use of the genre demonstrates the *relevance* or appropriateness of the values invoked.

Novartis (2008) addresses diabetes in ways that conform to Fisher's three remaining concerns as applied to features genres. As to consequences, the effects that these values might produce include "hope" (para. 6), progress in the form of the company's "commitment to innovative therapies" (para. 1), and "raising the standards for treatment" (para. 4). These values and those in the previous paragraph also illustrate *consistency* with values "confirmed or validated in one's personal experience, in the lives or statements of others whom one admires and respect, and in a conception of the best audience that one can conceive" (Fisher, 1987, p. 109). Novartis' efforts to fight diabetes, therefore, can be seen as "the ideal basis for human conduct" (p. 109), thus fulfilling the final concern for *transcendence* or idealism.

For the purposes of message design, then, practitioners may turn these five standards into message design questions so that values are better addressed when using features genres:

1. What are the values that should be present in the message, explicitly referred to, or implied?

2. What values are appropriate to the situation and to the issue(s) to be presented in the message?

3. If the organization and its publics were to follow these values, what would be the consequences for individuals, public behavior, human relationships, and communication ethics?

4. Are the values consistent with audience experience, those whom the audience admires and respects, their ideals?

5. Do these values constitute the ideal basis for human conduct? (adapted from Fisher, 1987, p. 109)

Incidentally, consistent with the traditional view of epideictic (i.e., "praise" and "blame"; see Chapter 2), features genres may address values that the organization stands against (e.g., ill health, fruitless research) in addition to those that it extols. The remaining epideictic functions are then easily fulfilled.

3. Epistemic Function

The epistemic function of features genres illustrates Fisher's (1987) main point that human beings are storytellers not merely to entertain but to inform and persuade audiences. The epistemic function for these genres is first and foremost educational (i.e., the educational dimension features messages that teach new ideas and encourages perceived linkage to audience values). The explanatory dimension is subordinate to education. However, there are times when explanation masks educational messages. Let's first cover the two dimensions in their purest forms.

When features genres are educational, they present audiences with information that the organization hopes the audience will accept and act on. They do so through associations with values or broad principles, not information the audience already knows. The National Paint & Coatings Association (2008a), in its backgrounder on environmentally friendly building practices, explains what green buildings are, the choices among rating systems for such buildings, and what is at stake for the paints industry. The message warns that a proposed revision in the Leadership in Energy and Environmental Design (LEED) rating system includes requirements for indoor paint that "are extremely limiting, from industry's view" (p. 3). For audiences unaware of the standards, the National Paint & Coatings Association cites its industry standards, which already had been tightened. In educating target publics, NPCA's message is designed to connect such industry efforts with the value of reasonableness. Such an argument reflects the classic epideictic appeal to common wisdom (Oravec, 1976), which is implicit in Fisher's standards of judgment just discussed under feature genres' celebratory function. If, however, the message were targeted only to members of the industry, such arguments would be explanatory, not educational.

The explanatory dimension occurs when messages connect with what the audience already knows as the basis for connecting it with something new. In such cases, organizational interests and audiences' interests should be served through communication by defining issues and fostering understanding (Condit, 1985). For example:

> We're all familiar with the growth rate of the public Web. Regardless of the metric used to measure its growth[—]attached networks, servers, users or pages[—]the growth rate continues to exhibit an exponential pattern. . . . However, the patterns of adoption differ by more than a simple lag. (King, 2000, para. 1)

The article details three orders of the effects of decreasing costs (citing Malone & Rockart, 1991). King ends his article with concerns for businesses to both securely access and protect databases as the World Wide Web continues to expand its impacts—concerns the audience likely shares as a result of reading his explanation.

In some cases, messages in features genres may appear explanatory on the surface but are actually educational. The Independence Institute's backgrounder on the increase of the number of local governments in Colorado (Longo, 2007) presents arguments for increasing that number and arguments against. However, the framing of the article, titled, "Is One Government Enough for Each Person in Colorado?," sardonically indicates the preferred position, underpinned by the value of smaller government. Of course, the ironic title may not be understood by some readers, thus reinforcing the position for some that more local governments serving fewer people is more effective. The values at stake, then, are effectiveness, efficiency, and economy. The message seems to provide information new to the audience (multiple sets of facts and figures, comparisons to other states, etc.), but its use of a literary trope (irony) serves to connect that information to known priorities of balancing public access to reasonable use of taxpayer dollars for bureaucracy.

4. Preservative Function

Features genres naturally fulfill the preservative function of epideictic discourse once the practitioner attends to the first three functions in designing messages. Good backgrounders, case histories, articles, and white papers simultaneously embody the preservative function's dimensions of cohesion and repurposing. Self-persuasion, it might be argued, naturally follows.

The way we have talked about cohesion in previous chapters brings new perspective to Fisher's concept of narrative probability. To fulfill epideictic's preservative function, use of features genres must maintain its cohesive dimension in order for the preservative dimension of repurposing to be possible. A story must hang together through its internal form *and* its relationship to other "stories" that the organization has told in the past, is telling during a campaign, or will tell in the future regardless of whether the story is told through a features genre or other genre (e.g., news). Audiences aware of an issue or already involved with it will compare one message with others in an organization's campaign and with those of other voices in public discussion about the issue.

Features genres build on previous narratives with which audiences may be familiar. For example, Hallmark's many special holiday ornaments capitalize on the popularity of various subjects (e.g., cartoon characters, television/film series). In a matte release produced by News USA (2005b), Hallmark introduces a miniature reproduction of the bell offered by Santa Claus in the movie, "The Polar Express," based on the book of the same name. The matte release therefore reminds readers of the book and promotes the coming movie. Similarly, a matte release from the North American Precis Syndicate (n.d.a, n.d.b) ties in to narratives that audiences can turn to for more information (e.g., the Proven Winners brand website) or support social issues linked to the organization mentioned in the feature. In this case, Proven Winners promises to "donate 5 cents from each purchase to the Breast Cancer Research Foundation" (para. 8).

Knowing that cohesion is central to narrative principles, it therefore becomes clear that features genres also lay the groundwork for later persuasion. Epideictic is ideally suited to this, as we have seen in our discussion of the epistemic function. Optivus (2006), for example, employs a white paper to address the high costs of proton beam therapy to combat cancer. Within it, the company lays out the key factors that doctors should consider when deciding to recommend a particular proton beam therapy machine manufacturer: device throughput, three standards for reliability, three criteria for safety, three considerations for future system upgrades, and so on. Although the white paper begins with facts and figures, some quite technical, these recommended standards are presented in a matter-of-fact manner, akin to friendly advice. In order to let stories create the possibilities for future opportunities to persuade audiences, then, a traditional concern of epideictic, *style*, comes into play.

With the issue of style, the relationship between literary concerns for figures of speech and rhetorical concerns of audience influence come to the fore. Obviously, practitioners use word choices to gain audience attention. Yet the capacity of stories to appeal to them and be remembered is part of the appeal of minor forms, such as metaphor, simile, reversal, and antitheses (see K. Burke, 1931/1968). Stylistic choices depend on the purpose a particular features genre is to accomplish. The Optivus (2006) example illustrates a more plain style that uses parallelism to provide decision makers with a balanced list of criteria to use (i.e., three criteria each for reliability, safety, and future system upgrades). In contrast, The Alliance to Save Energy's (ASE) case history titles employ testimonials (2008d; "We Did It. . . . So Can You!"), word play (2008c; "Margins for Profit, not Error"), and metaphors (2008e; for Mercury Marine, "Where Savings Float the Boat") to laud energy-saving companies. ASE's case study of Frito-Lay is laced with superlatives:

> Frito-Lay's corporate energy management (CEM) features aggressive energy reduction goals with a focus on results. This demands a high degree of monitoring, measurement, and communications. . . . Frito-Lay sought to achieve these ends by pursuing aggressive operational targets—"big, hairy, audacious goals" (BHAGs). The "BHAG" is a concept attributable to James C. Collins, author of Built to Last: Successful Habits of Visionary Companies. A BHAG is a clear and challenging organizational mandate. (The Alliance to Save Energy, 2008b).

Although they clearly fit the characteristics of features genres, ASE's messages are organized in the form of a printed transcript of an interview, questions followed by answers. ASE can play with wording and organizational pattern because of its third-person narrator role. Features genres thus provide the writer opportunity to engage in that most traditional offices of epideictic, to display stylistic skill with language.

Self-persuasion, therefore, occurs due to the other preservative dimensions and the epideictic functions discussed earlier. The role of the narrator/ hero allows for a confident tone that these narratives provide as accounts of what actually happened (or will happen). This suggests the reflexive quality of self-persuasion: The communicator reinforces his or her own beliefs. The connection to the audience made through the performative function's rhetorical dimension, the celebratory function's emphasis on values, the epistemic function's reliance on audience involvement, and the narrative's general appeal as form all increase the likelihood that the audience will be caught up in the message and thus moved by messages contained within features genres.

We have one final note regarding the preservative function, although it is not the case with all uses of features genres. Because Beale (1978) argues that "the typical home of literary epideictic is the special interest journal," which "lacks the concern for timeliness" (p. 240), we argue that using features genres for "evergreen" stories is the parallel case in organizational rhetoric. This suggests a subgenre that fulfills the preservative function in a unique way: Evergreen articles maintain in-reserve messages that may be used when an opportune occasion arises.

Features genres, thus, are vehicles for appealing to publics in particular ways that should resonate with audience experience, be consistent with an organization's established reputation (unless, of course, the situation requires image repair), and explicitly and implicitly address values that the audience already esteems. The use of features genres in public relations practice, therefore, must have more than just formal appeal (K. Burke, 1931/1968; see Chapter 3). The meanings that audiences bring to the reception of stories must be conveyed through the features genre's embodiment of audience experiences and contexts with which they are familiar. In addition to firsthand experience, today's heavily media-dependent environment affords publics windows to the world that expose them to a variety of such experiences and contexts.

Strategic Planning Implications

Features genres help raise an organization's visibility and tout its expertise on selected subjects to target audiences. As Beale (1978) puts it, "the 'feature story' [and, we would argue, features genres] often celebrate as well as report or inform about their subjects" (p. 240). Indeed, not just often; features genres always should celebrate, in this case, the organization, the values connected with the issues it addresses, and the audience's judgment as to what makes a good story. Although there is the storytelling dimension to features genres that make it both appealing to audiences and potent to organizations, at the same time there is an argumentative dimension that is concerned with making the case narratively. Strategically speaking, then, features genres give organizations ways to formally share and document what they are best at and explain why, with sufficient evidence and reasoning within the framework of familiar narrative structures and contexts.

Public relations professionals span many boundaries in their work, and doing so gives them invaluable access to the very pulse of what is going on inside and outside their organizations—employees/members and retirees/past members, customers, the communities[1] in which organizations operate, regulators and regulating bodies, stakeholders who stand to personally gain or lose depending on organizations' success or failure, the broader industry and market players in competition with organizations, suppliers and dealers/retailers for organizational outputs, and so on. This in-depth knowledge about what is on the minds of multiple publics is essential to planning communications efforts and, in particular, the key message platforms developed in the texts of selected genres to meet specified objectives. This knowledge also is important to identifying storytelling opportunities important to an organization and interesting to target audiences when one or more features genres can do the job required of them. This knowledge is vital to writing effective narratives that tell an organization's story in effective ways within a genre's framework for given audiences.

Both the formal and substantive features of the narratives in features genres contribute to making the public relations stories better in terms of their truthfulness, realisticness, and adherence to genre expectations. The strategic value of features genres, then, lies uniquely in the capacity of "compelling stories . . . [to] provide a rationale for decision and action. As such, they not only constrain behavior, they may also determine it" (Fisher, 1985, p. 364). When good stories "ring true" to audiences, they have important emotional and intellectual effects on audiences, and those are ideally the kind of reactions that public relations practitioners seek, which should be in response to the key message platform and are in tune with the objectives of a communications plan, which also is in tune with the organization's corporate strategic plan. That is, any story in a features genre must somehow help an organization get closer to achieving its goals, not just fulfill desired communication outcomes. Because features genres' potency relies on solid stories, the narratives must achieve a simple yet complex series of effects: attract attention, hold attention, build interest, add some knowledge, and inspire action. As we covered in the message design section, the epideictic functions of each genre can be employed well and ethically— especially emphasizing the problem-solution-added-value approach—to realize desired results while balancing organizations' needs with audiences' expectations.

Features genres provide organizations with additional discursive means to focus on particular matters, organizational strengths, and customer value. The narratives, when structured well, according to epideictic patterns we covered here, serve the interests of both organizations and their publics. When organizations want to put themselves more or even literally on the public stage, there is a collection of public relations genres to do that. These genres allow organizations to show off or "showcase" who they are, what they do, how well they do it, and why it is valuable. Showcase genres are the next set of genres we address.

Note

1. Community need not be just geographic. According to E. Burke (1999) and other writers on community relations, an organization's communities may be as abstract as "cybercommunity" and "world community" (Goddard, 2005).

References

The Alliance to Save Energy. (2008a). *Back to basics: Corporate energy management at Unilever.* Retrieved February 19, 2009, from http://www.ase.org/uploaded_files/industrial/Unilever%20Case%20v04.pdf

The Alliance to Save Energy. (2008b). *Big goals mean big success: Corporate energy management at Frit-Lay.* Retrieved February 19, 2009, from http://www.ase.org/uploaded_files/industrial/Frito%20Case%20v04.pdf

The Alliance to Save Energy. (2008c). *Margins for profit, not error: Corporate energy management at Dupont.* Retrieved February 19, 2009, from http://www.ase.org/uploaded_files/industrial/DuPont%20Case%20v08.pdf

The Alliance to Save Energy. (2008d). *"We did it. . . . so can you!": Corporate energy management at C & A Floorcoverings.* Retrieved February 19, 2009, from http://www.ase.org/uploaded_files/industrial/CollinsAikman%20v04.pdf

The Alliance to Save Energy. (2008e). *Where savings float the boat: Corporate energy management at Mercury Marine.* Retrieved February 19, 2009, from http://www.ase.org/section/topic/industry/corporate/cemcases

Beale, W. H. (1978). Rhetorical performative discourse: A new theory of epideictic. *Philosophy & Rhetoric, 11,* 221–246.

Booth, W. C. (1983). *The rhetoric of fiction* (2nd ed.). Chicago: University of Chicago Press.

Burke, E. K. (1999). *Corporate community relations: The principle of the neighbor of choice.* Westport, CT: Praeger.

Burke, K. (1968). *Counter-statement.* Berkeley: University of California Press. (Original work published 1931)

Cisco Systems, Inc. (1992–2008a). *Kabel Deutschland GmbH: Kabel Deutschland provides bundled digital communications services.* Retrieved February 19, 2009, from http://www.cisco.com/en/US/solutions/collateral/ns341/ns522/ns633/net_customer_profile0900aecd806db5fc.pdf

Cisco Systems, Inc. (1992–2008b). *Serbian ISP introduces tiered services and lowers operating costs.* Retrieved February 19, 2009, from http://www.cisco.com/en/US/solutions/collateral/ns341/ns525/ns537/ns549/net_customer_profile-0900aecd806208ba.pdf

Cisco Systems, Inc. (1992–2009). *Cisco, Microsoft and other IT leaders launch e-Skills Industry Leadership Board.* Retrieved February 19, 2009, from http://newsroom.cisco.com/dlls/2009/ts_020909b.html

Cisco Systems, Inc. (2006, December). *Enhancing application awareness for more services, greater efficiencies, and better control of mobile, wireline, and cable networks.* Retrieved February 27, 2009, from http://www.cisco.com/en/US/solutions/collateral/ns341/ns525/ns537/ns549/net_implementation_white_paper0900aecd80590c00.pdf

Cisco Systems, Inc. (2007, June). *Managing "over-the-top" web-based content and services.* http://www.cisco.com/en/US/solutions/collateral/ns341/ns525/ns537/ns549/ns746/net_implementation_white_paper0900aecd8066427b.pdf

Cisco Systems, Inc. (2008, January). *Cisco personalized subscriber management.* Retrieved February 27, 2009, from http://www.cisco.com/en/US/solutions/collateral/ns341/ns525/ns537/ns549/net_implementation_white_paper-0900aecd80745870.pdf

Commission of the European Communities. (2008, April 2). *WHITE PAPER on damages actions for breach of the EC antitrust rules.* Retrieved February 27, 2009, from http://eur-lex.europa.eu/LexUriServ/LexUriServ.do?uri=COM:2008:0165:FIN:EN:PDF

Condit, C. M. (1985). The functions of epideictic: The Boston Massacre orations as exemplar. *Communication Quarterly, 33,* 284–298.

Czubkowski, K. (2008, April 1). *Making a name for retail.* Retrieved February 26, 2009, from http://www.ocr.wisc.edu/newswire/featurearchives/?Id=40

De Grow, B. (2009, January). *Shining the light on Colorado school spending: The case for online financial transparency in K-12 education.* [Issue Backgrounder #2009-A]. Golden, CO: Independence Institute. Retrieved February 19, 2009, from http://www.i2i.org/files/pdf/IB2009A.pdf

Eagleton, T. (2008). *Literary theory: An introduction* (anniversary ed.). Minneapolis: University of Minnesota Press.

Eskin, S. B., Donley, N., Rosenbaum, D., & Mitchell, K. T. (2002). *Ten years after the Jack-in-the-Box outbreak—Why are people still dying from contaminated food? S.T.O.P. looks at the state of foodborne illness and the U.S. public health response.* Burlington, VT: Safe Tables Our Priority (S.T.O.P.). Retrieved December 19, 2003, from http://www.safetables.org/pdf/STOP_Report.pdf

Fisher, W. R. (1985). The narrative paradigm: An elaboration. *Communication Monographs, 52*, 347–364.

Fisher, W. R. (1987). *Human communication as narration: Toward a philosophy of reason, value, and action.* Columbia: University of South Carolina Press.

Frye, N. (1982). *The great code: The Bible and literature.* London: Routledge & Kegan Paul.

Goddard, T. (2005). Corporate citizenship and community relations: Contributing to the challenges of aid discourse. *Business and Society Review, 110,* 269–296.

Gronbeck, B. E. (1997). Tradition and technology in local newscasts: The social psychology of form. *Sociological Quarterly, 38,* 361–374.

Hauser, G. A. (1999). Aristotle on epideictic: The formation of public morality. *Rhetoric Society Quarterly, 29,* 5–23.

Hewlett-Packard Development Company, L. P. (2003). *HP IT Service Management (ITSM): Transforming IT organizations into service providers.* Retrieved February 27, 2009, from http://www.hoffmanmarcom.com/docs/hp_itsm_businesswp.pdf

Jarzinski, B. (2001, July). Thriving on uncertainty with an MPC system. *Strategic Finance, 83*(1), 60–63.

King, D. R. (2000, May). *Web warehousing: Business as usual?* Retrieved June 11, 2000, from http://www.dmreview.com/master.cfm?NavID=55&EdID=2179

Longo, J. (2007, August). *Is one government enough for each person in Colorado?* [Issue Backgrounder #IB-2007-F]. Retrieved February 27, 2009, from http://www.i2i.org/articles/IB2007F.pdf

Malone, T., & Rockart, J. F. (1991).Computers, networks, and the corporation. *Scientific American, 265*(3), 128–136.

Messaging Architects. (2008a). *EWI: Managing shared folders in GroupWise.* Retrieved February 19, 2009, from http://www.messagingarchitects.com/en/testimonials/ewi

Messaging Architects. (2008b). *Santa's Best: Simplifying GroupWise folder management.* Retrieved February 19, 2009, from http://www.messagingarchitects.com/en/testimonials/santasbest/

Mitchell, B. (2008, July 1). *It's not easy being green.* Retrieved February 19, 2009, from http://www.ocr.wisc.edu/newswire/featurearchives/?Id=38

Moffitt, M. A. (1994). Collapsing and integrating concepts of "public" and "image" into a new theory. *Public Relations Review, 20,* 159–170.

National Paint & Coatings Association. (2004). The public policy solution to runaway asbestos litigation. *Issue Backgrounder, 12*(1). [Online]. Retrieved February 19, 2009, from http://www.paint.org/pubs/background.cfm

National Paint & Coatings Association. (2007). Public nuisance lawsuits: The new public enemy for legal products? *Issue Backgrounder, 15*(2). [Online]. Retrieved February 19, 2009, from http://www.paint.org/pubs/background.cfm

National Paint & Coatings Association. (2008). Focus: The paint industry: Doing its part for a green building consensus. *Issue Backgrounder, 16*(3). [Online]. Retrieved February 19, 2009, from http://www.paint.org/pubs/background.cfm

News USA. (2005a). *College students—don't forget about auto maintenance.* [Matte release]. Retrieved October 15, 2009, from http://about.newsusa.com/corporate/print_samples.asp

News USA. (2005b). *Hallmark hops aboard "The Polar Express."* [Matte release]. Retrieved October 15, 2009, from http://about.newsusa.com/corporate/print_samples.asp

North American Precis Syndicate. (n.d.a). *In the garden: How hydrangeas can heighten enjoyment of your yard.* [Matte release]. Retrieved October 15, 2009, from http://www.napsnet.com/pdf_archive/49/49index.html

North American Precis Syndicate. (n.d.b). *Pointers for parents: A new horizon for children with hearing loss.* [Matte release]. Retrieved October 15, 2009, from http://www.napsnet.com/pdf_archive/63/63index.html

Novartis AG. (2008, March 19). *NVGH blazes a trail: Effective and affordable vaccines for the developing world.* Retrieved February 26, 2009, from http://www.novartis.com/newsroom/news/2008-03-19_nvgh.shtml

Optivus. (2006). *The path to protons: Business considerations for a proton beam therapy treatment center.* Retrieved February 27, 2009, from http://www.hoffmanmarcom.com/docs/optivus-business-issues-cancer-treatment-white-paper.pdf

Oravec, C. (1976). "Observation" in Aristotle's theory of epideictic. *Philosophy & Rhetoric, 9,* 162–174.

Poulson, B. (2008, September). *Amendment 59 gives the education lobby a blank check.* [Issue Backgrounder #IB-2008-C]. Golden, CO: Independence Institute. Retrieved February 19, 2009, from http://www.i2i.org/articles/IB_2008_C.pdf

Special Olympics. (2009). *Special Olympics: Corporate case studies.* Retrieved February 19, 2009, from http://www.specialolympics.org/case_studies.aspx

Symantec. (2002). *The value of information security.* Retrieved February 27, 2009, from http://www.hoffmanmarcom.com/docs/value_info_security_paper.pdf

Symantec. (2007). *Managing information storage in healthcare.* Retrieved February 27, 2009, from http://www.hoffmanmarcom.com/docs/symantec-healthcare-information-storage-white-paper.pdf

Tompkins, J. P. (Ed.). (1980). *Reader-response criticism: From formalism to post-structuralism.* Baltimore, MD: Johns Hopkins University Press.

6

Conversations

The Genetic Core

Public relations discourse is many and varied, as we have been explaining, and practitioners should be competent in them, especially those used more frequently than others. Those genres include both oral and written discourse. The most familiar kinds of public relations discourse are those that are published or the kinds we covered in the preceding chapters. These discourse forms are also among the most favored in textbooks about public relations writing. Perhaps the least familiar are oral texts—those texts that reflect primarily, if not completely, patterns of oral discourse.

In this new age of Web 2.0, organizations participate in and perpetuate certain oral traditions through selected discourse genres. Among them are the usual genres of in-person conversations, interviews, pitch calls, meetings, speeches, and podcasts. These genres are truly the basis for more literate traditions in public relations practice that reflect oral strategies such as letters and e-mail, correspondence to customers and publication editors, and social media sites, especially blogs and wikis.

Ong's (1971, 1982) analysis of the evolution and interplay of oral and literate traditions applies particularly well today. For Ong (1982), "primary orality" concerns cultures "totally untouched by any knowledge of writing or print" (p. 11). Indeed, he foresaw technology's role in what he called a "'secondary orality' of present-day high-technology culture, in which a new orality is sustained by telephone, radio, television, and other electronic devices that depend on for their existence and functioning on writing and print" (Ong, 1982, p. 11; see also Ong, 1971, p. 285) has come true thanks to the Internet, Web-based systems, social media, and wireless communication through text messaging. This chapter explores and explains the conventions for public relations discourse that tend to be more conversational in form, whether oral or written. The chapter then moves beyond prescriptions for effective conversational discourse (like those given in textbooks) to reveal deeper rhetorical and practical dynamics that are essential to their effective use and—most important—their strategic value and application in public relations.

Genres and Their Conventions

For oral cultures, "formulary materials" or "formularly devices" (Ong, 1971, pp. 285–287) are absolutely essential in discourse because they function as the means for organizing and presenting the ideas so they can be easily recalled and spoken by speakers and easily followed and remembered by listeners. Examples include:

> heavily rhythmic, balanced patterns, in repetitions or antitheses, in alliterations and assonances, in epithetic and other formulary expressions, in standard thematic settings (the assembly, the meal, the duel, the hero's "helper," and so on), in proverbs which are constantly heard by everyone so that they come to mind readily and which themselves are patterned for retention and ready recall, or in other mnemonic form. (Ong, 1982, p. 34)

As much as formulary devices are essential in oral discourse, they are just as essential in literate discourse. These devices amount to what we have called "discourse conventions," and they are the rules by which people create and use spoken and written texts.

Our understanding of the second orality and its application to public relations genres may be best understood through Ong's first orality. Indeed, public relations in sub-Saharan countries have used the earliest forms of communication to reach tribal audiences (Pratt, Silva-Barbeau, & Pratt, 1997): song, theatre, and dance. Dance in the second orality becomes a metaphorical means for communication. In public relations, there is a kind of dance that practitioners do within their organizations and among the organizations' publics. For public relations professionals, their oral and literate work must be in step with the needs and expectations of their organizations, publics, stakeholders, and the public relations profession. The written word—especially its technological incarnations from Gutenberg's press to social media—does not supplant the spoken word. Humans have always been primarily oral communicators, and the technologizing of language in the forms of writing, much later printing, and currently the Internet, reinforces and transforms oral language, in which degrees of formality and informality are relative to cultural values and communicative purposes (Ong,

1982). Such is the case in public relations, in which practitioners can rely on both purely oral and written genres that reflect largely oral tendencies.

Oral Genres and Their Conventions

The responsibility to inspire cooperation between an organization and its publics, even to the extent of celebrating an organization in any respect (for better or for worse), is a heady challenge that requires great competence in multiple forms of communication. Although public relations is considered a writing-intensive profession because of the great need to physically document what is going on for an organization and how it and its members think, feel, and act, oral communication genres play an important role. Indeed, fictional characterizations of public relations and public relations professionals on television and in the movies tend to showcase public relations people talking about, pitching ideas for, or otherwise discussing matters of some importance with clients.[1] We know that much of what public relations professionals do to get things done is to talk with people internally and externally, along with writing things down and disseminating them appropriately. In the daily business of public relations, oral genres—conversations, pitch calls, interviews, meetings, speeches, and podcasts—are especially important because they forge the kinds of personal connections between people that are necessary to establishing relationships, inspiring cooperation, and celebrating milestones.

Conversations (telephone, face-to-face, real-time video conference calls, and Internet chats and discussion forums) take place with representatives of media, publics, or stakeholder groups to comment on an issue, answer specific questions on a topic, arrange personal interviews with corporate leaders or experts, or are done to fulfill some other *ad hoc* purpose. Conversations are the most basic of human communication, and they entail personal and professional savvy about the topic, the situation, public audiences, one's self, and other contextual factors. The mediated forms of conversations—chats and discussion forums—that are held on the Internet pose interesting implications because they present the texts of conversations input there by users, and entire conversations may be saved as files locally on one's desktop or in other data storage. For Internet chats (including chat rooms within websites, instant messaging, and potentially text messaging over cell phones), what someone types is immediately shown and ready for immediate response. For discussion forums (sometimes referred to "message boards"), individuals input texts in an area of a website that specifically allows for messages to be posted and responded to over time. If everything works well, conversations can be fruitful, interpersonal ways to learn about ideas, attitudes, and information. They can also help build rapport and support. They also can be the beginning of the end if conversations take an ugly turn because of careless communication.

Pitch calls are placed by telephone to garner interest among editors and reporters about a particular story and the news appeal it will have on audiences. Such calls often precede and follow the sending of material information related to the story idea being pitched. In the span of a few minutes, a public relations person states the story idea that fits the journalist's and his or her audience's interests, gives at least one compelling example or explanation, argues why the story would be valuable, and asks for the journalist to cover it with or without the public relations person's help. Pitch calls, in effect, require public relations professionals to lay all their cards on the table and invite the journalist to play into the hand. Note that the cards being played have to fit the game the journalist plays at his or her table, and if they do not fit, the game is over before it started.

Interviews are arranged for an organizational official to comment on something that has timely news appeal for a mass media outlet, typically television, radio, print, or Web news organizations. Whether you are seeking news coverage or the news media seek you out, knowing how to manage media opportunities will serve you well before, during, and after interviews. You may prepare a spokesperson for an interview on the phone or in front of a video camera, or you may be the interviewee yourself. You may meet in a conference room at a news organization, or you may be on the scene of a news conference of which you are part. You should prepare a collection of standard source documents that can apply to almost any situation, and you will have to tailor other material for each opportunity because each story will be different yet a little the same. Plus you will put your knowledge and experience to work as you do some "thinking on your feet." Bear in mind that the reporter (and his or her editor or producer) has the final say in what gets printed or aired, and you can only do your best to make sure you provide the reporter with your story and relevant information. The difference between doing a "good" job and doing a "great" job is that reporters, editors, and producers are more likely to call you back when you have done a great job. Being dull and uninformative puts you on the fast track to failure in any interview, especially if it is on television or radio.

Meetings gather people together to address some matter of importance. Meetings can involve only organizational members or they can involve members of publics and stakeholder groups. Meetings can also range in size from very small (e.g., editorial management meetings) to very large (e.g., rallies or shareholder meetings). They typically are convened at a predetermined place and time, and they follow an agenda of subjects that will be addressed and by whom. There may be time limits for each item on the agenda, which is a way to manage discussion during the meeting. The substance of meetings can involve a variety of communication discourse (verbal and visual), but the defining discourse is conversation/discussion among participants. Even in large meetings, a structured question-and-answer (Q&A) period may be included to allow for some dialog or give-and-take among meeting organizers and invited publics.

Speeches or presentations are written by or ghostwritten (in whole or in part) for organizational leaders to address key topics for specific public-speaking occasions. Speeches are more personal than mediated communication because they allow for interaction between an organization's representative and an audience. In this way, speeches represent special opportunities to humanize an organization because someone, presumably a top official, is standing up for it. Speeches and presentations are written to be heard, not read, so that listeners grasp the meaning effectively, are moved emotionally, and are inspired to act purposively in tune with the speaker's thesis. Visual aids may be included to enliven or illustrate verbal content. Matters of both substance and style are vital, including verbal and nonverbal messages. What someone says must be true, compelling, timely, logical, and other factors that make for strong arguments. How someone presents him or herself and the message must include good personal character, good posture, appropriate gestures, and audible and understandable statements that are conversational in tone. As with interviews, you may be coaching a spokesperson regarding these matters.

Podcasts are single audio or video files created and maintained on a unique website or "blog" (see the next section) by one or more people who produce episodes of content for people to download to their computers and listen to. Podcasts are similar in content to blogs, which will be addressed momentarily. The big difference is podcasts' reliance on oral texts presented as only audio or as video and audio combined. Podcasts exist on the Internet and tend to mimic radio or television news stories or short documentaries about specific topics. Podcasts are produced, findable, social, viral, conducive to syndication, and linkable. Effective podcasts have clear and distinctive sound/video quality without mistakes, have proper and informative introductions and closings for every episode, are downloadable from websites to one's own computer and in turn to a portable playback device such as an iPod, present timely and relevant content with any pertinent analysis and action steps, complement a blog or website to allow listener responses, link to other sources referred to in episodes, and are ethical in content, ownership, and operations.

Literate Genres and Their Conventions

The bulk of the genres we cover in this book are written, literate forms of discourse. Selected literate public relations genres, however, tend to reflect certain aspects of oral discourse because the specific purposes behind them rely on oral discourse conventions related to one-on-one communication. The oral-based literate genres for public relations are pitch letters, written correspondence, Web logs ("blogs"), and wikis. It is important to note that the last two genres (and podcasts) have received much attention over recent years as public relations people have been quick to ascertain the potential value of these media because of their newness and, especially, usefulness with certain audiences.

Pitch letters are either hardcopy or electronic and are meant to persuade journalists that a particular story is compelling and worth covering in specific ways that should appeal to their audiences. These letters typically have included or linked with them other documents (e.g., press releases, fact sheets, articles, graphics) presented in a package or online news room (see Chapter 7) depending on the purpose. Hardcopy pitch letters are a formal way to ask for a journalist to tell an organization's story. It is prepared like a traditional business letter on letterhead and presents a concise and compelling argument in several short paragraphs. For example, the first paragraph gets the journalist's attention and lets the journalist know you know the news organization and its readers and what news fits them all. The second paragraph presents the story idea, covers the five Ws and the H, provides compelling data or evidence, and offers at least one expert source for personal information or interview from the organization. The third paragraph suggests illustrative material—photos, graphics, or video. The fourth paragraph asserts when and how the journalist can contact you and that you will follow-up in a few days. Attachments should be used sparingly and purposefully, such as sample illustrations and background information.

E-mail pitches are similar yet different. They are similar in purpose to pitch letters but different in most other ways. They should be used only if a journalist is known to accept pitches by e-mail. The e-mail must be personalized and sent only to single journalists whenever possible. (Mass e-mail "blasts" risk losing professional relationships with journalists, except in cases that involve broad news, such as announcements about quarterly financial and market performance.) The subject line should be short, descriptive, and precisely focused on the core news, not merely stating the obvious, such as "press release," a company's name, "information for you," or "a story idea." Because of the nature of the medium, e-mail requires an even shorter argument to tell your story—not more than a single screen of text without scrolling. Assuming the subject line has inspired a journalist to open your e-mail, the first two sentences must grab his or her attention and define the story. The remaining few sentences (not paragraphs) must argue why a journalist's audience would care. Add a link to your organization's website, especially an online press room, so no attachments are needed. Make sure your personal contact information is given.

Written correspondence may be prepared in advance (i.e., form letters) to consistently send key messages on one popular issue to individuals or prepared as needed to address individuals' specific concerns or to fulfill particular communication purposes for public relations assignments. Written correspondence reflects patterns of formal letter writing in business so that, no matter how long the argument is, the text politely, authoritatively, and ethically presents information on a specific topic that fulfills a particular communication purpose for one person or a whole group. Indeed, "it may be argued . . . that official correspondence has had a key role in setting written language norms in many language communities" (Nevalainen, 2004, p. 182). If an organization must respond to multitudes of similar inquiries from publics received over various channels, a form letter may be an appropriate way to respond—provided that each copy is individually addressed to a specific person or group and, if possible, hand signed by the appropriate corporate official. In unique, *ad hoc* situations, a similar approach should be used, but it must be much more tailored to the receiver's original argument.

Wikis (pronounced "wee-keys") are simple websites that include one or more pages on specific topics that are open to anyone who would like to post information that pertains to the purview and purpose of a given wiki. The word *wiki* is Hawaiian for "quickly," which is the essence of these websites—they are quick and easy to create and, especially, to maintain with information from anyone who wants to add it. Simple and special software is needed to create wikis, and most are free and available for download from credible Internet sources. In this way, wikis do not have restrictions on content or organization, but they do possess technology to track exactly who posted or revised what and when, including any visual and verbal information. This capability is critical when trying to uncover errors or changes. Discussions about content can be facilitated or policed on wikis so that disagreements over wiki content can be resolved. So many wikis are used for external audiences; however, wikis are created and maintained to facilitate internal communication among organizational members. In these cases, internal wikis, like their external cousins, present updated and accurate information about any subjects of interest to both an organization and its members. Information that is posted in internal wikis is governed by people or teams with the authority and responsibility for all information shared.

Weblogs (usually called "blogs") are single, self-contained websites created and maintained by one or more people who want to post text entries and photos/graphics about topics important to them on some broad subject(s). Blogs are perhaps the single largest realm of self-expression and free speech on the Internet, and many are high-traffic websites. The essence of blogs is dialog—blogs invite people to engage in a conversation about myriad topics, and dialog occurs over time as one person's post builds on others that preceded it. (Discussion forums may seem similar to blogs but are not because they are built into an existing website, whereas blogs are self-contained.) So many blogs exist now (the sum total of all blogs is referred to as the "blogosphere") and cover vast arrays of topics that there are websites that index them by subject matter, such as GlobeOfBlogs.com, and websites that provide search engines about blogs, such as Technorati. com and PubSub.com. Anyone with the savvy to create and maintain a blog can publish his or her ideas, to which all the world can access and respond. Like podcasts, blogs are publishable, findable, social, viral, syndicatable, and linkable on the Internet. Effective blogs have an attractive visual design that complements an organization's brand and is easy to navigate, include an initial posting that welcomes visitors and discloses the blog's purposes, present timely and relevant content with any pertinent analysis and action steps, feature easy and effective ways for visitors to post messages, link to an organization's website and podcasts, link to other sources mentioned in postings, and are ethical in content, ownership, and operations.

Certain blogs have been responsible for breaking stories that turned out to be big news, such as the DrudgeReport's story about President Clinton's escapades with Monica Lewinski (Bogosian, 2001). Others set the public record straight, such as the bloggers whose own investigations proved Dan Rather's report on President Bush's National Guard service wrong (Bacon's Information, 2005; Holland, 2005; Kirkpatrick, Roth, & Ryan, 2005). Yet most blogs are not so "successful" because they tend to lack the kind of broad appeal to or interest among readers, post infrequently, link to other blogs sparingly, and offer weak opinions that are wanting of passion, evidence, and other hallmarks of credibility (Levy, 2005).

All told, there are four basic types of public blogs, according to Bacon's Information (2005), all of which public relations can partake. Later in the chapter, we focus on the organizational context for these blog types, which grows out from their more common uses but refrain from spelling out specific things that could be done with each type. To lay out such specifics would take away from the fun of designing blogs for proactive public relations purposes; however, we mention some general ideas along the way.

Personal blogs—Someone creates and maintains a blog to express her or his personal convictions, observations, suggestions, and other matters about selected topics that interest her or him. Prime topics from an organizational standpoint would include a company and its performance, management and its decisions, corporate culture, recent news, product/service offerings, employee benefits, comparisons to the competition, and others. Personal blogs can be created by anyone, including organizational members, who are typically below those in top management (Haskel & Martin, 2004; Kirkpatrick et al., 2005; Zeller, 2005). Most frequently, a personal blog is set up and run independently—all by someone on her or his own time and nickel. Sometimes organizations, such as Sun Microsystems, Microsoft, and Maytag, encourage employees to become bloggers "for debate, free association, and collecting input about projects" (Roush, 2005, p. 38). The content is virtual word-of-mouth communication that is typically opinionated and replete with links to other Internet sources. These characteristics make personal blogs perhaps the most potent type because, depending on the blogger's agenda and attitude, subjects covered in the blog could be helpful or hurtful to the company's image, reputation, news, and other aspects.

Topic or industry blogs—These blogs focus on the nature, history, developments, trends, and players in a given subject area or industry. These bloggers tend to be authoritative and influential representatives of a subject area or an industry, with a credible track record of experience, knowledge, and success. They also have a strong following of disciples who actively follow and pass along the bloggers' thinking. These bloggers can play an important role of guru or statesperson on issues that matter to those inside and outside the blogosphere. In this way, these blogs function nearly like an ongoing white paper or keynote speech—as if to impart sage wisdom to others who, for example, need or want to know what the state of the subject or field is, where it is going, and what stands to be gained or lost with or without proper action being taken.

Publication-based blogs—As outgrowths of established media outlets, these blogs foster dialog about subjects of interest to the parent publications' readers. Typical bloggers are editors, reporters, or freelancers who follow a subject area closely, use their blogs to augment and promote their work, and want to benefit from the greater knowledge of the masses who would be willing to share that knowledge (Beeson, 2005; Mitchell & Steele, 2005; Tanner, 2005; Wasserman, 2004). Immediacy of stories is key because these blogs serve news-gathering purposes. Bloggers may take advantage of other blog types to research and develop news stories, and, thus, these blogs help organizations (in part) to take the pulse of the news environment.

Corporate blogs—A hybrid of the personal blog, these blogs are fairly new and feature the insights, assessments, commentary, and other discourse devoted to a single company. Key bloggers are corporate executives, including board members (Clarke, 2004; Jones, 2005a; Nash, 2005; Steinert-Threlkeld, 2005). Of special note is the potential use of blogs for investor relations: Boards of directors could use the technology "to get their message out, and at the same time provide a forum for shareholders to offer informal input to their elected board representatives" (Jones, 2005b, p. 14). The corporate-blog communication is typically much less free-wheeling than personal blogs, but the presence of top management makes this blog type attractive and useful because it presents an "inside view from the top" of what is going on. In public relations' corner is the idea that the executive has the necessary ethos to speak credibly on behalf of and about the organization. Also in public relations' corner is the problem of bias. That is, even though the executive is credible, he or she has a vested interest in the propagation of the faith about the organization. Skepticism thus will always be a prevailing attitude toward any corporate/executive blog, and it may well be tempered by glee when corporate details (for better and for worse) come out.

The examples of blogs have all focused on those created and maintained for external audiences. At the same time, like wikis, it is equally important to recognize that blogs can be used for internal communication purposes. In such cases, because the genre fosters dialog, internal blogs run on an intranet, which allows organizations to facilitate two-way communication with their members in at least two ways: (a) individual blogs that leaders or other employees/members run, and (b) team blogs that focus on their specific work or products/services for which they are responsible. Such blogs can focus on anything ranging from benefits to new-product releases. Any internal blog faces an approval process that addresses the business case about why any blog should be created and maintained.

Message Design

With this foundation for the discourse conventions for oral and oral-based public relations discourse, the questions now are, "What next? How do we use them?" The answer to these questions is, as in previous chapters, in two parts: message design and strategic planning. In this section, we address how public relations officials should think about each genre so they can maximize the effectiveness of their language to inspire cooperation between an organization and its publics. Such effectiveness is driven by the epideictic functions of public relations discourse, with the celebratory and performative functions providing the foundation for the epistemic and preservative functions. The first two functions work in tandem to capitalize on the value-centered, ritualistic, rhetorical, and identity management dimensions native to two-way communication.

1. Celebratory Function

As noted earlier, the forms of communication in traditional oral cultures provide an important clue to understanding the role of conversation-based genres in public relations discourse. Indeed, the metaphors of music, dance, and theater are especially apt in appreciating the particularly ritualistic qualities of these genres when we use them in message design. Indeed, Hearit (2006) has noted the importance of ritual in corporate *apologiae*. It comes as no surprise, then, that interviews, speeches, and corporate blogs have become important components to crisis communication plans. Likewise, business conversations, pitch calls and letters, podcasts, and wikis all serve as opportunities to invest in the values behind topics of discussion with nobility and dignity (see Aristotle's *Rhetoric*, I.9.40). For celebratory message design, attention to style, organizational patterns, and commonly shared, ritualized behaviors and values become the "music" of conversational genres in public relations message design.

Consider the appropriateness of word choices in the preparation of copy points for pitches, interviews, and speeches. Stylistic choices must focus on the conversational qualities of letters, podcasts, and blogs—but not so much so that messages become overly casual. Certainly the epideictic, celebratory qualities of these genres invite vividness (see Pratkanis & Aronson, 2001), but not to the point of letting the characterization of themes or core values overwhelm the main point of the message. For example, CEO Michael Hyatt of Thomas Nelson Publishers reacted on his blog in December 2008 to the hyperbole of news coverage of the economic recession:

> I'm tired of the relentless torrent of bad news coming from the media. I feel like I am stuck in a recession version of *Ground Hog Day* [sic]. The names and places change with each story, but underneath the veneer, it's the same story-line:
>
> - "We're in a severe recession."
>
> - "It's the worst economic downturn since the Great Depression."
>
> - "It's going to get worse before it gets better."
>
> - "There's very little you can do about it."
>
> I don't know about you, but this is not having a healthy impact on my psyche. Last night, after waking up again at 3:30 in the morning, I thought, *Enough is enough. I don't need the additional worry and fear that this is creating. It's time to turn off the news.*

Vividness, therefore, need not mean mere "colorful" style: "To insure [sic] the power of this shared experience, the speaker must create a vivid picture of the shared definition, not merely a clear and rational case" (Condit, 1985, p. 292). Hyatt countered the language intensity of the news with his seemingly more reasonable thoughts.

Beyond vividness, the deliberate choice of words or phrases that evoke particular mental images can be powerful, particularly as they resonate with publics. Kenneth Burke (1931/1968) referred to this notion about word and phrase choice as "the Appeal of the Symbol." Its importance lies in the fact that, " 'to be part of a community' means in large part to identify oneself with the symbols, values, myths, or 'heritage' of that community" (McGee, 1975, cited in Condit, 1985, p. 289). According to Burke, symbols have several possible functions: (a) interpretation of a situation; (b) favoring acceptance of a situation; (c) corrective to a situation; (d) means of stirring up audience recall of past experience; (e) giving freedom to the audience through relabeling of a situation or experience ("indolence" becomes "leisure," "stinginess" becomes "thrift," etc.); and, of course, (f) vehicle for aesthetic appeal. Symbols represent patterns of experience with which the audience is familiar. For example, Whirlpool's (2008) "American Family" podcasts have covered topics as diverse and mentally arresting as how women plan their household routines around menstrual periods, "Flu Vaccines," "Decorating for the Holidays," and engaging "kids" in the 2008 election, *Scholastic Magazine*'s Kids' Press Corps, and volunteerism.

Patterns of experience are grounded in the everyday world and couched in terms of specific, relevant values. Conversational genres are at once a celebration of shared experience within a community (here defined as the environment in which organizations and their publics interact) and an enactment of participation within that community, including living up to its values. Speeches serve this function quite well: "the story of the speech is told for the sake of the ritualistic need for communal sharing . . . and thus it is performative" (Condit, 1985, p. 292). For example, CEO Greg Wolf (1998), prior to Humana's merger with United Health Care, addressed the National Hispanic Leadership Summit and informed the audience about Humana's efforts in the Hispanic community. Obviously, Humana's programs for health care have definite appeal to Hispanics' needs, but Wolf combined the celebratory and performative aspects of epideictic with an interesting reference to Babe Ruth, who "learned a valuable lesson at an early age: Figure out what you're good at and put all your energy into it" (p. 2). Wolf did not need to state the connections between America's favorite pastime and its relationship to Hispanics. Wolf, through the example, linked Humana's character with the values embodied in Ruth. Implied in the baseball connection are roles for the speaker and the audience as lovers of the game and what it stands for, and Wolf developed his persona in the speech as a community leader expressing community held values. He attempted to manage his identity and that of the audience, and thereby establish common ground between them. All this was accomplished through the shared experience of baseball.

Therefore, the conversational quality of letters, blogs, and wikis—not just speeches and other oral genres—relies on more than word choices to accomplish the celebratory function. The stylistic differences between writing for news and writing conversationally are obvious, but Ong's idea of a second orality would emphasize the holistic need for verbal and nonverbal (even visual, including illustrations and layout/design) content working in concert within the epideictic situation. Write like you talk, but think of it as heightened conversation. As Aristotle, Cicero, and Quintilian prescribed, the language of discourse must match the dignity of the occasion. The ideal would be ritual that creates communion. "Instead we can define it [epideictic] rhetoric as the experience of members of an audience who find that the speaker is saying exactly what needs to be said, who find that they are being caught up in a celebration of their vision of reality" (Sullivan, 1993, p. 128). These examples suggest that conversational genres are ideal ways to foster identification in relationships with key publics.

2. Performative Function

If symbols (e.g., talking points) are the music of conversation, dyadic communication is the dance. Social scientists theorize that both music and dance promoted social cohesion in ancient cultures. However, Hagen and Bryant (2003) argue that the forming of groups and coalitions based on these art forms results in perceptions beyond sexual compatibility and social cohesion. In their study, Hagen and Bryant found that how well the music and dance worked together increased perceptions of coalition quality. Metaphorically, the dance of communication between an organization and its publics can be said to be an interaction with the words and symbols chosen and used in such a way as to increase perceptions of identification and relationship quality. Thus, conversation genres focus heavily on the identity-management and rhetorical dimensions of the performative function. For performative message design, some of these conventions invite opportunities to engage the political dimension, but practitioners must use the proper steps to avoid appearing fully engaged in policy advocacy (or coach spokespeople to follow the proper "dance" pattern). Overall, however, the first two dimensions are the more important.

Rhetorical dimension. For example, Dell Inc. built its reputation for consumer service through innovative mediated communication (Allen, 2008). The company developed two-way communication through its corporate blog, Direct2Dell. Its success led to further development of social media. Such moves suggest rhetorical adaptations to use new media to tailor messages with particular audiences in mind. According to Caroline Dietz, Dell's manager for its online community:

The experience of introducing [*Direct2Dell*] got us excited about the possibilities of having even more two-way conversations with our customers online. . . . There were a lot of ideas shared during the [CES roundtable]. These two driving forces led to Michael Dell's decision to launch *IdeaStorm*. (Allen, 2008, para. 6)

Wikis operate in a similar fashion, but most we have found are used by employee stakeholders, changing the way the organization engages with its human resources and conducts business (see the example of Sun Microsystems' blog practices in McKee & Lamb, 2009). At the telecommunications powerhouse Nokia and the German investment bank Dresdner Kleinwort, wikis were begun by the employees but have become vital to company operations (Carlin, 2007). In 2007, Nokia estimated that "at least 20% of its 68,000 employees use wiki pages to update schedules and project status, trade ideas, edit files, and so on" (Carlin, 2007, para. 4). Dresdner Kleinwort's Socialtext program originated with employees and was so successful that the bank launched its own wiki with great success: "By October, 2006, the bank's 5,000 employees had created more than 6,000 individual pages and logged about 100,000 hits on the company's official wiki" (Carlin, 2007, para. 7). Such developments build strong ties between the organization and its members.

Yet conversational public relations genres do not always result in the ideal relationship with publics. Letters, speeches, and electronic forms of conversation often provide the illusion of interactivity. Organizational transparency easily becomes a phantom when one-way communication masquerades as two-way. When conversational genres are used in the name of increasing dialogue but fail to do so, the theatrical side of orality can become a negative. The music of the words may not ring true, and the dance partners can become less intimate and out of step when publics recognize that the organization's persona may be but a mask. Publics readily recognize that the emperor, in the name of changing wardrobe, actually has no clothes. Of course, in today's mass-mediated age, some audience members may accept the illusion (in theater, this is called the suspension of disbelief).

Identity-management dimension. The first orality's communicative mode of theater provides a strong metaphor to recognize the potential downside of organizational attempts at conversation. Crable (1990) has rightly argued that today's public relations discourse—indeed much of public discourse in general—is stage managed. The scene is set, spokespersons have numbers of people behind the scenes to make them look good, and they speak on behalf of others. With the Humana example, we saw how Wolf attempted to build identification through discussion of common concerns and cultural experiences. We suspect that what Crable observed applies: that Wolf did not write the speech alone and likely was assisted in obtaining the appropriate occasion to address his audience of Hispanic opinion leaders. In this way, he enacted (i.e., performed) his own role—and Humana's—as a community leader.

Such opportunities for leaders to be perceived as similar to the audience can be blown without proper strategy. Such was the case for Illinois Governor Rod Blagojevich when he was interviewed for Comedy Central's *The Daily Show* (Stewart & Corn, 2006). The show's segment covered the state's legal requirement for pharmacists to provide prescribed contraceptives even if they personally objected to birth control methods. The governor clearly was unaware about the show's humorous treatment on news of the day, and the segment for which he was interviewed was to lampoon the issue. At one point, Blagojevich asked someone (we assume one of his aides), "Is he teasin' me, or is that legit?" and then became flummoxed when asked whether he was the "gay governor." The next day, Blagojevich's press officer claimed that the governor did not know that *The Daily Show* was a comedy program; the day after that, he reversed himself. Unintentionally, the governor separated himself from potentially friendly publics.

The same risk occurs with the illusion of two-way communication. Best Buy's Geek Squad blog (Geek Squad, 2007–2008), and many corporate blogs like it, are not truly dialogic. Best Buy's technology staffers sometimes answer questions from consumers but often provide consumer tips strictly from the organization's point of view. Other uses of conversational genres give the appearance of interactivity but still are one-way communication. *Parasocial communication* is mediated communication that imitates conversation by the way the speaker or spokesperson addresses the audience as if speaking to each person, one at a time. What makes it parasocial is that the receiver comes to feel as if she or he knows the spokesperson (much like how television audiences feel as if they know a celebrity, athlete, or soap opera character as a personal acquaintance). Of course, the consumer may not desire true dialogue. However, parasocial communication and the epideictic capacity to build ethos can work for great success, such as the case with famed Chrysler executive Lee Iacocca (Seeger, 1994). Parasocial communication works not just because the audience functions in the traditional epideictic role of observer, but as judge of the speaker's rhetorical skill to invoke values and inspire cooperation: "It is through 'appraisal' of the events, person, and objects in our lives that we define ourselves. We constitute ourselves as good (necessarily) by ranging ourselves against 'the bad'" (Condit, 1985, p. 291).

Political dimension. Although "the speaker must avoid dividing the community as far as possible" (Condit, 1985, p. 292), the juxtaposition of venerating the good and vilifying the bad in epideictic may address controversy (Hauser, 1999). This can work to the organization's disadvantage or advantage. In the case of Wal-Mart in 2004, it gave CEO H. Lee Scott an opportunity to address its customer-critics for paying employees too little, removing "offensive" material such as Jon Stewart's book *America*, which contained nudity, and consumer resistance to the entry of Supercenters in their communities (Saporito, 2004). Although Scott might not have persuaded some, he invoked values that Wal-Mart stands for, avoided the appearance of making a political stand by appealing to community standards, and perhaps reached others not so critical of the company, especially the loyal Wal-Mart customer.

We end our discussion of the political dimension of conversation genres with one caveat: The political dimension should be engaged with caution. Public policy concerns are most naturally suited to speeches from high-level organizational spokespeople (e.g., BP CEO Lord John Browne's [2003] address to the Institutional Investors Group and the British Carbon Trust), and interviews (e.g., *Der Spiegel*'s interview with BASF CEO Jürgen Hambrecht regarding the company's position on global warming) (Ramspeck & Mahler, 2007) and particular conversations (e.g., those held as part of involvement in a local nonprofit organization as a board member or volunteer) can be opportunities to state organizational positions on issues. Various types of blogs also may be used. The key is to recognize the salience of the issue to the target publics being addressed and the timeliness of the issue. Humana's outreach to Hispanic audiences and Hyatt's attitude toward negative news coverage illustrate legitimate attempts to talk about issues that audiences care about and, we suggest, foster identification with them.

Epideictic messages, thus, can serve as ways to reach audiences more favorable to an organization's position even while addressing some audiences through direct conversation. Inevitably, the balance of the three dimensions of the performative function of these genres can become strained. In such cases, disagreement becomes a dramatic event (Van de Vate, 1965): When it appears that an argument fails to persuade one public, it may be used to draw support or adherence from others. Our next example illustrates such a balancing act.

Cynthia McKinney, the outspoken 2008 Green Party candidate for president, seems to juggle rhetorical, identity-management, and political imperatives with mixed success in interviews. In 2006, while running in Georgia for reelection to Congress, McKinney could not seem to shake media interest in an altercation she had with a District of Columbia police officer, who did not recognize her when she attempted to go through a Capitol Hill security checkpoint without a special identification pin she was required to wear to indicate her role as a member of the U.S. Congress. McKinney allegedly struck the officer ("McKinney's Softened Image," 2006).

At a community center, McKinney was insulted when an Atlanta reporter asked her about the incident again, and she walked off with her microphone still live. She then returned to tell the reporter that her comments were only on the record when she was sitting in the chair opposite the reporter (WND, 2006). Her efforts to keep the comments off the record boomeranged—the story made national news ("Station Catches McKinney," 2006). Although some sided with McKinney, who called the police officer's actions "racial profiling," reactions were mixed, although some supported her attitude toward the media ("Cynthia McKinney's Capitol Offense," 2006), and she lost her reelection bid. McKinney's interview juxtaposed core values to which different publics might ascribe, presenting a polarizing persona that many bloggers criticized (e.g., gttim, 2006; Rangelife, 2006). However, supporters for her presidential run in 2008 saw her as someone ready to challenge the status quo.

3. Epistemic Function

Conversation genres can build on celebration and performance to explain and educate publics about an organization, its positions on issues, and its attitudes toward publics. Pitch calls and letters, op-ed pieces, podcasts, and in-person conversations, such as the Chicago Federal Reserve Bank's "Charlie Chats" (Crescenzo, 2008), weekly informal meetings with the CEO, most obviously are explanatory in character, although the last example has its educational dimension as well. In a sense, conversation's celebratory song and performative dance are followed by the display of explanations and knowledge that organizations deem important for their publics. Innovations in social media illustrate the explanatory and educational dimensions of conversation's epistemic function.

For epistemic message design, these genres may place explanation first, although education may be a close second. For example, Eastwick Communications used its Eastwiki 2.0 as the central communication hub for information regarding Fujitsu's "Going Green" event (McAdams, 2008). All material normally distributed through a press kit (see Chapter 8) was handled through the wiki. In fact, every document associated with the event was posted on the wiki, giving "Fujitsu communications staff access to the documents as they were developed" (para. 15) and providing the media with everything needed to explain the significance of the event.

Social media offer prime opportunities for education. Chicago's Federal Reserve Bank has a weekly blog, "Live Wire," by which organizational members, management, and other employees alike, learn what their peers are thinking (Crescenzo, 2008). The head of the bank's communications team, Catherine Cummings, says, "Each week, we pick a different employee to write the blog column. . . . We pick people who have something to say, but we don't tell them *what* to say" (para. 11). Not only does this blog perform a rhetorical "sense of community" (para. 12), but "it raises issues that might not otherwise get raised" (para. 13). H&R Block's (2003–2008) MySpace website offers direct access to tax information, explaining to site users all sorts of topics and educating them with tax tips for the 2008 tax year.

4. Preservative Function

Like the genres of the first orality (song, dance, and drama), the oral and oral-based conversation genres serve functions for more than their immediate audiences. Communicators can use these genres to bring coherence to seemingly disparate messages, especially with social media, which gives varying degrees of control over what is written. Audience participation through responses to blogs, contributions to wikis, and interaction during open meetings make possible a greater sense of identification with the organization, thereby functioning as a form of self-persuasion (see Burks, 1970). Finally, putting organizational messages in forms that can be referred to by organizational members, media contacts, and other interested individuals makes for a rhetorical storehouse of discourse preserved for future use.

For example, Chicago's Federal Reserve Bank communicates openness with employees with the previously mentioned "Live Wire" and "Charlie Chats" as well as a weekly e-mail newsletter, "The Skinny," and the "Grapevine," informal editorial advisory boards that provide feedback to management from employees about the bank's various communication programs (Crescenzo, 2008). In addition to bringing coherence to the bank's internal communication messages, employee participation programs such as "Live Wire" generate a sense of ownership among employees (see Holtz, 2004; Jablin, 2001; Quirke, 2008) and function as a form of self-persuasion (see Tompkins & Cheney, 1985).

For good or ill, speeches, interviews, and op-ed pieces become part of the public record and may be used by the organization's personnel or by others, for or against it. For example, the Gun Owners of America (GOA), in its written statement (i.e., a letter) to the U.S. Senate regarding Barack Obama's nominee for attorney general, Eric Holder, used Holder's own words from a *Washington Post* editorial, regarding the need for a universal requirement for all gun sales to be recorded, against him: Mr. Holder stated, " 'Congress should also pass legislation that would give the Bureau of Alcohol, Tobacco and Firearms a record of every firearm sale,' in spite of laws in place that prohibit gun owner registration" (Velleco, cited in Isler, 2009). Similarly, German officials reacted strongly in 2008 to an op-ed piece by U.S.

Ambassador to Sweden Michael Wood in the Swedish daily *Svenska Dag-bladet*. According to *Der Spiegel* (Beste & Meyer, 2008), Wood "wrote that the pipeline represents 'a special arrangement between Germany and Russia' that 'bypasses the Baltic States and Poland,' which are 'potential customers.' Wood calls for the EU to speak 'with a single voice to counteract the power of Russia's energy weapon'" (para. 3). Such words become part of history and shape news coverage for the record and affect international relations.

In these last examples, GOA leader John Velleco, then Deputy Attorney General Holder, and Ambassador Wood clearly illustrate all four epideictic functions in operation in genres of conversation. The "music" of celebration, through the various rituals of formal letters, op-ed pieces, and the like, invoke values held by the message source and the organization they represent. The music may be strident to some, but the dance of the performative function clearly establishes the source's identity, attempts to forge a relationship with audiences (and sometimes risks alienating others), and may become involved in public policy discussions (the final examples are most obviously political in purpose). Such sources dramatically generate public knowledge through explanation and education, and their words live on in print and via electronic media, or at least in the memories of those who have been part of the conversation.

Strategic Planning Implications

All conversational public relations genres, in today's expanded view of epideictic discourse, constitute special occasions in which we memorialize (celebrate) organizational and cultural values, condemn those in which cultural norms are violated, and unify organizations and publics as part of a larger community in which both play important roles. Conversational genres, thus, rely heavily on celebration of shared values and efforts to influence audiences through expression of shared interests and experiences. The image-building opportunities afforded through such epideictic discourse should not be minimized. However, the conversational qualities of these genres invite some of the best opportunities for interaction with publics among the genres covered in this book.

The dominant strategic implication among the conversational genres we address in this chapter is interpersonal communication. For example, the February 2009 issue of *Communication Theory* focuses on the role and importance of literal conversations in communication campaigns. The literature on interpersonal communication is vast, and we do not review it here, but we believe there is an especially useful and usable orientation to understanding interpersonal communication that can be used effectively in public relations (see Coombs, 2000). Basically, organizations are treated like individual people (Cheney, 1992; Cheney & Dionisopoulos, 1989; McMillan, 1987). Organizations today are as concerned about the same issues of effective communication as individuals are in their conversations: openness, disclosure, transparency, trust, respect, and so on. Understandably, individuals and organizations have things they are willing and not willing to share with others. The strategic implications for conversational public relations genres can be, then, effectively viewed through the lens of self-disclosure in relationships.

No organization is an island, and the successful management of an organization's relationships with its various publics is essential to its livelihood. Just like it is with individuals, organizations must be willing to share much of themselves with others while not sharing other things. The willingness to disclose information within and without the organization, just like with individuals, breaks down everything about an organization into four areas:

1. Open—information known to an organization is known to others

2. Blind—information known to others is unknown to the organization

3. Hidden—information known to an organization is unknown to others

4. Unknown—neither an organization nor others know

These areas make up the Johari Window (Luft, 1969), shown in Figure 6.1, which is a useful way to account for organizational self-disclosure.

This model reveals strategic implications of public relations' conversational discourse genres that enable organizations to self-disclose to individuals and publics. In the first quadrant, organizations and publics participate in open, transparent communication about each other. Information flows relatively freely about matters known well to all parties. The opposite of this quadrant is the fourth one, where all parties do not know what they do not know, so information is not shared. The trickiest quadrants are the remaining ones because they are characterized by privileged information one party has but the other does not. These are the quadrants that test the concept and practice of transparency. Although ethics is involved in all quadrants (as it is in all communication), it is especially noteworthy in the second and third quadrants. The second quadrant concerns situations where publics have something in mind but do not want

	Known to organization	Unknown to organization
Known to others	1 Open	2 Blind
Unknown to others	3 Hidden	4 Unknown

Figure 6.1. Johari Window.

an organization to know, such as litigation, protests, and other surprises for better and for worse. Public relations practitioners would do well to anticipate the possible issues that could arise and devise strategic contingency plans to address them. The third quadrant covers situations where an organization is in possession of information that it does not want others to get because it may compromise its competitive position or other matters, such as product development, market penetration outlooks, future performance projections, and so on. Public relations practitioners would be wise to ensure that all information is properly safeguarded—that what is disclosed is as important as what is not. These four dimensions for organization self-disclosure, then, provide practitioners with a framework for thinking strategically about the kinds of conversational discourse that may be used when appropriate, especially to fulfill audiences' expectations about organizational transparency.

The message design considerations given earlier play out when, strategically speaking, organizations identify that certain publics must get certain messages in certain discourse at a certain time for certain purposes. Moreover, an organization recognizes the risks in disclosing *and not disclosing* information, the relevance of any information that is disclosed or not, the probability information would inspire cooperation, and the effectiveness of the selected discourse and the messages it contains. Organizational self-disclosure, then, is something that public relations' conversational discourse genres enable. Self-disclosure does not occur instantaneously or easily, but rather it is something that occurs between an organization and its publics when such communication is given at the right places and the right times and in constructive ways. The epideictic nature of public relations, as realized through conversational discourse genres, takes ethical advantage of self-disclosure because, like interpersonal communication, it is characterized by revelations realized through candor; reciprocal communication; clarification of beliefs, attitudes, values, and so on; validation of beliefs, attitudes, values, and so on; management of information and impressions about one's identity; maintenance and enhancement of relationships through open and, perhaps, transparent communication; control of one's self in situations and the situations themselves over which one has control; and understanding of one's motives for disclosure (see Adler, Proctor, & Towne, 2005).

Remembering that organizations are created by people is important, too, because people make up those organizations and engage in daily organizing behaviors through their use of language and symbols with each other and others outside. As corporate officials make certain choices about controlling what and how to communicate with their publics, ethics becomes bound together with public relations. "'Eloquence' is the combination of truth, beauty and power in human speech" (Condit, 1985, p. 290), and, based on Burke (1968), it is through symbols that we "stretch our capacities and identities in the human quest for improvement" (Condit, 1985, p. 290). At the heart of an ethical stance about public relations are issues related to the equivocality of responsibilities, values, and rights of an organization's internal and external publics that may be at odds with the organization's own values and goals (Seeger, 1997). The objective, then, is to reduce "ethical equivocality"—the very stuff of organizations' hidden and blind selves—as much as possible so that practitioners make the right decision and do what is right and just. Accordingly, communications with internal and external publics should conform to and uphold ethical principles, in which the ideal ethic is that of dialogic, or two-way, communication (Johannesen, 1990).

This and the preceding chapters have revealed the ritualized nature of communication and the intimate role that discourse conventions have in the use of individual public relations genres. This chapter, in particular, revealed how certain genres allow for a heightened informality that is part and parcel to the kind of quasi-interpersonal communication that organizations have with their publics. The next chapter focuses on what we call "showcase" genres, and they possess even higher expectations of formal ritual and symbolic action than others we covered thus far.

Note

1. We lament, of course, the stereotypical (albeit shallow) depictions of the public relations profession found in popular culture (e.g., in television, *Sex in the City*; in literature, M. C. Beaton's "Agatha Raisin" mysteries).

References

Adler, R. B., Proctor, R. F. II, & Towne, N. (2005). *Looking out, looking in* (12th ed.). Boston: Wadsworth.

Allen, J. (2008, January 4). *Dell's* IdeaStorm *uses social media to tap customer ideas.* Retrieved January 4, 2008, from http://www.ragan.com/ME2/Audiences/dirmod.asp?sid=&nm=&type=MultiPublishing&mod=PublishingTitles&mid=5AA50C55146B4C8C98F903986BC02C56&tier=4&id=F938CA6F44B44AF7A5438C3F234EE86B&AudID=3FF14703FD8C4AE98B9B4365B978201A

Bacon's Information Inc. (2005). *Introduction to blogs: A quick guide to understanding and maximizing communication efforts in the blogosphere.* Chicago, IL: Author.

Beeson, P. (2005). The ethical dilemma of blogging the media. *Quill, 93*(3), 18–19. Retrieved June 4, 2005, from EBSCOhost.

Beste, R., & Meyer, C. (2008, September 22). *German-US tensions grow over Baltic pipeline.* Retrieved October 28, 2010, from http://www.spiegel.de/international/world/0,1518,579677,00.html

Bogosian, T. (Writer, Producer & Director). (2001). *The press secretary: A fascinating all-access look inside Clinton's White House press office.* [Television broadcast]. (Available from WGBH Educational Foundation, 125 Western Ave. Allston, MA 02134)

Browne, J. (2003, November 26). *BP CEO Lord Browne's speech.* Retrieved December 11, 2008, from http://www.pewclimate.org/companies_leading_the_way_belc/company_profiles/bp_amoco/browne.cfm

Burke, K. (1968). *Counter-statement.* Berkeley, CA: University of California Press. (Original work published 1931)

Burks, D. M. (1970). Persuasion, self-persuasion and rhetorical discourse. *Philosophy & Rhetoric, 3*, 109–119.

Carlin, D. (2007, March 12). *Corporate Wikis go viral.* Retrieved October 28, 2010, from http://www.businessweek.com/technology/content/mar2007/tc20070312_476504.htm

Cheney, G. (1992). The corporate person (re)presents itself. In E. L. Toth & R. L. Heath (Eds.), *Rhetorical and critical approaches to public relations* (pp. 165–183). Hillsdale, NJ: Erlbaum.

Cheney, G., & Dionisopoulos, G. N. (1989). Public relations? No, relations with publics: A rhetorical-organizational approach to contemporary corporate communications. In C. H. Botan & V. Hazleton, Jr. (Eds.), *Public relations theory* (pp. 135–157). Hillsdale, NJ: Erlbaum.

Clarke, A. (2004). What content should be in leadership blogs? *The Business Communicator, 5*(4), 1. Retrieved June 4, 2005, from EBSCOhost.

Condit, C. M. (1985). The functions of epideictic: The Boston Massacre orations as exemplar. *Communication Quarterly, 33,* 284–298.

Coombs, W. T. (2000). Interpersonal communication and public relations. In R. L. Heath (Ed.), *Handbook of public relations* (pp. 105–114). Thousand Oaks, CA: Sage.

Crable, R. E. (1990). "Organizational rhetoric" as the fourth great system: Theoretical, critical, and pragmatic implications. *Journal of Applied Communication, 18,* 115–128.

Crescenzo, S. (2008, March 14). *Chicago's Federal Reserve gets creative with communication.* Retrieved March 14, 2008, from http://www.ragan.com/ME2/Audiences/dirmod.asp?sid=&nm=&type=MultiPublishing&mod=PublishingTitles&mid=5AA50C55146B4C8C98F903986BC02C56&tier=4&id=F113E2884A6D4F1B9D48921B79D6CAC0&AudID=3FF14703FD8C4AE98B9B4365B978201A

Cynthia McKinney's Capitol offense. (2006, April 8). Retrieved December 11, 2008, from http://www.pressaction.com/news/weblog/full_article/mckinney04082006/

Geek Squad. (2007–2008). *Geek Squad blog.* Retrieved December 12, 2008, from http://www.geeksquad.com/news/default.aspx

gttim. (2006, April 24). Cynthia McKinney caught on tape! In *Better inhale deeply.* [Personal blog]. Retrieved December 12, 2008, from http://betterinhaledeeply.blogspot.com/2006/04/cynthia-mckinney-caught-on-tape.html

H & R Block. (2003–2008). *H & R Block: The tax pro team.* Retrieved January 18, 2009, from http://www.myspace.com/hrblock

Hagen, E. H., & Bryant, G. A. (2003). Music and dance as a coalition signaling system. *Human Nature, 14,* 21–51.

Haskel, J., & Martin, J. (2004, March). Back the blog? *Hospitals and Health Networks,* p. 30. Retrieved June 4, 2005, from EBSCOhost.

Hauser, G. A. (1999). Aristotle on epideictic: The formation of public morality. *Rhetoric Society Quarterly, 29,* 5–23.

Hearit, K. M. (2006). *Crisis management by apology: Corporate responses to allegations of wrongdoing.* Mahwah, NJ: Erlbaum.

Holland, K. W. (2005). Welcome to the blogosphere: Get the skinny on web logs from an association's perspective. *Association Management, 57*(5), 22–28. Retrieved June 4, 2005, from EBSCOhost.

Holtz, S. (2004). *Corporate conversations: A guide to crafting effective and appropriate internal communications.* New York: AMACOM.

Isler, E. (2009, January 17). *Gun owners of America opposes AG nominee* (Phoenix, AZ). Retrieved January 18, 2009, from http://americandaily.com/index.php/article/203

Jablin, F. M. (2001). Organizational entry, assimilation, and disengagement/exit. In F. M. Jablin & L. L. Putnam (Eds.), *The new handbook of organizational communication: Advances in theory, research, and methods* (pp. 732–818). Thousand Oaks, CA: Sage.

Johannesen, R. L. (1990). *Ethics in human communication* (3rd ed.). Prospect Heights, IL: Waveland.

Jones, D. (2005a, May 10). CEOs refuse to get tangled up in messy blogs. *USA Today.* Retrieved June 4, 2005, from EBSCOhost.

Jones, D. (2005b). Is boardroom blogging for you? *The Corporate Board, 26*(152), 14-18. Retrieved June 4, 2005, from EBSCOhost.

Kilpatrick, D., Roth, D., & Ryan, O. (2005). Why there's no escaping the blog. *Fortune, 151*(1), 44-51. Retrieved June 4, 2005, from EBSCOhost.

Levy, S. (2004). The alpha bloggers. *Newsweek, 144*(25), E16-E17. Retrieved June 4, 2005, from EBSCOhost.

Luft, J. (1969). *Of human interaction.* Palo Alto, CA: Natural Press.

McAdams, S. (2008, February 26). *Wiki improves internal communication at PR firm.* Retrieved February 26, 2008, from http://www.ragan.com/ME2/Audiences/dirmod.asp?sid=&nm=&type=MultiPublishing&mod=PublishingTitles&mid=5AA50C55146B4C8C98F903986BC02C56&tier=4&id=0E729EE5399B4A69BAD372CDA7D8DA41&AudID=3FF14703FD8C4AE98B9B4365B978201A

McGee, M. C. (1975). In search of "the people": A rhetorical alternative. *Quarterly Journal of Speech, 61,* 235-249.

McKee, K. B., & Lamb, L. F. (2009). *Applied public relations: Cases in stakeholder management* (2nd ed.). New York: Routledge.

McKinney's softened image takes a blow. (2006, April 5). Available at http://www.usatoday.com/news/washington/2006-04-05-mckinney-image_x.htm

McMillan, J. J. (1987). In search of the organizational persona: A rationale for studying organizations rhetorically. In L. Thayer (Ed.), *Organization↔communication: Emerging perspectives II* (pp. 21-45). Norwood, NJ: Ablex.

Mitchell, B., & Steele, B. (2005, January 15). *Earn your own trust, roll your own ethics: Transparency and beyond.* Paper presented at the conference on Blogging, Journalism and Credibility: Battleground and Common Ground, Cambridge, MA.

Nash, J. (2005). Look who's blogging. *InformationWeek, 1029,* 47-52.

Nevalainen, T. (2004). Letter writing. *Journal of Historical Pragmatics, 5,* 181-191.

Ong, W. J. (1971). *Rhetoric, romance and technology: Studies in the interaction of expression of culture.* Ithaca, NY: Cornell University Press.

Ong, W. J. (1982). *Orality and literacy: The technologizing of the word.* London: Methuen.

Pratkanis, A., & Aronson, E. (2001). *Age of propaganda: The everyday use and abuse of persuasion* (rev. ed.). New York: Freeman.

Pratt, C. B., Silva-Barbeau, I., & Pratt, C. A. (1997). Toward a symmetrical and an integrated framework of norms for nutrition communication in sub-Saharan Africa. *Journal of Health Communication, 2,* 43-58.

Quirke, B. (2008). *Making the connections: Using internal communication to turn strategy into action* (2nd ed.). Burlington, VT: Gower.

Ramspeck, S., & Mahler, A. (2007, June 27). *Spiegel* interview with BASF CEO Jürgen Hambrecht: "I have a problem with the term climate change." *Spiegel Online International.* Retrieved December 11, 2008, from http://www.spiegel.de/international/business/0,1518,491075,00.html

Rangelife. (2006, April 24). Cynthia McKinney and Ronald Reagan grab the open mic and choke up. In *Rangelife: It's the way we're living, right or wrong.* Retrieved

December 12, 2008, from http://rangelife.typepad.com/rangelife/2006/04/open_mic_nite_f.html

Roush, W. (2005). Sun Microsystems: Blog heaven. *Technology Review, 108*(4), 38. Retrieved June 4, 2005, from EBSCOhost.

Saporito, B. (2004, November 1). *10 questions for H. Lee Scott*. Retrieved December 11, 2008, from http://www.time.com/time/magazine/article/0,9171,995531,00.html

Seeger, M. W. (Ed.). (1994). *"I gotta tell you": Speeches of Lee Iacocca*. Detroit, MI: Wayne State University Press.

Seeger, M. W. (1997). *Ethics and organizational communication*. Cresskill, NJ: Hampton Press.

Station catches McKinney bad-mouthing staffer: Congresswoman calls communications director a "fool" after interview. (2006, April 24). Retrieved December 12, 2006, from http://www.msnbc.msn.com/id/12464118/from/RSS/

Steinert-Threlkeld, T. (2005, March). CEO blogs: Silence of the lambs. *Baseline*, p. 10. Retrieved June 4, 2005, from EBSCOhost.

Stewart, J., Executive Producer, & Corn, K., Supervising Producer. (2006, February 9). Pill of rights. *The Daily Show*. New York: Comedy Partners. Retrieved February 11, 2006, from http://www.thedailyshow.com/watch/thu-february-9-2006/pill-of-rights

Sullivan, D. L. (1993). The ethos of epideictic encounter. *Philosophy and Rhetoric, 26*, 113–133.

Tanner, G. (2005, May 16). Joining the mainstream? A recent bloggers' conference emphasized traditional reporting tools. [Electronic version]. *InformationWeek*. Retrieved June 4, 2005, from http://www.informationweek.com/shared/printableArticleSrc.jhtml?articleID=163103882

Tompkins, P. K., & Cheney, G. (1985). Communication and unobtrusive control in contemporary organizations. In R. McPhee & P. K. Tompkins (Eds.), *Organizational communication: Traditional themes and new directions* (pp. 179–210). Beverly Hills, CA: Sage.

Van de Vate, D., Jr. (1965). Disagreement as dramatic event. *The Monist, 49*, 248–261.

Wasserman, E. (2004). Pressures force the emergence of a new journalism. *Nieman Reports, 58*(4), 60. Retrieved June 4, 2005, from EBSCOhost.

Whirlpool Corporation. (2008). *Whirlpool American family podcasts*. Retrieved December 10, 2008, from http://www.whirlpool.com/custserv/promo.jsp?sectionId=563

WND: WorldNetDaily.com. (2006, April 23). *Oh cr--! Cynthia McKinney caught using C-word: Democrat tells TV station her comments were off the record*. Retrieved December 12, 2008, from http://www.wnd.com/news/article.asp?ARTICLE_ID=49871

Wolf, G. (1998, June 16). *Remarks to the National Hispanic Leadership Summit*. [Speech]. Retrieved October 28, 2010, from http://www.mark-ray.com/samples/hispanic.doc

Zeller, T., Jr. (2005, May 8). A blog revolution? Get a grip. *New York Times*, Sec. 3, p. 1. Retrieved June 4, 2005, from EBSCOhost.

7

Showcases

Grabbing the Mic, Taking the Stage

If any of the discourse that public relations professionals use could be thought of as being the most suited to organizations' extroverted or gregarious side, advertorials, public service announcements, press conferences, satellite media tours, and press kits would be them.[1] These genres allow organizations to bask in the spotlight—admittedly their own spotlights. Not that other public relations discourse genres are suited to organizations' introverted needs, but these genres more than the others seem to put an organization foremost on a public stage, where it takes the microphone and commands attention.

Genres and Their Conventions

The "showcase" genres give public relations professionals unique ways to put an organization on stage prominently and advance the key messages directly to audiences. Like any genre, much planning and careful attention to detail during discourse development are key. Moreover, the focused attention on an organization's view of things within the context of its publics' burgeoning understanding of the same things favors the organization but still contributes to the desire to inspire cooperation among all parties, starting with the organization. Because, then, the organization has its opportunity to speak on the public stage, the discourse genres of advertorials, public service announcements, press conferences, satellite media tours, and press kits function well as the first statements in an organization's drama.

Advertorials

Advertorials are a cross between advertisements and editorials. Rather than traditional opinions written independently by a publication's editor, advertorials are journalistic stories prepared by or for an organization but paid to be placed in a publication where an advertisement would go. The content of an advertorial is strictly meant to advance an organization's messages on specific subjects, especially itself and its products/services. The characteristics of features genres, as discussed in Chapter 5, apply especially those for case studies and articles, and they may be combined to result in a piece that appears at once to be a regular article in a publication but also is noted on the top or bottom margin to be a "paid advertisement." This marginal notation is important to the publication so that it discloses that it is not responsible for the content, and the purposes are less journalistic and more sales- or issue-related. Advertorials' layouts are designed to complement a publication's style but not precisely—there may be some variations in typeface, color use, text-to-visual relationships—because advertorials are prepared as "camera-ready" pieces that would be used as is, like a prepared advertisement (note that these are different from image and issue advertisements; see Chapter 9).

Public Service Announcements

Public service announcements (PSAs; sometimes referred to as "public service messages" [PSMs]) assert informative, concise, and compelling statements that are of interest to the general population and are advanced over mass-media channels to assert an organization's interest in the public welfare on specific subjects. Indeed, PSAs promote issue positions and/or programs and services of voluntary or government agencies that are in the public interest. Under federal regulations, there is no charge to air PSAs because they are shared over the airwaves for the greater public good. However, some organizations purchase advertising time to place them strategically for specific publics (e.g., the Partnership for a Drug-Free America's 1987 "Fried Egg" message [Partnership for a Drug-Free America, 2006] and the United Church of Christ's diversity messages that two major networks declined to air for concern over controversy [Guess, 2004]). PSAs on the radio are often read by the station's talent or prerecorded by an organization for playback, typically lasting 10, 15, 30, or 60 seconds in length. TV spots are typically 20, 30, or 60 seconds.

PSAs' content depends on what is being promoted in the public interest. The style of the text is prepared in journalistic style but is looser; therefore, the language is conversational and allows for sentence fragments, run-ons, contractions, colloquialisms, and slang. Grammar rules can be broken, but this should not be overdone. When referring to people, it is best to use names that target publics know and, when necessary, use titles before names to signal the person's notoriety first. Quotes are tricky because audiences cannot see quotation marks like they would in printed material. So direct attribution of quotes is essential in these cases. Actualities add "color" to PSAs—on radio, actualities include background sounds of what is going on in the scenes related to the subject matter; in video (television or Internet), actualities come from the audiovisual context of the subject matter. Considerations about using acronyms, abbreviations, numbers, technical terms, names, and so on must also be made so that messages are as obvious and understandable for the audience as possible because PSAs are meant to be heard (or seen), not read.

PSA scripts for radio or video should show on the first page an organization's logo and location (letterhead works well), the phrase "PUBLIC SERVICE ANNOUNCEMENT," the date of preparation, the start and kill dates for broadcasting, the duration of the text in seconds, the PSA's formal text (including a statement about how or where to get more information), and the word "END" or "-30-" to show that no more text follows. Contact information must also be given either before or after a PSA's formal text so producers know whom to call if necessary. The formal text for PSAs is written for time and should be formatted in double-spaced, 12-point type (preferably Courier font) that is in "sentence case" or all capital letters. (The second author recommends the latter based on broadcast experience.) PSA copy should also be prepared in 60-character, 5-inch lines so that each line equals 3 seconds of speech: a 10-second PSA is 3 1/3 lines, a 30-second PSA is about 10 lines (70–80 words), and a 60-second PSA is about 20 lines (135–145 words). Paragraphs' first lines should be indented, pronunciation guides should be given for unfamiliar words or names, there should be no word hyphenations at the ends of lines of type, and there should be no page breaks within paragraphs. Ellipses, rather than periods, also may be used to indicate desired pauses in delivery.

Press Conferences

Press conferences (sometimes called "press briefings" or "news conferences") are held by organizational spokespeople to personally release information about, present an official view of, or provide an update about something (e.g., announcements or breaking news) and, if permitted, address questions and concerns that journalists might have about the subject or issue at hand. A press conference may include one or more organizations depending on the situation and organizations involved. Any press conference, however, is not the news (unless something bizarre happens during the event or it is a rare event for an organization)—it is an event where all media can hear from an organization's officials at the same time. Press conferences work best when an announcement affects a large number of people, is a matter of public concern, announces a new product or service, and provides access to key individuals and opportunity to answer questions and "go on the record." Press conferences should be scheduled with journalists' time pressures in mind depending on several factors (e.g., television/cable stations, radio stations, newspapers, weekends, holidays). Ideally, press conferences should be held in locations away from a client's office but close to or easy for media to access, include electrical outlets and telephone connections, and be on the ground floor and open well before the event for easy equipment access and setup. Journalists should be advised of a press conference through a media alert or other invitation. When journalists and their crews come, check their credentials.

Press conferences rely on a strong key message platform that focuses on a central idea or thesis and is supported by individual proof points for that thesis. This key message platform governs all official, prepared remarks and answers to journalists' questions. If possible, press conferences should be rehearsed with everyone involved but the journalists. Press conferences begin with an opening statement from a corporate spokesperson that lasts 3 to 10 minutes and summarizes the situation. The balance of the prepared remarks includes the actual, formal announcement, which includes any necessary data, reasoning, visuals, and support from other individuals involved. If a Q&A period follows, the corporate spokesperson must set reasonable ground rules. It is vital that officials understand that they speak for the organization and must keep language simple, avoid acronyms and jargon, and use bridging techniques to bring attention back to the key message platform if and when the event strays because of a journalist's question. Officials must also remember, as in interviews, that everything is "on the record" and there are no "do overs." So all press conferences must be prepared in detail and rehearsed if possible.

Satellite Media Tours

Satellite media tours (SMTs) primarily function as a way for public relations professionals to "virtually" gather people (i.e., journalists) from a vast geographical area all at once without those people having to come to the site of a PR opportunity. The featured event of an SMT is hosted live at a given location (studio or onsite anywhere) by the subject organization and broadcast via satellite link (including web-based transmission) to target people. The idea is to, in effect, bring the place and the event/news to people so they can learn about it, cover it, and share it with their audiences. SMTs in their optimum form are like brief, mini documentaries with multiple camera/site shots about something newsworthy for an organization and its publics. The participants in the SMT are interviewed by a host/interviewer, and there may be opportunity at the end for viewers to pose questions of the participants in a two-way question-and-answer (Q&A) session. In their simplest form, SMTs can be used for beaming interviews or press conferences to journalists. In the latter case, the term *satellite media tour* (emphasis on satellite) seems to be used in an overly generalized way that makes the discourse more befitting the B-roll for a VNR or video program. Either way the content of an SMT is meant to be used as a primary substance for any news story that may be told by a news organization. The material may also be used by the hosting organization in other internal and external public relations discourse.

Press Kits

Press kits (sometimes referred to as "communication packages") contain several documents and other support material (e.g., press releases, photos, graphics, fact sheets, speech transcripts, computer discs with electronic files of printed matter) pertaining to a subject in one folder for easy handling, reference, and use by journalists and other interested parties. The key is to think critically about the value to journalists for anything you might include so they can prepare a story effectively and accurately. Press kits can be distributed at a press conference, sent to journalists and others unable to attend, placed in a press room at a trade show, sent electronically via mail or posted online at a corporate website, and given to others as a "leave-behind."

Hardcopy press kits are the traditional form for this genre. They include a carrier for the discourse it contains, and the best carriers are simple two-pocket folders or a 9 × 12-inch envelope. Note that the carrier can be reasonably creative, but understand that impressing editors with the packaging is no guarantee of newsworthiness or, especially, coverage. In hardcopy press kits, content should be organized effectively. For example, in two-pocket folders, the right side is primary because, like a book, it is the first area seen. So in the right pocket, news releases, bios, and speech transcript or unpublished articles would be placed. The left side is secondary and contains support material (front to back) such as photos/graphics, technical information, and brief organizational background/history. In large envelopes, the material is organized in a single stack that is organized like it would be for a folder.

Press kits are meant to make it easy for journalists to access and use the information you provide for them. So hardcopy press kits should not put literature carriers inside envelopes, use sealed envelopes, bury news releases, omit dates, omit graphics, include too many news releases, reuse old kits, or include "nonessentials" such as a letter describing the *news release*, ad reprints, article reprints, four-color literature carriers and brochures, lengthy backgrounders, and other "eye-candy." Increasingly, portable electronic media, namely, CD-ROMs and USB memory sticks/"flash drives," are used to provide journalists with the files they need in ways that allow them to immediately access and use the very texts in press kits. All files must be easily identifiable by their file names. Organizing files into folders or using multiple links to items should be used cautiously because such an organizational scheme may not work well for all people and, especially, can make finding and remembering where files are difficult. Electronic media require that the files be compatible with Apple, Microsoft, Linux, and other operating systems and desktop software. Any graphics should be provided in high-resolution form when in hardcopy and in multiple levels of resolution in electronic form.

Online press kits are made available on corporate websites as special areas of company news. The web address for any online press kit should be given in hardcopy press kits and other communication with journalists so they can use that resource in their work. Online press kits—also referred to as online "press rooms"—must be designed, populated with information, and maintained with journalists' expectations and needs in mind, even though nonjournalists may use the resource. An effective online press kit is one that is linked from the homepage and is linked from every page in the site; features searchable archives of news and corporate documents for public use; lists or enables a search for experts, events, and reports/documents; contains a complete list of corporate contacts for the media; does not require more than two clicks to get to content pages; is the place where press releases are first published, not over wire services; includes dates and contacts on every press release; features a daily digest of announcements with links to supporting documents or webpages; includes links to announcements from other sections of the website; lists awards and recognitions; and provides company background in the forms of reports, articles, case studies, and other documentation about the organization's influence, success, and contributions to the common good. Online press kits should also include links to financial data (primarily for publicly traded companies), company history, executive bios, and downloadable images in various formats (TIFF, GIF, JPEG) in high and low resolutions. The most effective press rooms do not force reporters to register, should keep the information current and show it as such, and market the press room through opt-in e-mail of news for reporters, links from other webpages to the press room, and printing the press room's web address on any correspondence or public relations discourse.

Message Design

Showcase genres perhaps reflect the most traditional perspectives on epideictic discourse. Press conferences, for example, are a display of rhetorical expertise in the context of one speaker addressing a live audience in much the way Aristotle's speakers addressed ancient Greeks as part of ceremonial situations. Indeed, showcase genres in general are the most celebratory of the genres covered in this book, so we concentrate on that function first. Because these genres are part of the public record, their preservative function is second. Next follows the epistemic function. Showcase genres deal with focused matters. This is not to say that the relationship between speaker and audience, the genres' performative function, is much less important because it is placed last. Rather, all four functions are extremely important to the success of advertorials, PSAs, press conferences, SMTs, and press kits.

All epideictic functions are important, as we said in Chapter 2, and depending on the family of discourse genres, the importance of epideictic functions (and their individual dimensions) varies in ways (see Appendix 1) that explain why they work so differently and potently. In fact, the balance among organization, message topic, and audience is a key to making the most of the four epideictic functions. Wayne Booth (1963), in an oft-cited article in the field, argued that a *rhetorical stance* occurs when speakers address audiences in such a way that a message does not overemphasize one element more than another: "The available arguments about the subject itself, the interests and peculiarities of the audience, and the voice, the implied character, of the speaker" (p. 141). Applied to public relations message design, no topic is so intrinsically interesting that it need not relate to organizational or audience interests. Likewise, the message should not feature the organization's credibility at the expense of the other elements anymore than should the audience's wants and desires. At times in this section, then, we offer examples relevant to each function that illustrate effective and ineffective stances in message design.

1. Celebratory Function

Showcase genres feature the ritualistic dimension of epideictic celebration more so than other genres. Secondarily, its axiological dimension is of primary concern for, as Perelman and Olbrechts-Tyteca (1969) point out, epideictic discourse focuses chiefly on values—in this case, the values of the organization *and* those of its publics.

Formal patterns are the stuff of ritual. Showcases follow certain patterns, such as the opening of a news conference or the placement of a phone number or Web address at the end of a PSA. Ritual, however, must not become rote. Think of how often you have heard your local American Red Cross chapter's 10- to 15-second announcements about a shortage of O-positive blood donations. Short PSAs that state the same thing every 2 to 3 months get lost in the sea of today's message environment. In contrast, a Christian Aid (2009) advertorial invites the reader to adventure: "This overnight team challenge will test your physical endurance—you will trek 60 miles in 30 hours—and take you on a journey in one of the most beautiful places in the UK" (para. 1). In five short paragraphs accompanied by five photos, the message walks readers through a trek that Christian Aid hopes to persuade them to take for real: a 60-mile, 30-hour fundraising hike from the Scottish border to Holy Island off the coast of Northumberland. The message imitates the pattern of the pilgrimage.

Showcase genres particularly highlight the core values of their messages. In the preceding example, "by raising money for Christian Aid, you'll be giving poor communities the chance of a brighter future." A similar advertorial celebrates the 8th anniversary of Tubbs Snowshoes' (2009) "Romp to Stomp Out Breast Cancer." Value appeals, of course, are central to the work that PSAs' genre conventions accomplish. In "Sex and the Kitty," People for the Ethical Treatment of Animals (n.d.g) uses only four sentences in between scenes of cats mating while their owner has left the house (with rock music to set the mood, too) to drive home the need to spay or neuter your pet. In between different shots, white-lettered sentences on black backgrounds imply core values the audience should reject or espouse: "Over 2.4 million unwanted kittens are born each year" (neglect). "Most will be put to death" (cruelty vs. humaneness). "It's a problem you can fix. SPAY OR NEUTER YOUR CAT" (responsibility). This PSA illustrates an important tension between ritual and values. It can be tempting to use language, visuals, and music to gain audience attention yet overwhelm the content of the primary message. Such appeals to the audience qualify as Booth's (1963) *advertiser's stance.* PETA's "Sex and the Kitty" comes near to the edge of losing the proper rhetorical stance, but its attention to the message and to consistency with its reputation make this PSA balanced.

2. Preservative Function

The genres we covered in earlier chapters have placed this function third or fourth in priority. With showcases, however, epideictic's preservative function follows the celebratory. Only one other set of genres, reports, places the preservative function high in importance (see Chapter 9). Given the assorted media tactics that may be included in press kits and used during news conferences, its dominant dimension is cohesion. Showcase genres facilitate repurposing, but self-persuasion should occur primarily for the audience, not the organization.

As implied in the previous section, each showcase genre has specific formal demands. A good press conference includes a key message platform with strong proof points to support it. Like other showcase genres, press conferences provide a public record of the organization's perspective on a given situation. As such, organizations hope that the key message, or at least some of its evidence, becomes part of media reports of the conference, thereby becoming preserved through news retrieval and perhaps through audience memory. Philadelphia Eagles player Terrell Owens' November 8, 2005, attempt to be reinstated after the team's management suspended him (for blaming quarterback Donovan McNabb for the team's record and for calling it an embarrassment that there was no in-stadium announcement for his own 100th career touchdown) failed in part because he did not directly apologize for disparaging public comments (Brazeal, 2008). The crisis communication literature is filled with instances in which the key message should have been admission of guilt, thereby making a cohesive set of messages across genres difficult (for an exception, see Jerome, 2008).

In contrast, online press kits, like their hard-copy counterparts, bring cohesion to a wide set of messages in multiple discourse types. The Heritage Foundation's (2009a) "press room" provides links to the organization's news releases, blogs, experts, commentaries, event calendar, and timely graphics (e.g., a comparison of global averages to American corporate tax rates; see also Heritage Foundation, 2009b). Likewise, PETA's (n.d.a, n.d.b, n.d.d) more general PSAs against cruelty to animals support messages specific to particular campaigns—for example, "PetSmart: Stop Cruel Animal Sales" (PETA, n.d.f) and "McCruelty: I'm Hatin' It" (PETA, n.d.e), as well as to its anticruelty campaign in general (PETA, n.d.c). PETA's Media Center is less an online press kit and more of a clearinghouse for links to specific media tactics and to separate, specific campaign websites (the ones against PetSmart and McDonald's are but a few).

Showcase genres readily lend themselves to repurposing. Indeed, they often include some material repurposed from other discourse (e.g., bios, backgrounders, and article reprints in press kits). A good example of this is the American Dental Association's (ADA, 2009a) satellite media tour featuring an Iraqi War soldier who received extensive reconstructive surgery after a roadside bomb attack left him with serious head and facial injuries. Video of the SMT documents a dentist's various responsibilities in such situations.

These same copy points are also featured in a news release (ADA, 2009b) and a brochure (ADA, n.d.) and its online version (ADA, 1995–2009).

Equally important is repurposing in the form of providing messages that can or will be used in later discourse. Key ideas in a December 2009 news conference by U.S. attorney general for the northern district of Illinois, Patrick Fitzgerald, came from the 76-page complaint against now-former Governor Rod Blagojevich and naturally appeared when "Blago" went to retrial in 2011. Fitzgerald revealed one particular allegation during the press conference that became referenced frequently in the Illinois Senate's impeachment of Blagojevich:

> I'll give you two examples set forth in the 76-page complaint. One involves Children's Memorial Hospital, a hospital that obviously takes care of children. At one point, the governor awarded funding—reimbursement funding to that hospital to the tune of $8 million, but he also indicated privately that what he wanted to get was a $50,000 personal contribution from the chief executive officer of that hospital. In the ensuing weeks, that contribution never came, and Governor Blagojevich was intercepted on the telephone, checking to see whether or not he could pull back the funding for Children's Memorial Hospital. (C-SPAN, 2008; Sweet, 2008, para. 8)

Several state senators turned this allegation into an opportunity to address the need for children's health care during final comments explaining their votes against the governor.

Finally, showcase genres have a self-persuasion dimension that focuses on the preservative function's role in reinforcing attitude change and other potential audience effects. For example, R. J. Reynolds (1995), the maker of Camel cigarettes, placed a rather unusual advertorial in the *Village Voice* to highlight nightspots in New York City. The bulk of the ad looks like a listing of nightclubs, the bands that will be playing there, and so on. Yet the framing sets up the potential for the audience to participate in its own persuasion: "For a change of pace, we are giving you an overview of all the venues in the Camel Club Program. Take time to check-out these hot spots. Next week, things will be back to normal. (Meanwhile, define normal.)" (p. 27). All the audience has to do is select a nightclub in order to be exposed to more messages to smoke Camels.

Be careful, however, to beware of the self-persuasion element in terms of the organization itself. Certainly organizations, through any act of campaign communication, will reinforce in the minds of its members what the organization stands for. But recall Sun Microsystem and Google's nonevent of a press conference referred to in Chapter 2, which focused too much attention on the people involved in the event and in the merger, which had already been announced. This overemphasis on the speaker is called the *entertainer's stance* (Booth, 1963): "the willingness to sacrifice substance to personality and charm" (p. 144). The organization basically is saying, "Look at us. Aren't we something?" The same would be true of the nonprofit that pays more homage to itself in a PSA than attention to the cause that it allegedly champions.

In contrast, dynamism to make messages memorable to audiences can arrest their attention in dramatic ways. In preparation for its "Wild Reef: Sharks at Shedd" display at Shedd Aquarium in Chicago, several small advertising, marketing, and public relations agencies worked together to produce a variety of tactics, including a media kit on CD-ROM (Germann & Boutelle, 2003). The CD opens with a picture of a dive mask and sounds of scuba tank breathing. The animation within the mask's "glass" goes from the shore, down into Lake Michigan, through an underwater entry, and into the museum's display. The journalist can choose from a variety of links to pictures of fish, sharks, and corals, downloadable photos and news releases, interactive backgrounders and feature stories, an interactive map of the display, and even a "Build a Shark" computer program to install and play with on a computer.

3. Epistemic Function

As might be suggested by the examples offered thus far, showcase genres have both educational and explanatory dimensions. We address them in that order and then apply Booth's rhetorical stance to indicate their importance.

As mentioned in Chapter 2, showcase genres such as PSAs and advertorials present ideas in such a way to connect cultural virtues (and therefore values) within the minds of publics. For example, an organization as an award winner may be likely to associate the organization's prestige with an alternative to standard industry practices. Advantage Development Company (2009), an Asheville, North Carolina, building contractor, placed an advertorial in the Asheville *Citizen-Times* to inform readers of "an alternative to the conventional 'lump sum' or 'cost plus percentage' that most builders offer" (para. 1). Immediately following this notion, the company seeks to build credibility in this manner:

> Advantage Development Co. is known for their [sic] high level of craftsmanship and solid reputation in the area. They've won the Asheville Parade of Homes award five different years and their custom-built homes can be found in many of the premiere communities in and around Asheville. . . . (para. 2)

Likewise, the Shedd Aquarium (Germann & Boutelle, 2003) CD-ROM press kit informs media contacts regarding a variety of types of sea life, information that most are unfamiliar with. The core values of science, environment, and exploration become what provide the context for the viewer.

Showcase genres also use audience knowledge as a context for new knowledge. A press kit for Woodhead Connectivity (2003) illustrates the explanatory dimension quite simply. Used to reach attendees at an industry trade show, one of its news releases announces an adapter for connecting "your 1769 Allen-Bradley® Compact I/O™ to an Allen-Bradley® Remote I/O network." Of course, not all new information is as arcane as the intricacies of computer technology. For example, news conferences in professional sports depend on media representatives and fans who keep up with the context in which sports news is taking place. In the wake of revelations that New England Patriots staff had violated NFL videotaping regulations by the play-calling signals of five opponents in six games between 2000 and 2002 (National Football League, n.d.), Commissioner Roger Goodell made sure that all reporters attending a May 2008 news conference were familiar with the scandal's circumstances: "I think you all have seen the tapes. If you want to see them again, we'll do it right now. Anybody want to see them again? I guess not" (NFL, 2008, para. 2). He then reported two new developments in the investigation. In similar fashion, Black Box Media Group (2009) used the "Cash for Clunkers" government vehicle trade-in program as a springboard to alert consumers through an SMT to tax credits available for energy-efficient appliances and home improvements.

In terms of Booth's (1963) rhetorical stance, effective use of the epistemic function's educational and explanatory dimensions balances concerns for the message with attention to an organization's position and the interests of the audience. When crafting messages to educate publics, the values implied in them should be those that will resonate with audiences and also reflect positively on the organization in ways consistent with its reputation and actual business practices. This, of course, ties in to showcase genres' primary function of celebration and the axiological dimension. When building explanations, message designers must pay attention to audience perceptions of fact as a basis for extending knowledge.

4. Performative Function

When enacting epideictic's performative function, as Booth (1963) prescribes, its rhetorical and identity-management dimensions always should be balanced in message design. However, even in organizational crisis communication, with its emphasis on image repair and frequent use of press conferences and press kits to accomplish it, it should place concerns for audience adaptation first. We, therefore, place the rhetorical dimension first in importance under showcase genres' performative function, with identity management close behind. In both cases, we offer examples that illustrate Booth's stances to avoid as well as the proper rhetorical stance. We conclude this section with the political dimension, which depends a great deal on the nature of the situation and the issue being addressed.

Rhetorical dimension. For the message designer, audience adaptation should be foremost in relating the performative function along with the three other functions. As suggested by our earlier discussions, knowing publics and adapting to them is instrumental to the celebratory and epistemic functions of showcase genres. We offer two examples to illustrate.

In 1991, the Church of Scientology (CSI) offered a series of advertorials via full-page ads in *USA Today* as part of its effort to regain its tax-exempt status from the federal government. In contrast to earlier issue advertising that it used to attack the *Los Angeles Times* and *Time* magazine in response to exposés in those periodicals in 1990 and 1991, the *USA Today* advertorials used a villain in its scenarios with which audiences could readily identify: the tax man. The first advertorials in the series, "IRS: An Agency Out of Control," are reminiscent of reality programming reenactments (although lacking the vividness of video to accompany the text). The first ad (Church of Scientology, 1991a) described IRS raids in a Maryland Amish community, a Michigan day-care center, and homes in Idaho Falls and Houston. In the second advertorial (Church of Scientology, 1991b), vignettes include a victim who committed suicide, a senator whose IRS files were used as source material for an article accusing him of taking bribes, and an Alaska couple left "bruised and bleeding" (p. 8B), all as the result of IRS actions.

In contrast, Planned Parenthood's (n.d.b [2008] separate website for its campaign to adolescents, "Take Care Down There" (Planned Parenthood, n.d.a [2008]), features a PSA jingle that certainly will appeal to young men, but probably for the wrong reasons. The song employs more than 30 euphemisms for male and female genitalia to lead up to the main point: "Guys, guys. Look, whatever you call it, you gotta know how to take care of it. So check out TakeCareDownThere.org." If this PSA is used as a teaser via cable television channels, for example, to get teens to the website, all well and good—but the other PSAs found at that address are not the same. They have a more serious tone; use frank, specific language and slang; and suggest through camera shots different scenes of varieties of sexual activity (hetero- and homosexual). Conversations featuring teenagers in various scenarios are interrupted by the singer from the jingle PSA to drive home the serious message of protection during any sexual activity. The jingle PSA's use of slang, brightly colored graphics, and music may gain audience attention, but it all applies an advertiser's stance (Booth, 1963), risking focus on the real message and an authentic voice for the organization. Balancing humor and relevance is not easy.

Identity-management dimension. Source credibility is critical for showcase genres because the voice behind the message clearly represents the organization. Many of this book's readers recognize the importance of having a corporate official as a spokesperson for a news conference, particularly during crises. Indications of the source's ethos also have implications for the degree of success a message has. For example, Christian Aid's (2009) purpose of helping the poor and Tubbs Snowshoes' (2009) event to fight breast cancer most likely reflect positively on the organization and, in the case of the latter, Tubbs' corporate social responsibility, whereas Advantage Development's (2009) advertorial clearly has a profit motive that makes it a clear effort to persuade. Indeed, the Church of Scientology's (1991a, 1991b) advertorials would be suspect with audience recognition of the "National Coalition of IRS Whistleblowers." The group is one that readers are invited to join, but it does not exist, and the church at that time was seeking to regain its tax-exempt status, which reveals a clear self-interested motive for CSI.

Inattention to the identity-management dimension and its relationship to all four epideictic functions runs the risk of falling into the stances Booth (1963) recommends to avoid. Toncar, Reid, and Anderson (2007) found in an experiment that choice of PSA spokesperson may shift audience trust. Respondents rated messages featuring victims of Hurricane Katrina more trustworthy than those using nationally known celebrity spokespersons. Local celebrities also were seen as more trustworthy than national ones, although there was no significant different between ratings of local celebrities and victims. Using a high-profile spokesperson can make the celebrity the message, rather than a PSA's content, thus creating the entertainer's stance. For example, the comedian, Cedric the Entertainer, and the rap star, Nelly, bring a serious tone to their words as much as Morgan Freeman does in a series of PSA appeals for donations to complete the Martin Luther King, Jr., Memorial (National Memorial Project Foundation, 2006–2009a, 2006–2009b, 2006–2009c). However, the effect of a spokesperson's high credibility on audience recall may fade over time, according to research on the so-called "sleeper effect" (Larson, 2007), leaving the message content in memory but without its credible source referent.

Messages can become important for their own sake yet not adapted to speaker and audience. This is Booth's (1963) *pedant's stance*: "ignoring or underplaying the personal relationship of speaker and audience and depending entirely on statements about a subject" (p. 141). Such was the case with a Friday afternoon news conference to announce the finding of the legendary Sasquatch, also known as Bigfoot (McCarthy, 2008). Two Georgia men claimed they found its corpse while hiking, and Bigfoot hunter Tom Biscardi hosted the news conference but declined to display the beast, hurriedly showing two photos (Fox News, 2008) and asserting that "he had invited Fox News reporter Megan Kelly to show it on-air and that a number of scientists would be performing an autopsy on Monday" (para. 2), which resulted "in the skeptical audience . . . on the verge of heckling" (para. 3). As it turns out, Bigfoot tracker Biscardi and the two Georgians, Matthew Whitton and Rick Dyer, may have given the audience through other media channels the message that it wanted: two websites devoted to selling "Searching for Bigfoot" or "BigfootTracker.com" hats, caps, pewter belt buckles, and welcome mats (Matyszczyk, 2008). What seemed to be a message of intrinsic interest easily shifts to the advertiser's stance.

The identity-management function, therefore, depends on the rhetorical dimension because knowing how audiences respond to the persona behind the message is key for advertorials, press conferences, and PSAs. A simple message, such as that included in the U.S. Department of Agriculture Forest Service's (n.d.) PSAs, "We need forests," uttered by Bill Nye the Science Guy in wild, outdoor settings and 15, 20, 30, and 60 seconds in length, appropriately balance the needs of organization, target public, and message design.

Political dimension. The rhetorical stance for showcase genres depends largely on the situation when considering the degree of advocacy that is warranted. The key here is that the organization takes the role of community leader and the audience acts as observer and judge (Oravec, 1976). In contrast to advertorials, some advocacy efforts appear low key in PSAs. For example, the National Fatherhood Initiative (1994–2009) uses Tiger Woods, wild animals, and animation ("Big Daddy," featuring Godzilla and his son, walking together to Harry Nilsson singing the theme from TV's "The Courtship of Eddie's Father") to convey its messages of the importance of fathers spending time with their children ("Elephants") and "changing the world" through them, "one child at a time" ("Tiger"). In contrast, former Idaho Senator Larry Craig held a press conference in late August 2007 to deny being homosexual and to express regret for pleading guilty to disorderly conduct for a June 11 incident in a Minneapolis airport men's room and vehemently charged that the *Idaho Statesman* had conducted a "witch hunt" in its coverage of him (Capitol Hub, 2007). As events would later demonstrate, Craig may have told the audience what he thought they wanted to hear. Craig was admonished by the U.S. Senate on February 13, 2008 (Hulse, 2008), and did not seek reelection that fall. The *Statesman* claimed that it had engaged in ethical reporting of the events leading up to Craig's press conference (Manny, 2007).

Showcase genres, then, can be used in more or less political ways. What makes them rhetorically in balance must be weighed in terms of how the message reflects on the organization; its recognition of audience interests, knowledge, and values; and how the issue was addressed to meet the needs of both parties. Appropriateness to the situation, therefore, is key (see Chapter 2 on Bitzer's "rhetorical situation") because faulty message design may lead to the traps that should be avoided in Booth's (1963) three rhetorical stances.

Strategic Planning Implications

When an organization feels it must command attention on the public stage, public relations' showcase genres enable such appropriately selfish communication. "Selfish" in this regard is justified because of the need for an organization to call attention to itself, its messages, and its relationships with its audiences. An organization, however, is not the true originator of any communication—that is done by a person, a corporate speaker. Cheney (1991) asserts that a corporate speaker is "confined largely to the alternative(s) 'seen' or associated with his or her personal targets of identification [i.e., the process by which identity is 'appropriated'], in seeking to do 'what's best' for the organization" (p. 19). The targets for identification may well include multiple audiences, which is a common goal for corporate speakers. Those corporate speakers, in turn, become "the face" of an organization for all publics receiving information through showcase genres. The net effect of a corporate official's rhetoric enacted on an organization's behalf is that "the individual or self is to some degree decentered through self-definition and self-diffusion in corporate symbols, images, [and] messages" (Cheney, 1992, p. 176).

The need for an organization to call attention to itself, its messages, and its relationships with its audiences may be reactive or proactive, and it is always strategic. It is strategic because of the constant expectation that any communication must be in tune with the PR function's operating plan and, by extension, help an organization get closer to fulfilling its overall objectives, actualizing its mission, and realizing its vision. Public relations officials who use showcase genres effectively enact a literal drama for target publics about a matter an organization faces through a sound combination of a rhetorical stance about the matter and the epideictic functions for designing message content. Corporate spokespeople's messages became identified with both internal and external audiences—those people become the embodiment of the organization and do so with one or more audiences. Corporate speakers, then, tend to personalize their organizations' images because "some corporate messages become identified with individuals and those individual speakers become the embodiment of organizations" (Cheney, 1992, p. 178). Ultimately, the effective use of showcase genres helps publics' members see themselves somehow in or part of the matter and motivated to cooperate in some way, whether it is intellectually, emotionally, behaviorally, or some combination of these.

We should note that some organizations, particularly the kinds we used in the advertorial examples, may choose not to use a chosen corporate speaker/rhetor in showcase genres. Instead they use these genres because they allow an organization to exercise more control over its message holistically. Such control, for example, is easily obtained with the pay-for-placement nature of advertorials, which risk the loss of credibility because advertorials are typically labeled as "advertisements" in headers or footers to the main text. In the Church of Scientology examples, identification of itself is rather veiled because the labels of the pieces as advertisements are small and refer to their being paid for by the church. The Camel Club example, in contrast, is explicit due to the nature of the nightclubs as participating members. Still other examples (Advantage Development and Tubbs Snowshoes) from today's online news stories indicate advertorials clearly as such.

Regardless of type, the rhetorical stance of showcase genres works to maintain their celebratory character. It is somewhat like inviting publics to a party with the organization as the guest of honor. Think of epideictic message design like planning a birthday party of sorts. Because it is never a surprise party, you are the person who consults with the host regarding what would be appropriate and whom to invite. The cake (the message) should be something the organization (the figurative "birthday girl" or "birthday boy") really likes but something that the guests (the media and other publics) would enjoy (Booth's rhetorical stance). To make the design of the cake or the party decorations so attention-getting that they detract from the purpose of the party would be inappropriate (the pedant's stance). To draw attention to the party's honoree so much that the guests become bored and the reason for being there is less about the occasion than the person would be inappropriate as well (the entertainer's stance). The guests deserve attention, too, making them feel welcome, but they are not the main reason for the event either (the advertiser's stance). Everything should work together so that the party is about the reason for being there.

The strategic implications for showcase genres, then, are largely opportunistic and fairly grand in scale. Organization officials who believe that "grabbing the mic and taking the stage" is the best way to handle a communication opportunity do so with an understanding that the dramatic climate in which they and the organization will participate will be highly visible and subject everyone to heightened levels of scrutiny. The risk-reward potential is huge. The return on the investment (ROI) for proactive and reactive showcase discourse must yield dividends in terms of effective outputs (great public relations products), outtakes (immediate neutral-to-positive audience response to messages), outcomes (eventual attitude and/or behavior changes), and outgrowths (lasting attitude and/or behavior changes) about the matter at hand now and over the foreseeable future. Seemingly simple aspects, such as associating a celebrity with a product or service and, thereby, the organization offering the product or service, become profound because of the cost of securing and using that endorsement in public relations discourse. A way to anticipate ROI here are Q-scores for celebrities, which reveal publics' attitudes in this regard and aid organizations in making the best choices for celebrity endorsements, if they should be used at all.

Questions about the effects on publics' knowledge, opinions, and behaviors are key for the strategic and successful use of showcase (and other) genres. How may a matter facing an organization reflect on its image and reputation? Might the matter affect publics' good will toward the organization in any ways? Could publics significantly alter the ways they act toward the organization? Anticipating answers and actions to these and other questions are key to strategic planning and decision making that bear on the public relations function's performance vis-à-vis its discourse and its contribution to the organization's overall performance.

Showcase genres, by their nature, allow organizations to place themselves in a broadly visible light to audiences. This kind of play on the public stage means the conventions for these genres are fairly stable—the conventions for and, particularly, the production of, the literal discourse rarely change. Other genres, however, are more prone to change, especially when caused by new communication technologies. In Chapter 8, we focus on genres that "collect" and present information to publics in ways that are in tune with established discourse conventions, but the actual discourse media have changed over time, revealing life cycles for genres.

Note

1. Although there is a kind of theatrical sensibility about showcase genres, as we named the family of them here, we do not consider events a sufficiently specific genre for public relations. Indeed, we see events comprising numerous types that each could be defined as a genre. When public relations has any role to play in any event is a good thing, but the sheer number of possible event types that could be possibly created, plus the fact that events host many varied discourse types (public relations and not), places them outside the bounds of this book. We continue to use the word *event* in a general sense throughout this book.

References

Advantage Development Co. (2009, March 6). Advantage Development Co. plots new course. [Advertorial]. *Asheville* (NC) *Citizen-Times* [Online]. Retrieved March 7, 2009, from http://www.citizen-times.com/apps/pbcs.dll/article?AID=200990305062

American Dental Association. (1995–2009). *Dentists: Doctors of oral health.* Retrieved December 30, 2009, from http://www.ada.org/public/dentists_docs.asp

American Dental Association. (2009a, June 11). *Dentists: Doctors of oral health.* [Satellite media tour video]. Retrieved December 30, 2009, from http://www.ada.org/public/media/videos/vnr/smt_poole_broadband.wmv

American Dental Association. (2009b, July 9). *Satellite media tour emphasizes dentists' role on health care team.* [News release]. Retrieved December 30, 2009, from http://www.ada.org/prof/resources/pubs/adanews/adanewsarticle.asp?articleid=3645

American Dental Association. (n.d.). *Dentists: Doctors of oral health.* [Brochure]. Retrieved December 30, 2009, from http://www.ada.org/prof/advocacy/brochure_091204_dentists_drs.pdf

Black Box Media Group. (2009, November 2). *Cash for clunkers 2 satellite media tour.* Retrieved December 30, 2009, from http://www.youtube.com/watch?v=ecQciaLj4R8

Booth, W. C. (1963). The rhetorical stance. *College Composition and Communication, 14,* 139–145.

Brazeal, L. M. (2008). The image repair strategies of Terrell Owens. *Public Relations Review, 34,* 145–150.

Capitol Hub. (2007, August 28). *Sen. Larry Craig press conference.* [Video]. Retrieved March 9, 2009, from http://capitolhub.com/video/6325/sen-larry-craig-press-conference

Cheney, G. (1991). *Rhetoric in an organizational society: Managing multiple identities.* Columbia: University of South Carolina Press.

Cheney, G. (1992). The corporate person (re)presents itself. In E. L. Toth & R. L. Heath (Eds.), *Rhetorical and critical approaches to public relations* (pp. 165–183). Hillsdale, NJ: Erlbaum.

Christian Aid. (2009, February 28). *Advertorial: Holy Island midnight challenge.* Retrieved March 7, 2009, from http://www.outdoorsmagic.com/news/article/mps/uan/5864

Church of Scientology International. (1991a, September 3). "Don't you kill my Daddy!" [Advertisement]. *USA Today,* p. 8b.

Church of Scientology International. (1991b, September 4). "You will find my body . . . on the north side of the house." [Advertisement]. *USA Today,* p. 8b.

C-SPAN. (2008, December 9). *FBI press conference on Gov. Rod Blagojevich (D-IL) corruption charges.* [News conference/video]. Retrieved March 7, 2009, from http://www.c-span.org/Watch/watch.aspx?MediaId=HP-A-13273

Fox News. (2008, August 18). *Bigfoot hunters' press conference reveals . . . little.* Retrieved March 9, 2009, from http://www.foxnews.com/story/0,2933,404805,00.html

Germann, R. (Producer), & Boutelle, T. (Associate Producer/Writer). (2003). *Wild reef: Sharks at Shedd.* [Press kit CD-ROM]. Chicago: John G. Shedd Aquarium.

Guess, J. B. (2004, December 17). *Determined to reach a wider audience, UCC releases new pre-Christmas commercial on television networks.* [News release]. Retrieved December 18, 2004, from http://www.ucc.org/news/u121704.htm

Heritage Foundation. (2009a). *Press room.* Retrieved March 8, 2009, from http://www.heritage.org/press/

Heritage Foundation. (2009b, February 24). *#044—Tax burden hobbles America in global market—February 24, 2009.* Retrieved March 8, 2009, from http://author.heritage.org/Press/ALAChart/alachart-detail.cfm?customel_data pageid_244663=303263

Hulse, C. (2008, February 14). *Senate ethics committee admonishes Larry Craig.* Retrieved March 9, 2009, from http://www.nytimes.com/2008/02/14/washington/14craig.html

Jerome, A. M. (2008). Toward prescription: Testing the rhetoric of atonement's applicability in the athletic arena. *Public Relations Review, 34,* 124–134.

Larson, C. U. (2007). *Persuasion: Reception and responsibility* (11th ed.). Belmont, CA: Wadsworth.

Manny, B. (2007, August 27). *Statesman response to Craig news conference.* Retrieved March 9, 2009, from http://www.idahostatesman.com/1264/story/144418.html

Matyszczyk, C. (2008, August 16). *The Bigfoot press conference and the art of selling a website.* Retrieved March 9, 2009, from http://news.cnet.com/8301-17852_3-10018540-71.html

McCarthy, C. (2008, August 15). *Internet captivated by Bigfoot hunters' press conference.* Retrieved March 9, 2009, from http://news.cnet.com/8301-13577_3-10018290-36.html

National Fatherhood Initiative (1994–2009). *Television PSA archive.* Retrieved March 7, 2009, from http://www.fatherhood.org/media/public-service-announcements/television

National Football League. (2008, May 13). *Transcript of commissioner's press conference after Walsh meeting.* Retrieved March 7, 2009, from http://www.nfl.com/news/story?id=09000d5d8084d741&template=with-video&confirm=true

National Football League. (n.d.). *Timeline of events surrounding Patriots' videotaping scandal.* Retrieved March 7, 2009, from http://www.nfl.com/news/story?id=09000d5d8084899e&template=with-video&confirm=true

National Memorial Project Foundation, Inc. (2006–2009a). *Build the dream—Cedric the Entertainer.* [Video public service announcement]. Retrieved March 9, 2009, from http://www.mlkmemorial.org/site/c.hkIUL9MVJxE/b.4979521/k.E56F/Build_The_Dream__Cedric_the_Entertainer.htm

National Memorial Project Foundation, Inc. (2006–2009b). *Build the dream—Morgan Freeman.* [Video public service announcement]. Retrieved March 9, 2009, from http://www.mlkmemorial.org/site/c.hkIUL9MVJxE/b.1247189/k.3964/Build_The_Dream__Morgan_Freeman.htm

National Memorial Project Foundation, Inc. (2006-2009c). *Build the dream—Nelly.* [Video public service announcement]. Retrieved March 9, 2009, from http://www.mlkmemorial.org/site/c.hkIUL9MVJxE/b.1247191/k.59AC/Build_The_Dream__Nelly.htm

Oravec, C. (1976). "Observation" in Aristotle's theory of epideictic. *Philosophy & Rhetoric, 9,* 162-174.

Partnership for a Drug-Free America. (2006, October 24). *The Partnership's "fried egg" TV message.* [News release]. Retrieved March 8, 2009, from http://www.drugfree.org/Portal/About/NewsReleases/Fried_Egg_Message

People for the Ethical Treatment of Animals. (n.d.a). *Dennis Franz/cruelty to animals.* [Public service announcement]. Retrieved March 8, 2009, from http://www.petatv.com/psa.asp

People for the Ethical Treatment of Animals. (n.d.b). *Edie Falco/cruelty to animals.* [Public service announcement]. Retrieved March 8, 2009, from http://www.petatv.com/psa.asp

People for the Ethical Treatment of Animals. (n.d.c). *Helping animals.* Retrieved March 8, 2009, from http://www.helpinganimals.com/index.asp

People for the Ethical Treatment of Animals. (n.d.d). *Julie Benz/violence.* Retrieved March 8, 2009, from http://www.petatv.com/psa.asp

People for the Ethical Treatment of Animals. (n.d.e). *PETA takes on McDonald's: McCruelty.com.* Retrieved March 8, 2009, from http://www.mccruelty.com/

People for the Ethical Treatment of Animals. (n.d.f). *PetSmart cruelty: What's wrong with PetSmart?* Retrieved March 8, 2009, from http://www.petsmartcruelty.com/whats_wrong.asp

People for the Ethical Treatment of Animals. (n.d.g). *Sex and the kitty.* [Video Public Service Announcement]. Retrieved March 7, 2009, from http://www.petatv.com/psa.asp

Perelman, C., & Olbrechts-Tyteca, L. (1969). *The new rhetoric: A treatise on argumentation* (J. Wilkinson & P. Weaver, Trans.). Notre Dame, IN: Notre Dame University Press.

Planned Parenthood. (n.d.a) [2008]. *Down there song.* Retrieved October 29, 2010, from http://www.takecaredownthere.org/#/watch/down-there-song/

Planned Parenthood. (n.d.b) [2008]. *Take care down there.* Retrieved October 29, 2010, from http://www.takecaredownthere.org/

R. J. Reynolds Tobacco Company. (1995, October 10). *Camel page classifieds.* [Advertorial]. *The Village Voice,* p. 27. Retrieved March 7, 2009, from http://legacy.library.ucsf.edu/tid/nvv19a00/tiff

Sweet, L. (2008, December 9). *Fitzgerald press conference on Blagojevich: Transcript.* [Weblog]. Retrieved March 8, 2009, from http://blogs.suntimes.com/sweet/2008/12/fitzgerald_press_conference_on.html

Toncar, M., Reid, J. S., & Anderson, C. E. (2007). Effective spokespersons in a public service announcement: National celebrities, local celebrities, and victims. *Journal of Communication Management, 11,* 258-275.

Tubbs Snowshoes. (2009). *Advertorial: Tubbs Romp to Stomp Out Breast Cancer Snowshoe Series celebrates its eighth anniversary.* Retrieved March 7, 2009, from http://www.snowshoemag.com/view_content.cfm?content_id=493

U.S. Department of Agriculture Forest Service. (n.d.). *USDA Forest Service conservation education: PSA home.* Retrieved March 9, 2009, from http://www.na.fs. fed.us/SPFO/ce/content/pub_service_announce/index.cfm

Woodhead Connectivity. (2003, August–September). *Woodhead: Complete connectivity solutions.* [Press kit]. Northbrook, IL: Daniel Woodhead Company.

8

Collections

The Corporate Round-up

Organizations expend much effort to show their many dimensions and achievements. Key among organizational efforts to communicate what is going on that matters to internal and external audiences are genres that collect and present information in ways that make it easy and attractive to follow the news. These "collections," in effect, round up the timeliest and most relevant stories about an organization and share them in specific forms that balance a variety of information that an organization wants to give and the audiences want to have. This chapter examines the three "collections" genres used in public relations addressing internal and external publics.

Genres and Their Conventions

The "collections" genres of newsletters, magazines, and video news programs are longstanding discourse forms upon which organizations have relied for many decades. Newsletters are essentially concise newspapers whose content and distribution are controlled by PR officials, prepared on a periodic basis, and meant for specific groups of people. Newsletters' lineage technically goes back to the first small-town newspapers, and these publications actually function as a way to keep people in touch with the happenings among the people within an organization (see Brody, 2005; Hudson, 1998). Magazines go well beyond newsletters by emulating the design and content of mainstream magazines but adopt a focus completely on matters of interest to an organization and its target publics. With the advent of video technology—especially after the 1970s—organizational video programs gained much favor among public relations and corporate leaders because of the mass-mediated and timely way they could share news and information with employees/members at corporate locations. All three genres involve dedicated internal and/or external staff to produce them, and the larger the corporate budgets, the more elaborate the finished pieces can be. The influence of Web-based and other new technologies has helped public relations officials to adapt newsletters, magazine content, and video news programs to their organizations' communication needs. Here is a look at the basic conventions for newsletters, magazines, and video news programs.

Newsletters

Newsletters, with the full backing of organizational leaders, provide specific audiences (e.g., company employees, a professional organization's members, nonprofit organizations' volunteers, or special interest groups' supporters) with brief journalistic coverage in text, photos, and illustrations of organizational performance, happenings, issues, people, and other topics of interest. Depending on the communication mission of a newsletter, stories can be written by communication staff, by organizational members, or some combination. The key to quality control is centralized project management by a chief editor. Newsletters can be prepared in print or electronic media, and the latter is typically far less expensive and easy to prepare and fix. Interestingly, electronic versions rely on the conventions for printed newsletters for matters of layout, design, and readability. Verbal and visual elements must be carefully combined on the page space so what is told and what is shown work together to convey messages effectively. Ample sources are available for newsletter design, and graphic design professionals can help as well.

Printed versions are designed as one- or two-color publications (four or more colors may be used if budgets allow) and are typically printed on both sides of 8.5 × 11-inch paper or on 11 × 17-inch paper that is folded in half to be 8.5 × 11 inches in finished size. Other paper sizes can be used as well. Print newsletters also can be prepared in one to four colors and finished in PDF files that are sent to audiences by e-mail or posted on websites for viewing and downloading. These e-newsletters have been referred to as "e-zines," which is meant to capture their electronic nature and simple magazine-like quality. In electronic or print forms, newsletters can be "pushed" to audiences by regular mail, interoffice mail, or e-mail, but care must be taken that they not be considered junk mail or spam. E-newsletters offer an alternative, "pull" delivery method, where audiences choose to subscribe on their own (referred to as "opt in"). In this case, the publication or notification of its readiness for downloading is sent to subscribers when an issue is posted on an organization's website, eliminating the junk e-mail problem. Newsletters can be either "full," which means the content is the same for everyone and everyone gets the same content, or "filtered," which means a variety of content is prepared for electronic distribution and people get only the stories they want based on how a Web-based search system applies a subscriber's search criteria. E-newsletters may also be presented to audiences in e-mail or on web pages with only story titles, the first paragraphs of each story following the title, then link to the full story on the organization's website. This approach allows readers to review content quickly and choose which stories they want to explore in more depth.

Magazines

Magazines are periodic publications that organizations may use that reflect much of the characteristics of mainstream printed magazines. Mainstream magazines project a kind of approachability and audience focus that organizations want to use for their and their publics' mutual benefit. Like those in the mainstream, magazines used for public relations efforts include cover, feature, and sidebar stories. They also may include summaries of "breaking" news of interest to the organization and other content. The key, however, is that magazines are solely focused on the organization and its publics in every respect. This genre is meant to be more engaging and, in effect, more in-depth on matters that warrant such coverage for target publics. In this way, magazines could be seen as "newsletters on steroids" because they are longer (more pages), published less frequently, and much more sophisticated because of their planning, design, content, and writing style.

Video News Programs

Video news programs dynamically cover, like newsletters and with management's full support, an organization's news, announcements, environmental influences, and other topics for its members. These programs resemble local television news programs because they have one or two people as the "anchors," prerecorded news segments (perhaps with a field reporter covering a story), and other features common to broadcast news. Decisions must be made about the purpose of the program, what its "brand" will be, what its episodes will contain and how they will look (including the stage, graphics, camera framing, etc.), and who is going to host the program. Scripts are essential because they document both the program content and directions for the producer and editor for what the content must be and what audio and video elements go together.

Video news programs have the advantage of being the most lifelike and self-contained medium, which uses color, graphics, motion, sound, animation, and other techniques. Video news programs can be costly and resource-dependent to do well. They may be seen as a combination of information/news and entertainment (i.e., "infotainment") instead of useful, on-the-job information, and difficult to use for large audiences. A requirement is a playback system or, depending on an organization's makeup, scheduled viewing times for individuals or groups (e.g., break times or team meetings at a manufacturing facility). Web technology has made access to videos easier for organizational members so they can view programs online anywhere there is an Internet connection. Video news programs can be produced and made available online in single programs (sometimes referred to as "webcasts") or divided up into individual stories that are accessible through dedicated links to the video for each story. Either way, the fundamentals of the genre remain intact. Live programs, too, can be produced when needed and made available over a closed circuit for television viewing or on an organization's website. Chances are good that the online access for either recorded or live programs would be over a secured website so that access can be made only by authorized users; otherwise, secure access may only be possible on an organization's intranet, thereby restricting access outside an organization's firewall.

Message Design

Genres have life cycles (Jamieson, 1973), and they arise and dissolve in response to recurring situations and audience needs to accomplish particular purposes. In Chapter 3, we noted briefly how the print news release has spawned other news genres: audio news releases, video news releases, and media advisories. To use a metaphor from biology, we might say that the news release developed useful mutations. Likewise, collections genres seem to have evolved in response to the changing technological environment, enabling organizations to fulfill public relations and business objectives in more cost-effective ways. However, the fact that the form and delivery of newsletters and organizational news programs have changed, like other genres we have covered in this book, does not mean that collections genres' functions have. It is easy to let changes from print to electronic media suggest the contrary.

Although newsletters and organizational news programs have changed from being "push" media to "pull" (to a large extent), their formal constraints, message strategies, and epideictic functions have remained the same. In terms of formal patterns, collections genres always have been organized much like a patchwork quilt. The patches (i.e., the stories) may look different one from another, but the quilt (i.e., the discourse genre) has a particular pattern. For example, in the late 19th century, the second author's great-great-grandmother made a fan-patterned quilt on a black background. If she had used a white background, the variegated fans would have appeared less bright. Nonetheless, the organization of the patches to make the fan shapes would remain the same. At first blush, changes in media channels would suggest that the stories which comprise newsletters and corporate news programs have become less connected and, therefore, more fragmented through electronic presentation. On closer examination, this observation is not true. Actually, collections genres are well organized and apply three organizing principles, the last of which is the set of epideictic functions. The first two, equally important to understand, are easily explained.

First, we have the matter of form, which concerns the parameters and limitations of what can be created and how much of it. Organizational imperatives drive the second organizing principle of placement, which concerns the order of stories in the sequence of all stories to be told. In collections genres, the seeming haphazard manner in which stories may be read and organized in a newsletter or corporate news program follows a formal principle of the quilt that combines form and placement: the *patchwork*. The size of space available (page space for print and time for video) and the placement of the patches (beginning, middle, and end) constrain what stories may be used and how long or short they may be. That is, the stories are organized in a sequence that matters and in ways that literally fit the space. Matters of form and placement of stories traditionally were governed by internal communication specialists who made editorial decisions about content with the approval of management. On corporate websites and intranets, such decisions may be made by specialists called "webmasters." Moreover, the message strategies within the stories are driven by core values and themes associated with the organization's identity, what researchers today call organizational *topoi* (i.e., themes or topics based on Aristotle's principle of the same name). We maintain that proper usage of collections genres employ an organization's core values and themes to unite seemingly disparate stories into cohesive wholes that feature news, policies, achievements, and other matters important to people as employees/members of an organization and individuals working in a shared culture.

The third organizing principle—the genres' epideictic functions—are the threads that stitch things together for collections genres. In this section, we occasionally refer to print and electronic formats, but, more important, we focus particular attention on how organizational *topoi* may be used to fulfill these functions. In order of priority, we focus on collections genres' performative, epistemic, celebratory, and preservative functions.

1. Performative Function

A casual sampling of online newsletters demonstrates that organizations may provide Web-only material in print or video formats, downloadable versions of those formats, or both. Moreover, newsletters and corporate news programs not only may be accessed with one click or through several links to multiple stories, but they also may be targeted to various publics, not just employees or a nonprofit organization's (NPO's) volunteers. Such concerns for audience and format usability indicate that epideictic's performative function of collections genres should be uppermost in practitioners' minds when using them.

Rhetorical dimension. Our experience with and brief survey of organizational newsletters and news programs uncovered several different audiences: employees, investors, children and adolescents, and hot-issue publics such as environmentally friendly audiences. For example, General Motors' online newsletter, in addition to (typically) three lead stories, offers three links to other news stories about safety (2008a, 2008d, 2008e, 2009), diversity issues (2008e), education (2008b, 2008c, 2009), community and international relations (2008a, 2008b), and fuel economy (2008e, 2009). In a main article linked to the November 2008 newsletter's home page, GM links audience concerns for education and the environment together with a story about Meaghan O'Neill, a staff writer for Treehugger.com, who offered tips for greening the classroom as part of a webinar attended by the winners of General Motors and Discovery Education's "LIVE GREEN Teacher Grant Program."

Similarly, the U.S. Army's (2009) audio/video news program appeals to a variety of audiences through its news stories. The lead story on March 26, featured in a large video box in the upper left of the webpage, was unusual in length when compared with the individual stories the Army regularly changes as newer stories become available because it was a recording of President Obama's remarks on his policy in Afghanistan. The webpage typically features more than 30 news stories to choose from, varying in length from 1 to 4 minutes. Other stories featured on March 26 would appeal to audiences with a variety of concerns: programs for veterans' and soldiers' health issues, brigade charity programs, and operations with other organizations in helping flood victims in North Dakota. The U.S. Navy's (n.d.) magazine, *All Hands* (published under that name since 1945), addresses multiple concerns in a similar fashion.

Political dimension. The Army's news program webpage illustrates the performative function's political dimension in its purest form: the organization avoiding any appearance of acting politically but implicitly communicating, for example, support for the troops in Iraq and Afghanistan and honoring those returning home. (A March 25 news story welcomed the First Armored Division back to Germany.) The military families gathered at an elementary school to honor the "work and sacrifice" of their loved ones. An article in the Jesuit magazine, *Company* (Grace, 2009), implicitly advocates the need for affordable housing through the story of Br. Mike Wilmot, SJ, and Gesu Housing, a ministry devoted to turning renters into first-time homebuyers through building homes in Omaha, Nebraska.

The tendency to eschew public policy statements is particularly pronounced among for-profit concerns, unless the news is regarding company policies for which management would like employee support. In such cases, collections genres offer prime opportunities for organizations to advocate policy positions, so the message designer does not necessarily have to shun the political dimension of the performative function as we saw in earlier chapters. For example, in the September 2008 issue of its employee newsletter, *CatFolks*, Caterpillar reported on its efforts with environmental organizations and other businesses through the U.S. Climate Action Partnership (USCAP) to call for "a federal initiative to address global climate change" (p. 6). However, the article reassures employees that they are not advocating a particular position. Quoting Jason Lynn, Caterpillar Governmental Affairs manager for its Washington, DC, office, "USCAP is not endorsing any specific policy proposal. Rather, it is focused on educating policymakers on key elements of a comprehensive approach" (p. 6).

In contrast, trade associations and nonprofit organizations are much more direct in their use of newsletters to address key issues. The National Association of Insurance Commissioners (NAIC) "offered Congress the assistance of state insurance regulators in crafting legislation to address health insurance access and affordability" (para. 1), according to a March 27, 2009, news story. The organization's immediate past president, Sandy Praeger, is quoted: "State insurance regulators believe it is important to ensure that affordable, sufficient health coverage is available to small business owners, their employees and individuals" (para. 2). Such arguments give indications of who the organization is and what it stands for.

Identity-management dimension. Collections genres are ideal avenues for conveying, explicitly or implicitly, the organization's identity and the themes associated with it (i.e., its *topoi*). In this way, collections genres reinforce the organization's "brand" and culture among its people, who work together to fulfill organizational objectives and, very important, are ambassadors of the organization to friends, family, neighbors, and the community at large. Clearly, in General Motors' (2008a, 2008d, 2008e, 2009) newsletters referred to earlier, concern for safety, customer satisfaction, and community respect are core values highlighted. In another example, Leisureworld Caregiving Centres (Thompson, 2009a), a Canadian company with nursing homes in 27 locations, used the front page of its March 2009 newsletter to introduce its enhanced vision, mission statement, and core values of respect, commitment, teamwork, communication, and learning. In a separate article, the company informed or perhaps reminded employees that the

2009 business plan's two pillars of "people" and "quality" should be who they are and how they represent Leisureworld to residents and others: "I would term it employee branding," says vice-president of human resources, Josephine DesLauriers (Thompson, 2009b, para. 3).

An organization's identity, which includes those ideas most associated with an organization by its members, is grounded in organizational culture. Therefore, how an organization's identity is communicated (its corporate identity, or *persona*) (see Courtright & Smudde, 2009) and its *topoi* may be implied through message design, too. For example, Ameriprise Financial's (2005–2009) mission statement is reflected at various levels in its quarterly investor webcast. The setting for the program is like a news roundtable, featuring the company's "top experts" (Ameriprise Financial, 2009), who are "personable and approachable" (Ameriprise Financial, 2005–2009, para. 4) in demeanor and delivery. The officials focus on long-term opportunities as they advise investors how not to let fear and other emotions guide their financial decisions during the then-current recession. A friendly, comfortable tone and logically presented advice, along with the last 20 minutes of the 31½-minute program devoted to answering customer letters, are consistent with the mission's stated belief that "life—and financial planning—is about more than money. It's about people, opportunities and dreams."

2. Epistemic Function

As news, of course, collections genres communicate information. In terms of their epistemic function, such genres are first explanatory and then educational, just as news genres are (see Chapter 3). Newsletters and video news programs, particularly as internal discourse conventions, are key elements in any organization's socialization of members, be they employees, volunteers, or government agency staff (see Jablin, 2001).

In particular, through the explanatory dimension, collections genres associate new information with organizational values, thus providing a potentially strong foundation for teaching members what is most important. Like the role of information in shaping the organization's identity, as explained in the previous section, this often can be quite subtle. For example, an article in the newsletter, *Around Dow*, explains how The Dow Chemical Company (2008) has sponsored Habitat for Humanity house building in three Michigan communities for more than 25 years. The fact that employee volunteers are part of this effort conveys the message that employees should be involved in their communities. Moreover, Dow inculcates further commitments to community and, globally, to environmentalism, in the article's penultimate paragraph: "Dow's global partnership with Habitat directly impacts the Company's 2015 Sustainability Goals. By addressing the challenge of affordable housing in increasingly expensive markets and in emerging geographies, Dow is helping to create stronger, safer, communities" (p. 3). Such inculcation of motives also works for nonprofit organizations and external publics. Trout Unlimited (2008a, 2008b, 2009) features a quarterly e-newsletter that features legislative updates to encourage member action based on commonly shared values. Ameriprise Financial (2009), in the context of a major, worldwide recession, encourages its audiences to examine their own values and then follow its advice. Doug Lennick, executive vice-president and senior advisor for the company, offered two decision-making rules as part of Ameriprise's February 2009 webcast, "Questions, Answers & Actions for Unprecedented Times." Lennick says, "Always prepare yourself for the certainty of uncertainty" and "Always make your financial decisions after first reflecting on your personal values."

Collections genres also build on audience knowledge. Through the State Farm Insurance intranet, employees can receive a video-highlights program, the *News Hubcast,* that gives links to the week's top three news stories. The program features a news anchor and links to additional video, audio, or print stories, where some are explanatory but many are educational. In February 2009, for example, a story on Louisiana insurance plans informed employees how those plans were different from Florida's response, which led to State Farm's withdrawal from the homeowner's market there (State Farm, 2009a). A later story updated employees with news that Florida's insurance commissioner had tentatively approved State Farm's withdrawal (State Farm, 2009c). Another story built on common knowledge of the Lincoln birthday bicentennial to link the company's name as sole sponsor for a PBS program on the 16th president (State Farm, 2009b). Similarly, for NASA, its news program, *This Week at NASA* (NASA, 2009a, 2009b, 2009c, 2009d, 2009e, 2009f, 2009g, 2009h), relies on audience knowledge of previous shuttle missions and, through successive lead stories from January through March 2009, additional information in the lead-up to *Discovery*'s March 12 return to the International Space Station.

3. Celebratory Function

Such maxims and other lines of reasoning embody the core values that bond organizations and publics through collections genres—and they are the stuff of cultural and organizational *topoi.* Indeed, there is a celebration of corporate values, almost ritual-like in quality, in the use of newsletters and video news programs that make these genres a paradigm case for the traditional function of epideictic: to celebrate the values that are commonly held and denigrate those that the community is opposed to, both within a regular, ritualized context.

Collections genres' axiological dimension is easily recognized. In the Leisureworld (Thompson, 2009a, 2009b) newsletter's articles mentioned earlier, the organization's core values and its message to employees about its 2009 business plan reflect key ideas expressed by the CEO, David Cutler, in his message to website visitors: "Banish the word 'institution' from your vocabulary. While you're at it, toss the term 'nursing home' on the rubbish heap as well. Not only are the names old hat, so too are the ideas they represent" (Leisureworld Caregiving Centres, n.d.). State Farm's *Hubcast*s are filled with values, both "praised" and "blamed." In the final February edition, State Farm (2009d) extols "eco-friendly building" and "environmentally related insurance products" and reports a call during an underwriters leadership conference to focus on "the fundamentals of insurance." In contrast, its February 9 edition (State Farm, 2009b) alerts viewers to the company's insurance policies that combat identity theft.

The celebratory function's ritualistic dimension is a given with effective use of any collections genre. Good practitioners know that one of the keys to effective newsletter production is the regular, consistent appearance in format and timing (e.g., monthly, quarterly, biannually). The same is true of video news programs. *This Week at NASA* and State Farm's *Hubcast* are good cases in point, as is the quarterly Trout Unlimited (2008a, 2008b, 2009) e-newsletter. An interesting variation can be found in the January–February 2008 and 2009 issues of *USDA News*. The lead story for both features the swearing-in of a new Secretary of Agriculture, first Ed Schaefer (U.S. Department of Agriculture [USDA], 2008a), the second Tom Vilsack (USDA, 2009b). Not only does the layout of the newsletter stay consistent, but the titles of the articles are practically identical, and the new secretary's message to employees heads page 2 (USDA, 2008b, 2009a).

Incidentally, in contrast to news genres, collections genres prioritize the celebratory function over the preservative. Given their ritual qualities and their emphasis on organizational values, this priority is quite fitting.

4. Preservative Function

It is unsurprising, based on the ritual demand for consistency in form and delivery, that cohesion is first among the dimensions applicable to collections genres' preservative function. Note, however, that collections genres occasionally undergo "face lifts" to renew their appearances and content for improved audience appeal, but the fundamental purposes for form, placement, and epideictic functions remain intact. Although somewhat difficult to separate one from another, the three preservative dimensions follow a logical progression from cohesion to self-persuasion to repurposing. (This order reverses the priorities of news genres' preservative function.)

Our introduction of the classical concept of rhetorical *topoi* as applied to organizations is central to the cohesive dimension of newsletters and video news programs. The various examples we have used to illustrate the first three functions demonstrate these genres' ability to help an organization stay on message through the invocation of key *topoi*, whether they are organizational values, goal statements, appeals to beliefs and attitudes shared by an organization and its publics, and so on. As sources of socialization, they are instrumental in passing on the ideas embodied in *topoi* to future generations of employees and future publics. *This Week in NASA*, for example, serves as a vehicle to appeal to students from elementary school through college. Sometimes this appeal appears through example. The March 20 program (NASA, 2009i) reports a $1 billion partnership between NASA's Ames Research Center and the University of California, Santa Cruz, and Foothill-de-Anza Community College (to establish a sustainable research center to be opened by 2013). The program also features a story about NASA's work with the National Symphony Orchestra and the Corcoran Gallery to present events related to students, families, and NASA's exploration of the earth via satellite and of space itself.

Collections genres are prime genres for self-persuasion. NASA's video news programs reinforce organizational *topoi*, such as exploration and learning with its own employees, and inculcate those *topoi* with external audiences and, as indicated in the Ames Research Center story, future employees. News stories such as these emphasize the importance of gaining knowledge (e.g., scientists' and students' experiments in space [NASA, 2009e, 2009f] and through school programs for high school students [NASA, 2009e]). Newsletters and video news programs, therefore, establish premises for later persuasion as well as self-persuasion, building on cohesive messages and paving the way for later use of those messages through the preservative function's warrant-establishing dimension.

Collections genres clearly employ rhetorical premises for future communication efforts. Much more obviously than the genres covered in earlier chapters, however, collections genres demonstrate the repurposing component of the warrant-establishing dimension. For example, Trout Unlimited (TU) features a "Legislative Update" in its online newsletter, alerting members to proposed policy changes and government activities at the state and federal levels. These stories often become subjects for stories in the member magazine, *Trout*. In its September 2008 newsletter, TU reported progress by the Penobscot River Restoration Trust to remove three dams from the Maine River. The following winter, a story in *Trout* again reported the $25 million that had been raised for the effort, and it repeated and modified particular details (Trout Unlimited, 2008b, para. 6; see also "Pocket Water," 2009, p. 10). Our research and the first author's industry experience suggest that such repurposing is common with collections genres—repurposing material from other genres and providing news fodder for others. In the case of Trout Unlimited, among its core *topoi* are restoration and reclamation of trout streams and waterways.

In summary, collections genres may be focused on news, but they differ from news genres (Chapter 3) in functional emphasis because of their epideictic purposes. Both genres privilege the rhetoric dimension of epideictic's performative function first, but for collections genres its political function precedes identity management because, at least for internal news publications, organizations typically must avoid the appearance of advocating public policy positions to employees through an official house organ. Both news and collections genres naturally focus on epideictic's epistemic function because, after all, collections genres also present new information, sometimes based on previous audience knowledge. Most significant, collections genres place the celebratory function ahead of the preservative because newsletters programs extol the values of the organization, ideally on a metaphorically ritualized, regular basis. Newsletters and corporate news programs serve as a record of events, but their preservative function is in no way primary. Collections genres pay primary attention to audience and corporate voice because they are a potential means of increasing commitment among members (see Cannon, 2007), helping them feel a part of the organization through newsworthy information and shared values—communicated through the invocation of organizational *topoi*.

Strategic Planning Implications

Audiences for collections genres can be internal and external, which would drive decisions about content. Internal audiences could include employees/members plus, if the organization has a broad view of who is in its "family," retirees, dealers/retailers/distributors, suppliers, and stockholders. External audiences could include these latter groups (if they are not included as internal audiences) plus customers, prospective employees/members, news media, regulators/legislators, professional/industry organizations, community organizations, funding sources, and so on.

With this wide range of audiences for any collections genre, the question is not which genre works best for internal and external publics. The answer to that question must be obtained through effective audience research for every target audience. Such research would guide professional communicators in their decisions about which genre or genres to use, which stories to tell, and how to tell any story. But even before conducting an audience analysis to help identify genre and content preferences among audience members, communications professionals and management must settle on the overall purpose for any communication. Remember: Form follows function.

Strategically speaking, then, collections genres have certain implications for communications decision making on at least two crucial points: counseling management and delivering discourse. In terms of management counsel, organizational executives can often see more communication as a good thing, and the first thing they want is another newsletter or video news program. Of course that thinking is jumping to tactics, which we know is an ineffective approach. The first author had just such an experience during his industry career, where a vice-president of sales wanted a new, dedicated newsletter for his sales staff. It would have been another newsletter on top of the biweekly corporate employee newsletter that included a detailed section on sales performance, the weekly sales staff reports over e-mail, and weekly sales staff meetings held by conference call. These formal communications were in addition to the many other communication media from numerous external and internal sources that salespeople dealt with on a daily basis to do their work. The counsel given to the vice-president of sales was that people were already inundated by information from multiple internal and external sources every day, and one more medium they have to pay attention to would not add that much value. Plus, thanks to the results of an internal communications audit, the decision was to make more effective use of the media already in place and balance better the information sales people wanted and the information management wanted them to have.

If a decision is made to create one collections genre or another, the next strategic matter is how. Technology offers communicators and organizational leaders great flexibility in getting information to employees/members effectively and efficiently—at least in terms of production costs and delivery methods. Even so, whether a collections genre is created in hard form (i.e., print or videotape) or soft form (i.e., digital media), the design of content plus the access to finished pieces are important. Again, the first author's experiences in this area included systematic ways to produce effective communications. A communications audit revealed what information and in what forms employees/members wanted that balanced management's desires. Focus groups and secondary research on effective design for collections genres revealed the most effective ways to "package" content for employees/members. The process can be time-consuming, but the final yield is well worth the work.

Realize one important thing: The epideictic purposes for collections genres are the foundation for why any or all media may be used and, especially, what and how information would be presented. Generally speaking, collections genres enable public relations professionals to promote organizational identity and culture, build knowledge about what is going on in and around an organization, celebrate organizational values and achievements, and advance key messages that bear on past, present, and anticipated future organizational matters. Because of these epideictic purposes, collections genres offer excellent ways to reach any public about a wide range of subjects that bind the organization and its publics together. As our examples showed, organization-specific dimensions are evident in every story, but audience-relevant dimensions are also just as evident. So collections genres are much less about telling audiences what is going on and more about including audiences in some of the most pressing and interesting matters an organization faces at the time. In this way, the collections genres enable both organizations and publics to see that they are "all in this together."

When it comes time for an organization to bring the widest possible range of publics together, there is one family of discourse genres that has worked well for decades. Those genres are the "reports" genres, and they address the pressures of organizations to communicate about issues of legal/regulatory importance to publics and stakeholders. They also describe the sweeping, epideictic trend for organizations to tout how much good they do for the world at various levels and in various ways, from the environment to support of causes.

References

Ameriprise Financial, Inc. (2005–2009). *The Ameriprise Financial corporate mission.* Retrieved March 28, 2009, from http://financial-planning.ameriprise.com/ameriprise/ameriprise-competitive-advantage.asp

Ameriprise Financial, Inc. (2009, February). *Questions, answers & actions for unprecedented times: New financial ideas for the new year.* [Webcast]. Retrieved March 28, 2009, from http://budgeting-investing.ameriprise.com/planning-and-budgeting/webcast/2009-02-09.asp

Brody, E. W. (2005). The brave new world of public relations: A look back. *Public Relations Quarterly, 50*(4), 31–34.

Cannon, D. F. (2007). Church newspaper readership and faith community integration. *Journal of Media and Religion, 6,* 17–40.

Caterpillar, Inc. (2008, September). Coalition on climate: Cat helping to shape legislation. *CatFolks,* p. 6. Retrieved March 28, 2009, from http://www.cat.com/cda/files/1086857/7/CatFolksCORPSEPT08-2.pdf

Courtright, J. L., & Smudde, P. M. (2009). Leveraging organizational innovation for strategic reputation management. *Corporate Reputation Review, 12,* 245–269.

The Dow Chemical Company. (2008, November–December). Dow volunteers bring new life to an aging neighborhood. *Around Dow, 14*(9), 1–3. Retrieved April 13, 2009, from http://www.dow.com/PublishedLiterature/

dh_01ab/0901b803801ab9ba.pdf?filepath=news/pdfs/noreg/162-02480. pdf&fromPage=GetDoc

General Motors Corporation. (2008a, August). *Corporate responsibility newsletter* (Vol. 7, No. 8). Retrieved March 28, 2009, from http://gmdynamic.com/newsletter/archive/2008_Vol_7/cr_newsletter_august2008.html

General Motors Corporation. (2008b, September). *Corporate responsibility newsletter* (Vol. 7, No. 9). Retrieved March 28, 2009, from http://gmdynamic.com/newsletter/archive/2008_Vol_7/cr_newsletter_september2008.html

General Motors Corporation. (2008c, October). *Corporate responsibility newsletter* (Vol. 7, No. 10). Retrieved March 28, 2009, from http://gmdynamic.com/newsletter/archive/2008_Vol_7/cr_newsletter_october2008.html

General Motors Corporation. (2008d, November). *Corporate responsibility newsletter* (Vol. 7, No. 11). Retrieved March 28, 2009, from http://gmdynamic.com/newsletter/archive/2008_Vol_7/cr_newsletter_november2008.html

General Motors Corporation. (2008e, December). *Corporate responsibility newsletter* (Vol. 7, No. 12). Retrieved March 28, 2009, from http://gmdynamic.com/newsletter/archive/2008_Vol_7/cr_newsletter_december2008.html

General Motors Corporation. (2009, January). *Corporate responsibility newsletter* (Vol. 8, No. 1). Retrieved March 28, 2009, from http://gmdynamic.com/newsletter/archive/2008_Vol_8/cr_newsletter_january2009.html

Grace, E. (2009). One house at a time: Building quality low-income housing is a "justice thing" for this Omaha Jesuit. *Company, 27*(1), 14-16. [Online version]. Retrieved December 30, 2009, from http://www.companymagazine.org/v271/FA09.Profile.pdf

Hudson, H. P. (1998). *Publishing newsletters* (3rd ed.). Rhinebeck, NY: H&M.

Jablin, F. M. (2001). Organizational entry, assimiliation and disengagement/exit. In L. L. Putnam & F. M. Jablin (Eds.), *The new handbook of organizational communication: Advances in theory, research, and methods* (pp. 732-818). Thousand Oaks, CA: Sage.

Jamieson, K. H. (1973). Generic constraints and the rhetorical situation. *Philosophy and Rhetoric, 6*, 162-170.

Leisureworld Caregiving Centres. (n.d.) *Message from the CEO.* Retrieved March 28, 2009, from http://www.leisureworld.ca/Meet_Greet_CEO.html

National Association of Insurance Commissioners. (2009, March 27). Health reform: NAIC offers full support. *Insurance newscast: Headlines edition.* [Online newsletter]. Retrieved March 28, 2009, from http://www.insurancebroadcasting.com/today.htm#legislate

Pocket water: News bits and bytes. (2009, Winter). *Trout, 51*(1), 10-14.

State Farm Mutual Automobile Insurance Company. (2009a, February 2). *Hubcast.* [Corporate news video program]. Bloomington, IL: Author.

State Farm Mutual Automobile Insurance Company. (2009b, February 9). *Hubcast.* [Corporate news video program]. Bloomington, IL: Author.

State Farm Mutual Automobile Insurance Company. (2009c, February 16). *Hubcast.* [Corporate news video program]. Bloomington, IL: Author.

State Farm Mutual Automobile Insurance Company. (2009d, February 23). *Hubcast.* [Corporate news video program]. Bloomington, IL: Author.

Thompson, J. (2009a, March). Leisureworld introduces enhanced vision, mission statement and core values. *In the news.* [Online newsletter]. Retrieved March 28, 2009, from http://www.leisureworld.ca/PDFs/InTheNewsMarch2009web. pdf

Thompson, J. (2009b, March). "People" an integral part of Leisureworld's 2009 business plan. *In the news.* [Online newsletter]. Retrieved March 28, 2009, from http://www.leisureworld.ca/PDFs/InTheNewsMarch2009web.pdf

Trout Unlimited. (2008a, June). *TU Newsletter-June 2008.* Retrieved April 13, 2009, from http://www.tu.org/site/c.kkLRJ7MSKtH/b.4195989/k.7878/TU_Newsletter__June_2008.htm

Trout Unlimited. (2008b, September). Get involved: Legislative updates. In *TU Newsletter-September 2008.* [Online]. Retrieved April 14, 2009, from http:// www.tu.org/site/c.kkLRJ7MSKtH/b.4466557/k.3ECE/Dam_Removal_on_the_Penobscot_One_Step_Closer_to_Reality.htm

Trout Unlimited. (2009, March). *TU Newsletter-March 2009.* Retrieved April 13, 2009, from http://www.tu.org/site/c.kkLRJ7MSKtH/b.5015613/k.7FF8/TU_Newsletter__March_2009.htm

U.S. Army. (2009). *Army media player.* Retrieved March 28, 2009, from http://www. army.mil/media/amp/

U.S. Department of Agriculture. (2008a, January–February). Ed Schafer takes the helm as our 29th secretary. *USDA News: USDA's Employee News Publication-For and About You!, 67*(1), 1. Retrieved March 28, 2009, from Retrieved March 28, 2009, from http://www.usda.gov/wps/portal/!ut/p/_s.7_0_A/7_0_1OB?contentidonly=true&contentid=OC_USDANews_Vol67_No1.xml

U.S. Department of Agriculture. (2008b, January–February). Secretary of Agriculture Ed Schafer. *USDA News: USDA's Employee News Publication-For and About You!, 67*(1), 2. Retrieved March 28, 2009, from Retrieved March 28, 2009, from http://www.usda.gov/wps/portal/!ut/p/_s.7_0_A/7_0_1OB?contentidonly=true&contentid=OC_USDANews_Vol67_No1.xml

U.S. Department of Agriculture. (2009a, January–February). Secretary of Agriculture Ed Schafer. *USDA News: USDA's Employee News Publication-For and About You!, 68*(1), 2. Retrieved March 28, 2009, from http://www.usda.gov/wps/portal/!ut/p/_s.7_0_A/7_0_1OB?contentidonly=true&contentid=OC_USDANews_Vol68_No1.xml

U.S. Department of Agriculture. (2009b, January–February). Tom Vilsack takes the helm as our 30th secretary. *USDA News: USDA's Employee News Publication-For and About You!, 68*(1), 1, 7. Retrieved March 28, 2009, from http://www. usda.gov/wps/portal/!ut/p/_s.7_0_A/7_0_1OB?contentidonly=true&contentid=OC_USDANews_Vol68_No1.xml

U.S. National Aeronautics and Space Administration. (2009a, January 9). *This week at NASA.* [Online video program]. Retrieved March 24, 2009, from http://www. nasa.gov/rss/TWAN_vodcast.rss

U.S. National Aeronautics and Space Administration. (2009b, January 16). *This week at NASA.* [Online video program]. Retrieved March 24, 2009, from http://www. nasa.gov/rss/TWAN_vodcast.rss

U.S. National Aeronautics and Space Administration. (2009c, January 30). *This week at NASA.* [Online video program]. Retrieved March 24, 2009, from http://www.nasa.gov/rss/TWAN_vodcast.rss

U.S. National Aeronautics and Space Administration. (2009d, February 10). *This week at NASA.* [Online video program]. Retrieved March 24, 2009, from http://www.nasa.gov/rss/TWAN_vodcast.rss

U.S. National Aeronautics and Space Administration. (2009e, February 17). *This week at NASA.* [Online video program]. Retrieved March 24, 2009, from http://www.nasa.gov/rss/TWAN_vodcast.rss

U.S. National Aeronautics and Space Administration. (2009f, February 24). *This week at NASA.* [Online video program]. Retrieved March 24, 2009, from http://www.nasa.gov/rss/TWAN_vodcast.rss

U.S. National Aeronautics and Space Administration. (2009g, February 27). *This week at NASA.* [Online video program]. Retrieved March 24, 2009, from http://www.nasa.gov/rss/TWAN_vodcast.rss

U.S. National Aeronautics and Space Administration. (2009h, March 6). *This week at NASA.* [Online video program]. Retrieved March 24, 2009, from http://www.nasa.gov/rss/TWAN_vodcast.rss

U.S. National Aeronautics and Space Administration. (2009i, March 20). *This week at NASA.* [Online video program]. Retrieved March 24, 2009, from http://www.nasa.gov/rss/TWAN_vodcast.rss

U.S. Navy. (n.d.). *Navy News Service-*All Hands *magazine.* Retrieved December 30, 2009, from http://www.navy.mil/allhands.asp

9

Reports

Big Sticks for Corporate Image Management

Organizations function within a larger context of a social, political, economic, technological, and cultural environment. As organizations affect and are affected by the environment, they face coping with it symbolically to various internal and external constituencies. Such management of symbolisms is at the heart of public relations, which "suggests a foundation of common assumptions about an organization's resources for coping with its environment, while at the same time public relations holds open the prospect for adaptation, change, and the incorporation of new assumptions when that environment undergoes its inevitable changes" (Cheney & Vibbert, 1987, p. 173). Consequently, the general interorganizational role that public relations plays is that of recreating a changing reality symbolically in strategic and ethical ways amid environmental uncertainties and interdependencies—to rhetorically influence relevant constituencies about an organization's values, issues, identity, and image. Reports, then, fulfill an important need of constituencies for information about the organization because they are summaries of a company's view of its environment and relevant issues for a given year or other defined period of time.

Genres and Their Conventions

Taken together, annual reports, issue reports, and image pieces are the "big sticks" that organizations use to inspire cooperation with their publics. (As we'll see, they are also the "hubs" around which the PR wheels spin.) These reports tend to be published regularly but usually not much more than once or twice a year, which means they must have as much impact as possible for as long as they are useful to the organization, primarily, and its publics, secondarily. That impact from these "big sticks" is not taken lightly—it is painstakingly planned so that each genre fits the communication need and, especially, promises to deliver the kinds of results that are needed.

Annual Reports

Annual reports recount details about an organization's position, policies, and performance over a period of time (i.e., a calendar or fiscal year) and on particular subjects. The environment within which organizations work is what Emery and Trist (1965) describe as a "turbulent field" (p. 13). That is, organizations face pressure from many interconnected agents while much change is going on in the environment. Such high interconnectivity means that organizations must manage their boundaries, and public relations specialists function as "boundary spanners" who "are continually involved in making symbolic connections between organization and environment, even as they 'say' what each of the linked domains is" (Cheney & Vibbert, 1987, p. 178). Corporate annual reports, as an extension of a public relations strategy, are published for a company's constituencies in an effort to make sense of the turbulent environment over the preceding year. The U.S. Securities and Exchange Commission "compels more than 12,000 public companies to produce annual reports, but thousands of other organizations [not obligated to follow the Securities and Exchange Act of 1934 and its related regulations since then] *voluntarily* create glossy paperbacks to market their credibility and a rich casserole of products and services" (Poe, 1994, p. 17; italics added). Clearly, annual reports are seen to possess both great informational value as well as persuasive power.

At a minimum, however, publicly traded companies must follow a standardized pattern mandated by the economic oversight agency within their particular country. In the United States, under the Sarbanes-Oxley Act, a company's CEO and CFO must certify the accuracy of "the control structure of the company and the financial information contained in periodic reports" (Koonjy, 2002, para. 2). Organizations filing a Form 10-K (annual report) must discuss business matters, risk factors, properties, legal proceedings, issues to be brought to shareholders for a vote, the market, financial data in aggregate form, discussion and analysis of that data, and forward-looking statements based on the information reported in the previous items. Financial statements include an independent auditor's report, statements of operation, balance sheets, and other accounting reports and notes. Requirements in Great Britain have become increasingly more specific since March 2007, including reporting of social responsibility policies and results: toward employees, the community, the environment, and social issues (KMPG UK, 2009). Accounting requirements similar to those required in the United States under the Sarbanes-Oxley Act also have been introduced in Japan (Tohyama, 2008). The European Financial Reporting Advisory Group (2009) considers the United Kingdom, Denmark, France, Germany, Italy, Poland, Spain, and Sweden to be "the national standard-setters" for financial statements in Europe. Other countries (e.g., India) are working toward compliance with international financial reporting standards (KMPG UK, 2007).

Issue Reports

Public-interest reports, similar to annual reports, recount details about an organization's position, policies, and performance on particular subjects that matter to how an organization relates with its various spheres of operation and those in them. In recent years, many corporations have released specialty reports on community relations, corporate social responsibility, environmental initiatives, and so on. Much of the textual portion of an issue report is dedicated to explaining the organization's stance toward and action on selected issues that commanded its attention over a year-long period. Crable and Vibbert (1985) assert that "an issue is created when one or more human agents attaches significance to a situation or perceived 'problem.' These interested agents create or recreate arguments which they feel will be acceptable resolutions to questions about the status quo" (p. 5). Cheney and Vibbert (1987) state further that "issues are focal points in public discourse that never get 'solved' in the sense of an absolute termination of discussion, but they do become 'resolved' or managed" (p. 175). Because issues arise in the public domain, they often call for legislative action or public policy change. Consequently, the implications of an issue on an organization are broad, and as an agent on the social scene, organizations have rights similar to those of individuals to comment on issues, especially as greater information becomes available from which new or refined opinions can be formed, asserted, and adopted or rejected. Issue reports, then, serve as one way that an organization can voice its opinion on and assert what it is doing about issues in its environment that matter to its internal and external publics and stakeholders. Such reports often serve as the foundation material for issue advertising. Such advertising also serves to build organizational image.

Image Pieces

Corporate image pieces (e.g., brochures/pamphlets, websites, advertisements) that are meant to convey a limited number of key messages about an organization in specific, effective ways (e.g., sales-oriented language and ample visuals as part of an overall graphic design) fulfill certain communicative purposes and fit a selected medium. *Brochures* and *pamphlets* function as carry-away, leave-behind, or direct-mail discourse for almost any occasion. Brochures and pamphlets are printed on paper (and often made available electronically in portable document format [PDF] files), focused on a single topic, divide the topic into discreet parts that are explained verbally and visually, and are arranged on the paper in "chunks" of visual and verbal information. Those chunks divide the page space in ways that follow a cultural reading pattern (e.g., left to right, top to bottom) but allow readers to read sequentially or nonsequentially as they can glance at the headings and content of any chunk/section and skip to any other section. Brochures and pamphlets can cover a topic in concise and sufficient detail, then be published in multiple-column formats and folded between those columns, so a standard three-column brochure is folded twice. Brochures and pamphlets can also be longer treatments across multiple pages that are stapled/saddle-stitched. Front and back covers are important—the former identifies the subject of the discourse and the provider, and the back features full contact information, publishing date, and possibly brief summary text about the organization.

Websites are organizations' virtual presences for their publics. For many years, websites were used as electronic brochures and pamphlets, presenting online access to selected information divided into sections (webpages) that link to one another. Websites are much more sophisticated now, and they stand as important ways to manage people's impressions of and facilitate interations with organizations. Websites, then, are not just channels for communication. We believe websites possess sufficient characteristics (i.e., they have their own "grammar") to consider them a discourse genre. Even so, what is most interesting to note about websites is that the discourse conventions for them are not unique. Website design, when the Internet was very young, was a whole new thing. Anyone who had the skills and resources to design websites did so with vast ranges of effectiveness and creativity. Some sites were overly simplistic, whereas others were "over the top" with nearly every possible design element that could be put on a screen. Webmasters, which is a term that emerged later on after the Internet's popularity and usefulness solidified and the experts who designed and ran websites needed a title, quickly surmised that design standards were necessary. The guiding question was, "What makes a good website?" Much work went into answering this question, from graphic designers to human-factors researchers. What emerged was a flexible set of discourse conventions using printed documents as the analog. That is, the language of Web design was based on metaphors about printed material—websites have "pages," and so on. Even the name "website" is a metaphor for something physical but really isn't—it exists electronically, and we read light, not ink.

So web designers used the discourse conventions for brochures, booklets, indexes, and so on to fashion Internet-specific standards for how text and graphics would work together on the virtual pages of websites. Subjects from the most basic to the most complex are indexed and linked page after page. A key to good website design is effective navigation, which gives website visitors a clear sense of what's where, how to get to it, and how to get back to something seen before by clicking on links to specific webpages about particular topics. Websites begin with a homepage, which acts as a kind of cover to the rest of the sites' content. Standard content includes background information about an organization, links to topic-specific pages, contact information, and news, among others. Because websites are a visual medium, website design varies, but content usability is key. People's attention is overtaxed in today's society, and they expect to find and access the information they want on websites quickly and easily. In addition, people's eyes scan webpages nonsequentially for what they want, which underscores the importance of simple and effective design for pertinent content. Webpages are designed in chunks with short amounts of text and related visuals or icons that include areas for links to other website areas about specific topics (and subtopics). Use of embedded programs for animation, sound, video, and so on should add to a visitor's experience, not detract from it. Knowledge about any audience's technological capabilities is essential when designing a website because if an audience is not web-savvy or in possession of proper software and hardware, there's little point to having "all the bells and whistles."

Advertisements in print, broadcast, or electronic form provide organizations with opportunities to share single, ultra-focused messages on some topic. For public relations purposes, advertisements tend to be used mainly (but not exclusively) to assert a corporate image (either new or current) or assert a stance on an issue or a situation. The reason: The message about the focused topic is key, and its link to the organization is made visually and perhaps verbally. In such cases, an organization's brand figures importantly in an advertisement's design but may be subservient to the core verbal message. In general, advertisements are the single-most succinct form of reports genres an organization may use to assert its position on a defined topic. The text and graphics may take up any amount of space (e.g., full to partial page ads, online pop-up ads, or 60- to 10-second video or audio ads), which makes—as is true for all genres—message design critical. All these conventions mean that advertisements are very controlled in terms of paid-for timing and space utilization (e.g., print, broadcast, web) of messages, which contrasts with the unpaid editorial judgment exercised by editors.

Message Design

Public relations' role in strategic communication fundamentally balances organizational and constituency needs. Cheney and Vibbert (1987) assert that "it is important to note that many of the principles that apply to external persuasive campaigns apply to internal ones (and vice versa): Both types are directed at specific 'publics' and both represent the organization in particular ways" (p. 180). Public relations activities generally help an organization cope with the uncertainties of an organization's broad social, political, economic, technological, and cultural environment. Public relations activities also attempt to recreate through language and symbols, as guided by principles of ethical communication, a changing reality that rhetorically influences the thinking, attitudes and actions of relevant constituencies about an organization in all respects. Corporate reports, then, not only serve as reviews of a company's environment, operations, and financial viability over the preceding year, but they also seek to manage, presumably in an ethical manner, the issues germane to the company and its environment for that year and the year(s) ahead that are on the minds of its publics and stakeholders.

Based on these observations, a public relations practitioner might focus most on reports' preservative function, noting their primary role as part of the public record. This clearly is most important. Yet a report's emphasis on information might lead us to prioritize the epistemic function and its complementary dimensions of explanation and education as primary. Although important to all reports genres, however, we suggest that these surface-level emphases hide deeper concerns. Annual reports, issue reports, image pieces, and image and advocacy advertisements each should primarily lean on their preservative function for an organization and then immediately celebrate the organization and reinforce the identity-management dimension of epideictic's performative function. We therefore cover their functions in this order of priority: preservative, celebratory, performative, and epistemic.

1. Preservative Function

Both dimensions of the preservative function are impossible to place in an absolute rank order. We see them working simultaneously in reports genres because the function may operate in multiple ways for reports genres. For example, Ferrero Group seeks to maintain cohesion of its messages across three continents and websites in 19 countries. The progress of Toyota's environmental agenda can be traced discursively through its annual reports, advertising, and, on its website beginning in 2007, environmental issue reports (Toyota North America, 2008, 2009a, 2009b). General Motors'

(2008b) full-page issue advertisement about its dire financial situation need for a federal bailout was consistent with its news release (2008a) issued the same day and with the message its then chairman and CEO, G. Richard Wagoner, Jr., provided in testimony before Congress (2008c). Message cohesion may be the most important of reports genres' preservative dimensions, followed by repurposing/messages for future usage and then reflexive/self-persuasion. Because this chapter has amply demonstrated the first dimension, we conclude this section with the remaining two.

Reports genres, among all those covered in this book, most obviously afford practitioners possibilities for reusing messages, casting them in new forms (i.e., other genres) and in general providing a storehouse for message design at a later date. As with the cohesive dimension, the Toyota examples also illustrates this "repurposing" dimension. Indeed, the epistemic and preservative functions work together in an attempt to shape Toyota's green reputation. The company's "Why Not?" campaign (see e.g., Toyota Motor Corporation, 2009) also refers advertisement readers, as many messages do today, to another reports genre, the company's webpage (Toyota North America, 2009b) devoted to the campaign theme.

As reflections of the past, assessments of the present, and prognostications for the future, reports genres have an important reflexive dimension. The earlier annual report examples are indications of an organization's own self-persuasion as well as the invitation to publics to persuade themselves. Organizations use corporate history to reinforce a particular view of the firm; nothing could be more true than in the case of annual reports' narratives of the previous year's successes. Additionally, the outlook for the coming year functions as what Kenneth Burke (1937/1984) calls "the coaching of attitude" (p. 322): How we talk about how we want to be in the future and how we want it to look operates rhetorically as a sort of wish fulfillment or self-fulfilling prophecy. If the company's report serves as a map to the coming year, the company's members should be doing all they can to make the report's "dream" come true.

One final example illustrates this organizational self-persuasion and how it might occur in other publics as a result. "Lemonade Stand for Life" (Virtual Lemonade Stand, n.d.), a partnership between Alex's Lemonade Stand Foundation [ALSF] (2008a) and Volvo Motor Cars of North America (n.d.a), offers people the chance to purchase virtual cups of lemonade for $1 each. Each cup may be sent electronically to friends or family members, with all proceeds going to find a cure for pediatric cancer. Alexandra "Alex" Scott was diagnosed with neuroblastoma shortly after her first birthday (ALSF, 2008b). After leaving the hospital on her fourth birthday, she would have a neighborhood lemonade stand every summer, devoted to childhood cancer research. The foundation continues her work since her death at age 8. The foundation's website functions to reinforce what its staffers and volunteers already have—a commitment to fight pediatric cancer. A list of donors on a single-page website (Virtual Lemonade Stand, n.d.) links to Volvo's website (Volvo Motor Cars, n.d.a) and to the foundation's (ALSF, 2008a). Volvo's homepage also links to its page devoted to the cause, which of course links back to the single-page website where people can purchase the virtual cup of lemonade. Each step of the way, hitting links involves the audience in such a way as to reinforce the discursive appeals to become involved. (Incidentally, when the second author was investigating all the links, he found links "About Volvo," including a page devoted to a succession of frames about the company's commitment to child safety from pregnancy through 12 years old [see Volvo Motor Cars, n.d.b].)

2. Celebratory Function

As noted earlier, the formal constraints on reports genres stem from their focus on the centrality of organizational image and issue positions. Although their formats have become more varied through media adaptation (e.g., glossy annual reports can make the SEC's minimum amount of information a lesser percentage of a complete report; image pieces can be as small as a tri-fold 8½ × 11 take-away or as large as a website with many pages and links), they allow practitioners to ethically place an organization in the best possible light within a given context. Indeed, perhaps more so than any other genres, reports develop issues and shape image in marked ways to help build and sustain an organization's reputation. The framing of the situation thus primarily employs the ritualistic dimension of celebration in order to convey the organization's core values (i.e., the function's axiological dimension).

First and foremost, reports genres illustrate the essence of what the celebratory function's ritualistic dimension means. Among these genres, annual reports fulfill this dimension in an obvious fashion, with publicly traded companies fulfilling the legal requirements of financial reporting within their respective host countries. Some opt to do nothing more than this (e.g., Indian Oil, 2007). Others may follow the required form's information but dress it up with four-color formatting and interspersed pictures, as does Samsung's (2007) annual report. Regardless of how much production value is added to a piece, however, its key characteristics mentioned earlier reflect the ritualistic demands of the situation. Just as many organizations opt to go beyond regulatory requirements of their host countries, however, other companies do not. Private companies have the option to issue none at all. For example, the well-regarded Italian company Ferrero Group (2007) is family owned and, therefore, relies on its website and other reports genres to fulfill other epideictic functions. (Shortly we discuss Ferrero's website in the next subsection on the performative function.)

Depending on the particular situation and its associated communication demands, the ritualistic dimension of reports genres can be strict or fluid. Quarterly and annual reports are bound by the constraints of time. Indeed, the opening letter from the CEO focuses at first on the past. Toyota (2007) Chairman Fujio Cho opens with a rather standard-sounding statement: "In fiscal 2007, ended March 31, 2007, Toyota again posted solid business results," and he goes on to thank key stakeholders for "their constant support and understanding, which continue to underpin Toyota's growth" (p. 7). Similarly, Samsung Vice-President and CEO Yoon-Woo Lee begins the "2007 Results and Analysis" section of his annual report letter with, "We achieved our best-ever business results through a series of innovative management approaches" (Samsung, 2007, p. 5). The letter opens, however, with a paragraph to frame the past year's success and the company's plans for an innovative future. Toyota's Cho opts to leave reference to the future to his final paragraph, promising to follow founder Takichi Toyoda's precepts while "contributing to the development of the automotive industry and international society" (p. 7) and tackling environmental issues. More than just report the past year and forecast the coming one in specific sections alone, as certainly implied by government regulations, the two focuses on past and future typically work in tandem throughout such reports.

Other reports genres treat time more fluidly. Image and issue advertising, for example, reflect a more traditional view of epideictic time, a sort of eternal present (Perelman & Olbrechts-Tyteca, 1969) and, consequently, give somewhat less precise placement of the past and future. In contrast to the aforementioned annual report, Toyota North America's (2009a) advertising regarding its environmental efforts is indeterminate in time: "We've reduced raw material usage and we're recycling virtually every material, including paper, plastics, metal, and even waste water. And we're constantly looking for innovative ways to further reduce waste" (p. ii). Mutual of Omaha's (2008) image ad spans general periods in the human lifespan: "When Mom was my age. . . . Today you can prepare for what's coming. Our insurance will help take care of our bills later in life . . ." (p. ii). Our research suggests that reports genres may capitalize on the elasticity of timeframes, from the specific (e.g., issue advocacy advertising) on matters of immediate importance to evergreen publicity pieces (e.g., brochures) where the essence of time is most vague.

Annual reports and other reports genres also perform the celebratory function's axiological dimension. For example, ITT's 2007 annual report (ITT Corporation, 2008) devotes its cover and first 16 pages to full-page photographs interspersed with pages with captions and three- to five-sentence explanations of how the company implements its values: "speed and precision" (p. 1); "tapping alternative energy" (p. 2); saving the world's "precious resource," water (p. 4); "providing protection and security" (p. 6); and so on. Consider also the similarities and differences between the 2007 annual reports of the two Asian powerhouses referred to earlier, Toyota and Samsung. Both companies make extensive use of news genres, available in electronic press rooms on their websites. Both extol the value of innovation. In a 12-page special feature, Toyota (2007) features the core values of its philosophy and specific principles behind innovative approaches to production, product development, and so on: "We seek *kaizen* and *kaikaku*. *Kaizen* means continuous pursuit of incremental improvements. *Kaikaku* means revolutionizing for benefits on a bigger scale. Together, these two approaches help us to continuously and dramatically strengthen our competitiveness" (p. 22). Samsung, however, must be content in its 2007 annual report with promises of innovation. Toyota is able to report concrete results, such as "simpler, streamlined production equipment" (p. 28), a shift from plants dependent upon Japanese "mother plants" to "self-reliant overseas operations" (p. 29), and ongoing technological innovation.

3. Performative Function

Reports genres not only celebrate the organization and provide a public record of its activities, but they operate at a deeper level to build an organization's ethos and enhance its reputation with stakeholders. Such genres provide powerful opportunities to use the performative function's identity-management dimension to the best advantage. This concern for ethos is closely allied to, in order of importance, the function's political and rhetorical dimensions.

Identity-management dimension. Although reports genres allow an organization to celebrate its role and position in specific issues and situations, we find that reports genres' performative function builds on the celebratory with an emphasis on image and reputation. This function's identity-management dimension, in ways related to the scope of time associated with the celebratory function's ritualistic dimension, allows great flexibility in projecting various facets of how it wishes to be perceived—what McMillan (1987) and others have called organizational *personae* (see Chapter 3). Annual reports, for example, allow organizations to perform (in a dramatic sense) various roles with the presentation of the faces of a company. Websites afford the same opportunity, although we have observed that the provider of goods and services to consumers tends to predominate corporate homepages and links. Issue reports, brochures, and advocacy advertising communicate particular faces of an organization, ideally without creating perceptions of being political actors. We therefore place the identity-management dimension of the performative function first, followed closely by the political dimension. Although clearly intertwined with these dimensions, we place the rhetorical dimension last because audience considerations must take into account how an organization is to be perceived.

Within reports genres, identity management is fundamentally the projection of multiple *personae* or a particular *persona*. Let's return to Ferrero Group (2007), an organization with the highest corporate reputation rating in the Reputation Institute's (2009) Global Pulse rankings, and its use of the Web. The introduction to the Ferrero Group's homepage emphasizes its role as a purveyor of fine products: "Ferrero is *superior* because of its unique *quality* products which give *pleasure* to consumers WORLDWIDE." It then provides links to the homepages of its operations in various countries around the globe (e.g., Ferrero do Brasil, n.d.; Ferrero France, 2008; Ferrero USA, n.d.). Ferrero Group's (2007) website illustrates how organizational rhetoric is an *enactment* of a company. Campbell and Jamieson (n.d.) explain that *enactment* occurs when the speaker is the evidence for the message (i.e., the speaker embodies the argument). In this case, Ferrero Group has links on its homepage that do not take the viewer to other webpages. After the website introduction, which features products such as Nutella and Tic-Tac, these links reveal the large company "F" logo and text related to the group, its principles, its social responsibility efforts, and its online newsroom. For example, the "Group" link has five other links, each crafting a different persona: a family-owned company; a successful business; one based on solid principles such as "very high quality artisanal attention to detail, product freshness, selection of the finest raw materials, and respect and care for the consumer"; a global line of products, including its Kinder brand found in Europe and Latin America; and yet another set of text that positions Ferrero as a good employer.

Political dimension. Ferrero Group (2007) also illustrates the political dimension of epideictic's performative function. Its four subjects under "Social Responsibility" include one link to the company's five guiding principles of environmentalism. These principles state how Ferrero incorporates concern for the environment in all of its planning, through reduction of environmental impact and the use of renewable resources when possible, a commitment "to the responsible management of water resources," establishing and monitoring environmental objectives, and educating employees and suppliers. Note that Ferrero's listing of principles does not advocate that others do likewise. The organization simply leads by example (at least that's one interpretation). Although its "Environmental Management System conforms to ISO 14001:2004," Ferrero "promotes a global approach . . . to protect the environment," it does not seek to influence environmental policies or government regulations. The group's website, along with its websites for each country of operation, does not directly advocate the company's viewpoints on the environment, societal living conditions, healthy lifestyles, and responsible advertising. In the case of the latter, Ferrero Group merely mentions media education programs it supports in Great Britain and France and how it "respects the self-regulatory codes recognized by the ICC (International Chamber of Commerce)." Such messages, then, add to the organization's *personae* as a company that acts responsibly.

Rhetorical dimension. Whether audiences see Ferrero in this way depends on the audience and what website and links they navigate to, of course. Ferrero's websites, therefore, fulfill the rhetorical dimension of epideictic's performative function. As we mentioned in Chapters 2 and 3, messages within genres imply a desired audience and seek to establish a relationship with that audience. (You'll recall that Black [1970] called this implied audience the *second persona*.) A few examples suffice to demonstrate how websites, as reports genres, develop rhetorical connections with publics. Like many product- and profit-oriented companies' websites, those of Ferrero feature product lines on their homepages (the U.S. website is devoted to consumers alone) (see Ferrero USA, n.d.). The audience implied, of course, is the consumer. However, specific links may (and, we might add, should) reinforce the performative function's identity-management and political dimensions. Consider Ferrero France's strategic support of programs that promote a healthy lifestyle. The link to "Allez, on bouge!" (literally, "Go, we're moving!") leads the viewer to Ferrero France's (n.d.a) community website devoted to helping families find sports and leisure activities they can do together. Audiences interested in Ferrero's employment practices in France may link to testimonial videos from retirees (Ferrero France, n.d.b) and company officials in charge of policies such as hiring of the handicapped (Ferrero France, n.d.c).

Likewise, other reports genres develop links with audiences that support an organization's identity-management and political efforts. Government agencies and nonprofit organizations issue thousands of brochures that balance the three dimensions of reports genres' performative function. For example, the U.S. Department of Health and Human Services Centers for Disease Control's (n.d.) brochure regarding the West Nile virus shows pictures of everyday citizens taking simple precautions to avoid infection: applying insect repellent and draining standing water. The brochure provides basic information, statistics, and answers to questions that concerned citizens would want to know. The agency's voice is authoritative but not pushy, thus adopting a role appropriate to a federal agency that serves the people rather than political ends.

In terms of the performative function, then, reports genres are the enactment or embodiment of who an organization is. Projections of *personae* may range from multiple actors (to represent an organization over the course of an entire fiscal year or across the pages of a website) to a specific voice for its policy positions—without appearing to have an active role in public debate on various issues. These two dimensions, identity management and political, depend on how well the message is crafted to influence audience perceptions and, thereby, fulfill the performative function's rhetorical dimension. The organization's *personae*, the message content—the products, services, and issues it addresses—and how images are shaped in audience members' minds must fit together when using reports genres so that an organization's overall reputation is built and maintained. Figure 9.1 illustrates the guiding concern of identity management to build reputation with the support of the content concerns of public relations message design. Those concerns rest on the notion that an organization's overall (and specific) reputation constantly relates to and relies on more specific factors about the organization, its product/service offerings, public image, given issues/topics/situations, and so on. Like an umbrella, reputation covers these matters all at once and individually, and the performative function of reports genres is especially potent for projecting *personae* and beyond in effective, ethical messages.

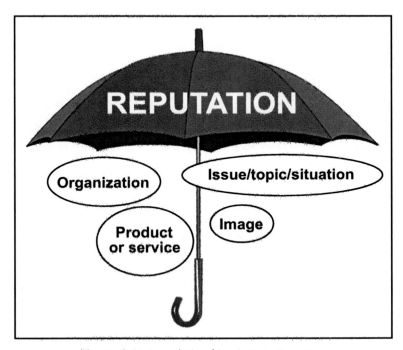

Figure 9.1. Key relationships in reports genres.

4. Epistemic Function

Among reports genres, issue reports best illustrate the function of building knowledge. Today, most issue reports available to publics are linked on organizational websites and focus on corporate social responsibility efforts (i.e., annual reports specific to the environment, community relations, diversity, or other issues vital to an organization's position as a good corporate citizen). Reports genres, first and foremost, must appeal to the audience beliefs and values (thus tying in with the axiological dimension of epideictic's celebratory function). Like annual reports and other reports genres, issue reports are primarily explanatory (i.e., they build on what the audience already accepts as fact). Perhaps more subtle is the inculcation of values and linkage to new information that the epistemic function's educational dimension affords.

Although issue reports (and the advocacy advertising that often is a byproduct of them) would seem to offer judgments about the past and make recommendations for the future—therefore making them fit Aristotle's other two categories of discourse, deliberative and forensic, respectively—these genres clearly have epistemic functions related to the purposes of epideictic. Toyota North America's (2009a) website includes its *2008 North America Environmental Report*. This webpage and its links build on knowledge that automakers increasingly must focus on product impact on the environment. Its opening page draws audience knowledge of issues in the news:

> Over the past year, we saw a convergence of will from industry, government and society to respond to climate change and to address our collective footprint on the planet. It is clear that the mix of limited resources, rising temperatures and an increasing global population that wants to be mobile demands an innovative and sustainable response. As an auto manufacturer, Toyota believes that "sustainable mobility" can be achieved through advanced technologies, key partnerships and creative people who are willing to take on this most important challenge. (para. 2)

Toyota thus builds on problem awareness on the part of its audience to assert its view of the environment and its resulting policies as correct.

General Motors (2008b), as we mentioned earlier, used an advertisement for its *apologia* to the American people after requesting $18 billion from the federal government in December 2008. The full-page advertisement, which appeared in major newspapers and trade media, illustrates how epideictic's epistemic function operates within deliberative discourse. The advertisement was an "open letter" that appealed to the audience's recognition of GM's history of service to consumers and the nation: "For more than 100 years, we have been serving your personal mobility needs, providing American jobs and serving local communities. We have been the U.S. sales leader for 76 consecutive years" (p. B3). It also appealed to common experience:

> Just like you, we have been severely impacted by events outside our control. U.S. auto industry sales have fallen to their lowest per capita rate in half a century. Despite moving quickly to reduce our planned spending by over $20 billion, GM finds itself precariously and frighteningly close to running out of cash.

Reliance on shared knowledge, therefore, functions not only epistemically but also as a way to foster identification between the company and its publics.

Many issue reports, of course, seek to inform audiences, in ways ranging from the most mundane to the most elegant. For example, the *Washington Post* in its *2004 Community Involvement Report* informs readers of the many rewards for community service that the newspaper has garnered. What is more subtle here is the inculcation of that knowledge through linkage to values the organization holds dear and, we might assume, hopes that its readers will, too. Certainly most readers support the value of education, but not all will value concern for ethnic heritage or the importance of the arts. These types of reports recount the organization's commitment to these efforts and, therefore, lead by example by (perhaps) instilling values in latent publics. Therefore, if reports genres foster a sense of organization-public equality and oneness through identification, they also seek to establish the organization as an authority with information that the audience does not have but may find important to the values they hold.

In our analysis, it should be clear that the dominant functions of preservation and celebration work in concert with the sometimes more subtle functions of performance and epistemology. We argued earlier that the performative function's identity-management dimension may be central to these genres, working in concert with the celebratory function. We now may state that the epistemic and preservative functions also are vital to the potential for building organizational image, identity, and reputation. As Aristotle argues, the principle of the enthymemes (and its contemporary counterpart, the organizational enthymeme) can be a potent way that reports genres can fulfill business strategies and communications objectives well.

Strategic Planning Implications

Perhaps more than the preceding chapters, this one illustrates the most aggressive application of multiple texts to create genres and for those genres to be, in turn, used to create other texts. In this way, reports genres can be thought of as the hub of public relations discourse because it is (a) in their creation that they assemble the extant, relevant knowledge about what is going on for an organization; and, subsequently, (b) in their use that they provide readers with authoritative sources of information about a range of organizational matters, from specific to holistic. Public relations managers and technicians alike recognize the strategic and tactical importance of reports genres as they preserve message consistency in ways that lend themselves to multiple situations at various times. So reports genres almost necessarily are among the most resource-intensive discourse types organizations can create and use because of a combination of the long-term permanence and lasting impact they will have as reference documents, high-profile argument presentations, and so on.

Understanding that multiple texts are used by communications professionals to create reports genres and that, similarly, reports genres beget other texts is essential to the public relations discourse-development process and strategic planning. This dynamic is addressed in the concept of "intertextuality," which has been addressed in organizational communication scholarship. Indeed, we caution readers strongly to avoid oversimplified views of the concept as, for example, matters of documents cross-referencing other documents, documents commenting on or quoting from other documents, and observing how the text of a document may be "embedded" in other documents and vice versa (see Cali, 2000; Phillips, Lawrence, & Hardy, 2004; Sillince, 2007). We are dealing with a much more profound sense and reference to the concept of intertextuality. Specifically, intertextuality

> was originally introduced by [Julia] Kristeva and met with immediate success. . . . The concept, however, has been generally misunderstood. It has nothing to do with matters of influence by one writer upon another, or with the sources of a literary work; it does, on the other hand, involve the components of a *textual system* such as the novel, for instance. (Roudiez, 1980, p. 15)

As Kristiva (1974/1984) defined it, intertextuality is the "transposition of one (or several) sign system(s) into another" (pp. 59–60), which means that the sign systems (e.g., language, symbols, discourse, discourse conventions, culture, etc.) used in a given situation rely on the sign systems from other situations. As she elaborates:

> If one grants that every signifying practice is a field of transpositions of various signifying systems (an inter-textuality), one then understand that its "place" of enunciation and its "object" are never single, complete, and identical to themselves, but always plural, shattered, capable of being tabulated. (Kristeva, 1974/1984, p. 60)

Culler (1975) further clarifies the concept this way: "A work can only be read in connection with or against other texts, which provide a grid through which it is read and structured by establishing expectations which enable one to pick out salient features and give them a structure" (p. 139). This idea of a grid (or network, or even a web) of interactions among texts is a useful way for public relations professionals to think about their work and the strategy behind reports genres.

The multiple texts that public relations professionals use "form a complex network of interaction, a structured set of relationships among texts, so that any text is best understood within the context of other texts. No text is single, as texts refer to one another, draw from one another, create the purpose for one another" (Devitt, 1991, p. 336). Reports genres, then, are historical documents that, as Fairclough (1992) would assert, intertextually transform in the present what has gone on for an organization through "existing conventions and prior texts" (p. 85). The strategic value of Figure 9.1 now becomes clearer: The holistic view of an organization (i.e., its reputation) is an intertextual phenomenon for which public relations discourse can influence change at various levels—intellectual, emotional, and behavioral, within and beyond organizations about salient topics. The examples we gave in this chapter, especially those from Ferrero Group, show how much reports genres depend on other texts and, more important, become the foundation for other texts. Strategically speaking, reports genres function as the "big sticks" organizations can use epideictically to great effect and be the hubs around which the wheels of corporate communication turn.

The strategic role that intertextuality can play is an important one: It allows public relations professionals to tend to both the macro- and microlevels of discourse development in message-specific ways. At the macrolevel, a public relations professional engages the concept of intertextuality as he or she considers what has been said for and about the organization, the exact topic at hand, related topics, and other things—whether or not he or she or other organizational insiders prepared that prior discourse. Also at a macrolevel, a public relations professional understands how the discourse he or she is creating contributes to the larger "*text*ture" of and about the organization and the topics of direct and indirect concern. This macrolevel should also involve all other organizational discourse about the organization (e.g., marketing advertisements, website, investor relations, speeches, news interviews, recruitment material, etc.). At this level, too, any development of public relations discourse must be accounted for in the strategic program of the public relations function (i.e., resource allocations and performance measures) and how it helps the organization to achieve its overall corporate objectives. At a microlevel, a public relations professional engages intertextuality as he or she applies the knowledge of the macrolevel of discourse to the specific discourse type(s) and, especially, the key message platform that will be enacted in any public relations effort for target audiences. This microlevel of intertextuality also gives public relations professionals a way to link the specific work they must do to manage messages for an organization's other communication demands that fit into the larger, macro "texture."

One thing to recognize, however, is that intertextuality may direct too much attention to the preservative function of reports genres. On the one hand, intertextuality leans on the interconnectedness of texts with one another, which is in keeping with our notion of repurposing. But, on the other hand, intertextuality is more a matter of all epideictic functions working simultaneously in terms of message consistency, which is a top priority for any communication professional. During political campaigns, "staying on message" is vital to any candidate's or issue's success. With the various discourse types that public relations professionals can use and the number of corporate officials who may be asked to comment on an organization's dealings, message consistency and coherence is an intertextual matter of great importance. In this way, what we call the "dramatic durability of messages" is a key to successful strategy. Prior messages take on even greater importance as *resources* for future message design. Much of what an organization does and says is on the public stage, and the elements of a drama—the scene (i.e., time and place), the act that took/takes place, the actors involved (organizational members or not), the means for the actors to take action, and the purpose for the actors' action—all roll into the messages that have been said in the past, can be said in the present, and may be said in the future, if things work out in certain, anticipated ways. Familiarity with audiences and their views of the drama are vital to make sure messages are durable (consistent and cohesive) over the period during which a situation is managed.

The strategy behind reports genres rests largely on the idea that these discourse types are textual forms that lend themselves to special applications of specific and holistic messages that possess high degrees of durability for an organization and its publics and stakeholders (see Smudde, 2007). Intertextuality is a theoretical construct that has highly practical implications for public relations professionals to ensure reports genres fit in the big picture and that the big picture has the clues about what and how reports genres can and should be enacted best in situations. The strategy, then, is to harness the explanatory power of intertextuality for both the effective development of public relations discourse and the effective management of public relations activities at the macro- and the microlevels.

With this chapter, we close our analysis of the families of public relations discourse genres, but at the same time we recognize how much this chapter reflects and builds on the others. Reports genres certainly are the most thoroughly epideictic of all public relations discourse genres. Taken as a whole, our analysis in this book is but a preface to the first statements in a larger conversation about public relations discourse and how strategy and generic conventions intertwine for successful communications.

Note

1. Conversations (blogs), showcase genres (press kits), collections genres, and reports all have award-mills. The Webbys (The Barbarian Group, n.d.), the Stevie Awards (2009), also known as the American Business Awards, and the 2008 winners live up to the sense of occasion.

References

Alex's Lemonade Stand Foundation. (2008a). *Alex's Lemonade Stand Foundation: Fighting childhood cancer, one cup at a time.* Retrieved July 5, 2009, from http://www.alexslemonade.org/slideshow

Alex's Lemonade Stand Foundation. (2008b). *Meet our founder: Alexandra Scott.* Retrieved July 5, 2009, from http://www.alexslemonade.org/about/meet-alex

The Barbarian Group. (n.d.) *Webby nominees.* Retrieved April 21, 2009, from http://www.webbyawards.com/webbys/current.php?season=13

Black, E. (1970). The second persona. *Quarterly Journal of Speech, 56,* 109–119.

Burke, K. (1984). *Attitudes toward history* (3rd ed.). Berkeley: University of California Press. (Original work published 1937)

Cali, D. D. (2000). The logic of the link: The associative paradigm in communication criticism. *Critical Studies in Media Communication, 17*(4), 397–408.

Campbell, K. K., & Jamieson, K. H. (n.d.). Form and genre in rhetorical criticism: An introduction. In K. K. Campbell & K. H. Jamieson (Eds.), *Form and genre: Shaping rhetorical action* (pp. 9–32). Falls Church, VA: Speech Communication Association.

Cheney, G., & Vibbert, S. L. (1987). Corporate discourse: Public relations and issue management. In F. M. Jablin, L. L. Putnam, K. H. Roberts, & L. W. Porter (Eds.), *Handbook of organizational communications: An interdisciplinary perspective* (pp. 165–194). Newbury Park, CA: Sage.

Crable, R. E., & Vibbert, S. L. (1985). Managing issues and influencing public policy. *Public Relations Review, 11,* 3–16.

Culler, J. (1975). *Structuralist poetics: Structuralism, linguistics, and the study of literature.* Ithaca, NY: Cornell University Press.

Devitt, A. J. (1991). Intertextuality in tax accounting: Generic, referential, and functional. In C. Bazerman & J. Paradis (Eds.), *Textual dynamics of the professions: Historical and contemporary studies of writing in professional communities* (pp. 336–357). Madison, WI: University of Wisconsin Press.

Emery, F. E., & Trist, E. L. (1965). The causal texture of organizational environment. *Human Relations, 18,* 21–32.

European Financial Reporting Advisory Group. (2009, March 25). *EFRAG and European national standard-setters publish a discussion paper on performance reporting.* Retrieved July 2, 2009, from http://www.efrag.org/news/detail.asp?id=339

Fairclough, N. (1992). *Discourse and social change.* Cambridge, UK: Polity Press.

Ferrero do Brasil. (n.d.). *Ferrero Brasil* (Ferrero Brazil). Retrieved July 3, 2009, from http://www.ferrero.com.br/

Ferrero France. (2008). *Ferrero France: Confiserie et goûter au chocolat* [Ferrero France: Candy maker and chocolate taste]. Retrieved July 3, 2009, from http://www.ferrero.fr/

Ferrero France. (n.d.a). *Allez, on bouge!: Le site communautaire des activités sportives de loisir en famille* [Go, let's get moving!: The community site for family sport and leisure activities]. Retrieved July 3, 2009, from http://www.allezonbouge.net/

Ferrero France. (n.d.b). *Les anciens collaborateurs–Nelly Gandon* [Former employees–Nelly Gandon]. [Corporate video]. Retrieved July 3, 2009, from http://www.ferrero.fr/ferrero_webtv_detail.php?flv=http://ferrerovideo.farm.inrete.it/ferrerofr/NellyGandonv2_FL9_604x340-v4.flv&sectionId=0&itemId=1

Ferrero France. (n.d.c). *Intégration de personnes en situation de handicap* [Integration of handicapped persons]. [Corporate video]. Retrieved July 3, 2009, from http://www.ferrero.fr/ferrero_webtv_detail.php?flv=http://ferrerovideo.farm.inrete.it/ferrerofr/handicapdefv2_FL9_604x340.flv&sectionId=0&itemId=0

Ferrero Group. (2007). *Ferrero Group.* Retrieved July 3, 2009, from http://www.ferrero.com/eng/index.html

Ferrero USA, Inc. (n.d.). *Ferrero.* Retrieved July 3, 2009, from http://www.ferrerousa.com/

General Motors Corporation. (2008a, December 2). *GM submits plan for long-term viability to the U.S. Congress.* [News release]. Retrieved July 5, 2009, from http://media.gm.com/servlet/GatewayServlet?target=http://image.emerald.gm.com/gmnews/viewmonthlyreleasedetail.do?domain=74&docid=50755

General Motors Corporation. (2008b, December 2). *GM's commitment to the American people.* [Advocacy advertisement]. *Wall Street Journal,* p. B3.

General Motors Corporation. (2008c, December 4). *Examining the state of the domestic automobile industry: Part II. Testimony of G. Richard Wagoner, Jr., Chairman and Chief Executive Officer, General Motors Corporation, before the Committee on Banking, Housing, and Urban Affairs, United States Senate.* Retrieved July 5, 2009, from http://media.gm.com/servlet/GatewayServlet?target=http://image.emerald.gm.com/newspublisher/support_file/12-04-2008/38/081204wagoner.pdf

Indian Oil Corporation Ltd. (2007–2008). *Financial performance.* Retrieved October 2, 2008, from http://www.iocl.com/Aboutus/FinancialPerformance.aspx

ITT Corporation. (2008). *Extraordinary focus: 2007 annual report.* Retrieved April 21, 2009, from http://www.itt.com/docs/investors/financial-statements/annual-report/2007_annual.pdf

KMPG UK. (2007). *Corporate governance in India–trends in financial reporting and auditing practices*. Retrieved July 2, 2009, from http://www.nfcgindia.org/presentations/presentation_kpmg.pdf

KMPG UK. (2009). *Financial reporting 2009 UK GAAP checklist*. Retrieved July 2, 2009, from http://www.kpmg.co.uk/services/a/pubs.cfm

Koonjy, D. (2002, November 1). *SEC reporting requirements for public companies*. Retrieved July 2, 2009, from http://www.allbusiness.com/human-resources/employee-development-leadership/1080884-1.html

Kristiva, J. (1984). *Revolution in poetic language* (L. S. Roudiez, Trans.). New York: Columbia University Press. (Original work published 1974)

McMillan, J. J. (1987). In search of the organizational persona: A rationale for studying organizations rhetorically. In L. Thayer (Ed.), *Organization↔communication: Emerging perspectives II* (pp. 21–45). Norwood, NJ: Ablex.

Mutual of Omaha. (2008). *How do you sleep?* [Image advertisement]. *National Geographic, 214*(3), i–ii.

Perelman, C., & Olbrechts-Tyteca, L. (1969). *The new rhetoric: A treatise on argumentation* (J. Wilkinson & P. Weaver, Trans.). Notre Dame, IN: Notre Dame University Press.

Phillips, N., Lawrence, T. B., & Hardy, C. (2004). Discourse and institutions. *Academy of Management Review, 29*(4), 635–652.

Poe, R. (1994, May). Can we talk? CEOs speak frankly in the new breed of annual reports. *Across the Board*, pp. 17–23.

Reputation Institute. (2009, May 6). *Ferrero, Ikea, Johnson & Johnson rank as most reputable companies in the world on Reputation Institute's Global Reputation Pulse study*. [News release]. Retrieved July 3, 2009, from http://www.reputation-institute.com/events/Global_Reputation_Pulse_Release_2009_06may2009.pdf

Roudiez, L. S. (1980). Introduction. In J. Kristeva (Ed.), *Desire in language: A semiotic approach to literature and art* (T. Gora, A. Jardine, & L. S. Roudiez, Trans.). (pp. 1–20). New York: Columbia University Press.

Samsung. (2007). *Samsung Electronics annual report*. Retrieved October 2, 2008, from http://www.samsung.com/us/aboutsamsung/ir/financialinformation/annualreport/downloads/2007/00_SEC_07AR_E_Full.pdf

Sillince, J. A. A. (2007). Organizational context and the discursive construction of organizing. *Management Communication Quarterly, 20*(4), 363–394.

Smudde, P. M. (2007). Public relations' power as based on knowledge, discourse, and ethics. In J. L. Courtright & P. M. Smudde (Eds.), *Power and public relations* (pp. 207–238). Cresskill, NJ: Hampton Press.

Stevie Awards, Inc. (2009). *The American Business Awards: The Stevies*. Retrieved April 21, 2009, from http://www.stevieawards.com/pubs/awards/403_2436_17718.cfm

Tohyama, A. (2008). *Understanding J-SOX requirements: An IT perspective*. Retrieved July 2, 2009, from http://www.itpolicycompliance.com/what+s_new/thought_leader_articles/read.asp?ID=39

Toyota Motor Corporation. (2007). *Annual report 2007: Building a platform for growth*. Retrieved January 10, 2010, from http://www.toyota.co.jp/en/ir/library/annual/pdf/2007/ar07_e.pdf

194   Inspiring Cooperation and Celebrating Organization

Toyota Motor Corporation. (2009). *Can you do more for the earth by putting less into it? Why not?* [Issue advertisement]. *National Geographic, 215*(3), i–ii.

Toyota Motor North America, Inc. (2008). *2007 North America environmental report.* Retrieved July 5, 2009, from http://www.toyota.com/about/environment-2007/

Toyota Motor North America, Inc. (2009a). *2008 North America environmental report.* Retrieved July 5, 2009, from http://www.toyota.com/about/enviroreport2008/

Toyota Motor North America, Inc. (2009b). *Toyota why not?* Retrieved July 5, 2009, from http://www.toyotawhynot.com/#/home

U.S. Department of Health and Human Services Centers for Disease Control and Prevention. (n.d.). *West Nile virus is a risk you can do something about.* [Brochure]. Washington, DC: Government Printing Office.

Virtual Lemonade Stand. (n.d.). *Virtual lemonade stand: Support pediatric cancer research.* Retrieved July 5, 2009, from http://www.lemonadestandforlife.com/

Volvo Motor Cars of North America. (n.d.a). *Volvo cars.* Retrieved July 5, 2009, from http://www.volvocars.com/us/Pages/default.aspx

Volvo Motor Cars of North America. (n.d.b). *Volvo child safety.* Retrieved July 5, 2009, from http://www.volvocars.com/us/campaigns/Misc/ChildSafety/Pages/default.aspx

10

Introduction

We believe this book has drawn new attention to the day-to-day dimensions of public relations discourse, which we maintain is celebratory in character. Public relations professionals need to pay attention to the celebration, the party, to which they invite publics. To do this, public relations pros must understand the core values of the organizations, causes, and so on on whose behalf they write and speak. They must understand their publics' values if they are to fulfill the practice's discursive function—"to [adjust] organizations to environments and environments to organizations" (Crable & Vibbert, 1986, p. 394)—all ultimately to inspire cooperation between organizations and their publics.

This final chapter ends our book literally, but we see it metaphorically as the beginning (thus the title, "Introduction") of the long-term practical and academic discussion and action about the strategy behind public relations discourse genres. We have shown how different sets of public relations genres may be understood through the four epideictic functions. Moreover, within each of those genres, we have argued that each type prioritizes those functions differently. These prioritizations arise from the intersections of situation and content with the purpose of any given discourse convention. (For the convenience of the reader, we have summarized these priorities in Appendix 1, "Families of Public Relations Discourse Genres.") Additionally, we have provided particular prescriptions for the strategic use of genres within each chapter to aid the understanding of each family of discourse (e.g., concepts of *personae* for news genres, schema and perception theory in summaries genres, narrative for features genres, the Johari window for conversations genres, intertextuality for reports genres, etc.). This chapter therefore serves as a starting point for public relations students and practitioners not only to take concepts that researchers heretofore have used in case analyses and campaign evaluation, but also apply them to issues central to strategic planning and message design.

The central question to this book has been, "How much may thinking about and enacting generic public relations change the practice and study of public relations for the better—to be more *prospective* (i.e., forward-looking and strategic) than retrospective (i.e., backward-looking and a matter of 20/20 hindsight)?" Based on the preceding chapters, we begin the conversation with initial answers to this question through four principal topics: discourse competency, ethics, power, and strategy.

Discourse Competency

Discourse competency is a core concept to this book, and it concerns someone being both streetwise and book-smart about genres and message design. In other words, a person possesses a holistic understanding of any discourse's potential and limitations—from conception to creation to coherence to comprehension (e.g., see Blakemore, 2003; Eggins & Martin, 1997; Fairclough, 1992; Halliday & Hasan, 1976; Kinneavy, 1971, for treatment of individual concepts pertaining to this view). Our view of discourse competence parallels Hymes' (1972) concept of "communicative competence," which concerns how well someone recognizes whether and to what degree discourse is grammatical, appropriate, feasible, or actionable (Jaworski & Coupland, 2006; see also Hudson, 1980; Jablin & Sias, 2001). The preceding chapters present what we believe are the fundamental factors of discourse competence in public relations. Instrumental in it all is the strategic framing of messages to fulfill specific purposes and adapt to specific audiences.

Note, however, that people can possess varying degrees of discourse competency, such that individuals can be identified along a continuum ranging from those who are especially good to those who are terribly inept. Discourse competency can be viewed also as field-dependent so that we can say, for example, that those who are unfamiliar with the principles and practices of public relations (e.g., students beginning study in public relations and new hires of public relations organizations from another profession) may be discourse incompetent to a degree merely because of their ignorance of the discourse practices and genres in the field. In this section, we extend our examination in the preceding chapters by being concerned with the *prospective* framing of messages to (a) manage the relationship of form and function in the use of media channels; (b) address audiences epideictically; (c) link matters in terms of past, present, and future messages; and (d) build organizational character through strategic message design.

As you will recall from Chapter 1, any genre is defined by its purpose, form, and situation. In terms of public relations, these concerns also relate to matters of audience because audiences to some degree judge the fitness of a message in terms of the immediate situation and their perceptions of what forms of discourse are best suited—indeed, most typically used, based on past experience—for a given occasion. Moreover, the audience will judge the legitimacy of the organization's purpose(s) in communicating through the genre's use. In turn, audiences also evaluate the credibility of the source behind the message, thereby generating an image of the organization (see Moffitt, 1999) and a judgment of how much trust they ascribe to that source. When combined with judgments of the truth and intelligibility of the message (see Burkart, 2004, for further discussion of such judgments), attention to such considerations make for a potent approach to message design. In our view, then, public relations practitioners must attend to each one *individually* and, most important, balance each one with the others *simultaneously*. These interrelationships are depicted in Figure 10.1.

To illustrate, consider again the comparison of the annual reports of Samsung (2007) and Toyota (2007), which we mentioned in Chapter 9. In terms of the *media channel*, both companies produced annual reports not only in keeping with government requirements in the countries in which they operate, but also in the form and for reasons (i.e., functions and purposes) that audiences have come to expect (as described at the beginning

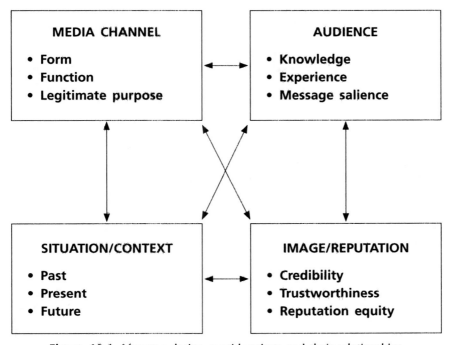

Figure 10.1. Message design considerations and their relationships.

of the previous chapter). Consistent with epideictic's epistemic function, the annual reports' form and purpose(s) were designed to appeal to the *audience's* knowledge, past experience, and salient needs to acquire new information about the particular companies. At the same time, both annual reports are adapted to past, present, and future *situations* and audience awareness of them. Publics who follow the companies most closely would know that Toyota has an *image* or *reputation* for innovations documented through prior messages. These audiences would know that Samsung could not make the same claim. Both companies, however, consistent with the genre and standard practice in writing annual reports, have paved the way for future messages with promises and predictions of future innovations.

These first three parts of media channel (genre), audience, and situation/context make audience expectations and adaptation central to message design (see Courtright & Smudde, 2009). Figure 10.1 reminds us, however, that concern for organizational image and reputation also are important in all public relations messages. Although audiences may not be conscious of the judgments they make when receiving messages, practitioners must take into account the need for honesty and transparency (as both Toyota and Samsung appear to have done in their annual reports). Such efforts should increase the credibility of the voices implied in the various sections of the report, be they specific company officers (e.g., the CEO, the CFO), a more ambiguous corporate voice, or that extremely flexible pronoun, "we." Additionally, audiences, at least implicitly, evaluate the message source based on previous organizational messages, past experience, and projections about the future.

Thus, all four—media channel, audience, situation/context, and organization image and reputation—must fit together to create a more cohesive and comprehensible message design effort. When one of these considerations does not seem to fit, less than "good" public relations is recognizable. Even when a stakeholder cannot put his or her finger on what is wrong, there is at least an implicit sense of unease due to miscues in using a genre, missing the target in terms of audience interests or needs or other considerations highlighted in Figure 10.1. To better appreciate the utility of our approach to discourse competence, we next take a look at each aspect of the figure in turn.

Form AND Function

Contrary to what many people believe, the medium is *not* the message— medium *and* message work together in rhetorical ways that organizations use to inspire cooperation with their audiences while also inviting them to celebrate their common ground. As McLuhan (1964) argues, "the message of any medium or technology [itself] is the change of scale or pace or pattern that it introduces into human affairs" (p. 24). The medium and message are necessarily bound together, as the medium/form of communication follows from the reason/function for what is said. Messages and their purposes affect media choices, and media literally shape the messages in space and time. This point is key to the "media channel" portion of Figure 10.1. The key here is how people read forms (see Langer, 1942/1979). For example, we process form as a whole, say, a news release. This is *presentational form*. Based on Ware and Linkugel (1973), this is the *de facto* labeling of a genre. We recognize it as a news release because of its overall appearance. We also process form *discursively*. We read a news release just as we would a painting, following its component parts in some recognizable pattern of consumption. Ware and Linkugel would recognize this as a *structural approach* to genre classification because we are labeling a genre based on its pattern of organization.

A central tenet to this book is that the genre/type/form of discourse used in public relations is in direct response to the purpose/reason/function behind why an organization wants or needs to communicate something to its audiences.[1] As Louis H. Sullivan (1918/1979), modern architect around the turn of the 20th century, said:

> It is the pervading law of all things organic, and inorganic, of all things physical and metaphysical, of all things human and all things superhuman, of all true manifestations of the head, of the heart, of the soul, that the life is recognizable in its expression, that *form ever follows function*. This is the law. (p. 208; italics added)

For something to be created begs the question of why it was created. Whether we look at architecture, manufacturing, communication, or any other human endeavor, form *and* function necessarily go together.

The forms and functions of public relations discourse also, as we have argued in other ways in this volume, allow us to focus on both the particulars that make them work (i.e., conventions, message design, and strategies) and the generalities of how they may be best used across situations.[2] On the one hand, an atomistic view is valuable because it allows us to engage in an analysis of the details of the very stuff of particular public relations discourse and practice. On the other hand—and most important—a gestalt view of public relations genres in context allows us to achieve a synthesis of principles about the nature of effective public relations in general. For example, in the *Mona Lisa*, the figure of the woman is present over the ground of the rest of the painting. The relationship between figure and ground are vital and pronounced. In public relations, the figures of particular discourse genres are always given within the ground of the greater context of what was, is, and will be going on in, around, and for an organization and its audiences. Managing the gestalt of public relations' form and function is made possible through acute discourse competency for epideictic audiences.

In terms of strategy, an astute public relations professional would recognize that the epideictic functions of public relations discourse allow her or him, based on particular purposes, to use genres that will fulfill particular objectives and, perhaps, to use them in a sequence that builds one on the next. It should be noted at this point that strategic use of public relations discourse genres takes place within the context of communication campaigns. Any of the 39 genres we have highlighted may be used to increase awareness, change attitudes, and/or obtain certain behaviors. Any genre also may be used in combination, for example, in crisis communication. Each retains its prioritized epideictic functions, yet each operates within a broader rhetorical genre at the campaign level (i.e., corporate apologia). Product introduction campaigns, too, utilize many of the individual genres featured herein, but may together enact the characteristics and functions of utopian campaign rhetoric to heighten awareness about a product, inspire favorable opinions about it, and induce people to buy it. Even a combination of the traditional genres we have reviewed and a nontraditional set of campaign strategies (e.g., protest events with placards, masks, etc.) may serve organizations such as People for the Ethical Treatment of Animals (PETA) or Greenpeace in a campaign genre that Weaver (2010) has termed "carnivalesque activism." At both individual message and campaign levels, then, managing the gestalt of public relations' form and function is made possible through acute discourse competency. Such efforts must be tailored to epideictic audiences.

The Epideictic Audience

As discussed in Chapter 2, the audience figures prominently in epideictic's performative and epistemic functions. Audience is the next part of Figure 10.1 that we explain. Public relations' audiences do not serve as mere spectators who appreciate the values invoked through epideictic discourse (i.e., the traditional view of epideictic as speeches of "praise and blame"). The performative function entails making a substantive connection with the audience—identification—in order to inform, persuade, or other purpose. Assuredly, epideictic rhetoric is a rhetoric of display or entertainment, but it also serves to foster mutual understanding and to shape and share a sense of community (Condit, 1985). (Prime examples of organizations that are known for doing this exceedingly well include Harley Davidson, John Deere, Special Olympics, and many religious organizations.) Public relations discourse therefore invites audiences to make judgments about the stylistic choices found within the message, the accuracy of the ideas the message presents, and recognition and support of the "advice" recommended within it (Oravec, 1976). As indicated previously, stylistic choices begin with issues of form; the ideas and appeals that organizations make relate to the purposes or functions for which genres are used.

But to which audience(s) are messages directed? As we take a discourse-oriented approach that takes into account a genre to be used, the situation in question, and the organization's prior reputation and the image to be projected, demographic and psychographic analyses are but a beginning to targeting an audience. According to Black (1970), every message implies how the speaker (in our case, an organization) wishes the audience members to view themselves in relationship to the speaker. Clearly public relations practitioners use specific genres for the purpose of influencing segmented audiences or discourse communities. Yet such market orientations are not always useful. Moreover, two potential problems arise. First, many of the genres illustrated in this book are designed to appeal to multiple audiences (e.g., news releases, annual reports). Second, narrow conceptions of audience run the risk of alienating other, often unintended, audiences (Perelman & Olbrechts-Tyteca, 1969).

Because the availability of multiple media sources to today's publics complicates communication, a more comprehensive solution is needed— one that allows organizations to address multiple audiences in ways that reinforce the ability to stay on message. This addressing of multiple audiences may be done in one of two ways. First, messages may include multiple topics, lines of reasoning, or pieces of evidence (depending on the amount of discourse afforded by a given genre) such that different audiences may be moved for different (as well as overlapping or multiple) reasons. An audience need not accept all parts of a message to identify with it and, by extension, the organization. For example, some audiences for Toyota's annual reports may find particular innovations more salient than others. At the same time, environmental audiences may identify with messages contained in both Toyota's and Samsung's reports.

A second possibility is to use language at a higher level of abstraction (i.e., with less specificity) when adapting the message to a genre (media channel) and audience. Such appeals are typical of epideictic rhetoric because values, by definition, are abstractions. Thus general appeals to "going green," for example, more likely will invite cooperation with multiple stakeholders than specific green practices, such as wind farms, biodiesel fuels that may increase the cost of soybeans or corn, or extreme positions on global warming. Although some use of ambiguous language might raise ethical concerns, appropriate stylistic choices can induce identification with multiple publics and, thereby, facilitate stronger relationships between organizations and publics. Indeed, reputation platforms are necessarily broad (see Eisenberg, 1984) to maintain a consistent organizational story with which audiences may identify (see Fombrun & van Riel, 2004). Such identification is essential for matters in the present and how it stems from the past and extends into the anticipated future.

Situation as Transcendent Present

Organizations, like individual people, consider today in light of what they did yesterday and will or may do tomorrow. This capacity to conceive, cogitate, and construct on events within and across time is unique to humans. Korzybski (1921/1950) called it "time-binding" because humans uniquely

> select, gather together, and combine into something new the various elements that belong to different periods of time [past, present, and anticipated future]. They combine them, transform them, and make out of them something that did not exist before. They can repeat this operation as often as they wish, each time creating a modification, an enlargement, a complexification of the world in which they live. (Bois, 1978, p. 122)

All cultures view and use time as circular or rectilinear (Caillois & McKeon, 1963). No matter what view of time one uses, inventions, discoveries, and creations lead to other inventions, additional discoveries, and new creations. Public relations is a time-binding function for organizations that links the past and the future in the now. This point is the substance of the "situation/context" part of Figure 10.1.

This time-binding capacity spells a special timeliness and timelessness to the epideictic discourse of public relations. That is, in parallel fashion to Campbell and Jamieson (1986), public relations discourse transcends the present by bringing into it messages about that which was and that which will or may be. The result is that relationships between organizations and their publics are ever-present or eternal, allowing for messages to be reenacted at other times in other ways. The epideictic character of public relations discourse, then, possesses a potency "that can be realized when rhetors and audiences cooperatively create a vision that defines and celebrates the community's values but leave open the possibility that those values can be creatively reinterpreted in response to new challenges" (Agnew, 2008, p. 153). In this way, epideictic discourse accommodates rectilinear, Western views of time (i.e., past, present, and future as discrete points in time) and circular, oriental, or tribal views of time (i.e., the use of a genre at a given point in time reflects previous occasions when similar patterns of discourse occurred and implies future uses of the same patterns).

One particular facet of writing for online media is an example of future thinking and affects both process and product, with the potential to do so adversely. The application of search engine optimization (SEO)—the use of key terms in and "meta tags" to online texts (e.g., documents, images, web pages) to influence how Internet search engines find texts and place them higher in a search above others so they are seen first—can dominate writing for online media for the worse not the better. That is, because SEO places emphasis on key terms, the primary objective is to, based on the organization and the subject matter, identify and use key words that will obtain prominent placement for public relations discourse in web searches. After that, messages would be defined and a text would be written to fit those terms and, coincidentally, fulfill certain objectives—not the other way around, which is the more potent issue in message design within a strategic framework. SEO, then, reverses the process for creating effective messages in genres that fulfill strategy. A new view of discourse emerges here as the binding of space and time through language and symbols. For example, reports genres show the transcendent present in public relations. Their content necessarily binds what has, is, and will happen in time for an organization and its publics. (Annual reports perhaps provide the most obvious example of a genre's timeliness and timelessness.) Most important, content can be reused (and likely edited or revised if needed) in other genres for other purposes and audiences (see Courtright & Slaughter, 2007). In particular, what is presented in an annual report can be transliterated into another genre, say an article or a brochure, that enables an organization and its publics to co-create "a new vision of the world," one in which "audiences and speakers who enter epideictic moments with a genuine commitment to learn from each other, even as they respectfully acknowledge their differences, will be uniquely prepared to respond to a world in which difference is often seen as a divisive force" (Agnew, 2008, p. 161). Such mutual learning and cooperation between organizations and their publics is instrumental to building organizational character.

Organizational Character Building

Regardless of message genre, audience, or situation, we regard reputation building (the last part of Figure 10.1) to be one of the important purposes of public relations message design. Although many public relations writing texts are organized by media channel and discourse forms associated with them, how messages imply how the organization desires to be perceived and what image(s) audiences may form as a result must be taken into account.

Corporate reputations "reflect how companies are perceived across a broad spectrum of stakeholders" (Fombrun & van Riel, 2004, p. xxvii). Positive and negative events in the life of any organization reflect on its reason for being as well as direct people's attention to salient matters about what and why an organization does what it does (e.g., financial reporting, product safety, employee satisfaction, customer relationships, etc.). Reputations, then, are earned through organizational action—primarily communicative action— with various stakeholders. Although scholars have given some attention to communication's role in reputation management (e.g., Brønn & Berg, 2005; Schultz, Hatch, & Larsen, 2000), that role has been, in the main, broadly construed. We have argued that genre theory may be employed to deepen our understanding of how messages may shape identity to influence stakeholders' images and change or sustain corporate reputation (Courtright & Smudde, 2009).

Message design, then, is at the heart of reputation building. Two central concepts—trust and credibility—are important to reputation. Credibility is more than just the character of the organization as represented in the message (i.e., ethos) but a judgment based on audience perceptions and interpretations prior to, during, and after message delivery. Trust is but one factor of credibility but a precious commodity that organizations can lose in an instant. As Kiley and Helm (2009) stated in *BusinessWeek*, "Trust is the most perishable of assets. Polling in recent months shows that increasing numbers of consumers distrust not just the obvious suspects—the banks— but business as a whole" (p. 38). Indeed, reputation is typically seen as a function of trust, and both are simultaneously cultivated by public relations activities and supported by marketing efforts. When built over time through the use of many discourse genres, the result is reputation equity—a rhetorical bank account of credibility that may sustain an organization's good name in times of trouble (see Fombrun & van Riel, 2004). Reputation equity therefore also functions as a source of prior credibility when audiences receive new messages.

In summary, just as all messages imply an audience, they also imply the character of the source (*again*, Aristotle's concept of ethos) (see Black, 1970). Selection of discourse genre and an appropriate media channel therefore communicate a desired *persona* of the organization just as much as the content of the message (see Courtright & Smudde, 2009). Audiences interpret these messages and form, reinforce, or alter the images they hold in their minds. In relation to epideictic's transcendent present, audiences also make evaluations of organizations relative to the situations their messages address. It behooves public relations practitioners, then, to think seriously about the image(s) they project in selected genres through the messages they craft on behalf of organizations. Reputations rise and fall based to a great degree on what the organization says and does (see Williams & Moffitt, 1997). Thus, judgments of credibility, trustworthiness, and legitimacy hearken back to Aristotle's original concern for ethos—the character of the speaker as implied in the message. We therefore turn to a topic related to that ancient Greek word, ethos: ethics.

Ethics

Ethics involves thinking about morality, moral problems, and moral judgments. Frankena (1973) asserts that such philosophizing arises when we are directed by traditional rules and beyond a stage when those rules are internalized such that we are "inner-directed" to think in critical and general terms, thereby achieving "a kind of autonomy as moral agents" (p. 4). Whether informing employees about policies, managing an issue, publishing an annual report, or setting up a blog, organizations continually weigh ethical considerations about their communicative actions (see Curtin & Boynton, 2001). As Conrad (1993) points out:

> It is through discourse that individuals develop their own views of morality; through discourse that organizations develop and inculcate core values and ethical codes; and through discourse that incongruities within individual and organizational value-sets are managed and contradictions between the value-sets of different persons are negotiated. (p. 2)

Theories about organizational communication ethics would at least help people sort out what is ethical communication and what is not. Organizations are often seen and treated (even legalistically) like individual people (see Cheney, 1992). Organizations face "complex interrelationships between values, ethics, and organizational decision making, the matrix of concepts that comprise the 'ethical nexus'" (Conrad, 1993, p. 2) for communication. Therefore, organizations, as interconnected participants in an environment, cannot plan for, take action, or manage their own boundaries without considering their stakeholders and other organizations.

Character of Good Speakers

There is a strong link between giving a speech (or creating any other discourse form) and the character of people as communicators (and the audience) involved in it. To address this idea about character, which is as good for organizations as it is for individual people, we must begin with Aristotle because he gives us the best foundation on which to build. As Aristotle (1991) argues in his *Nicomachean Ethics*, individuals seek the highest good for not only themselves, but also for others and the state, primarily in the civic context of public address. Aristotle argues that rhetoric falls under politics, generally, and ethics, specifically. The reason for this division is that, for Aristotle, politics is the *archetechne* (master art) of the good for people, and ethics is part of politics that concerns ideas about virtuous actions and habits to achieve the good. Aristotle's *Rhetoric* benefits from his *Nicomachean Ethics* in at least two ways. The characterizations of the good person in the *Nicomachean Ethics* carry over into the *Rhetoric* in the descriptions of a good speaker. Indeed, the same root word, *eth*, is shared between *ethos* and *ethike*, referring to individual moral character. The *Rhetoric* also borrows from the *Nicomachean Ethics* ideas about virtuous actions and habits such that one's discourse must be crafted in accordance with virtuous ends for the audience.

The central question in the *Nicomachean Ethics* is what is the nature of the good—the highest good—and by what means and character can humans attain that good, which is happiness? The good person possesses attributes of riches, honor, strength, beauty, good fortune, worldly success, and so on (*Ethics* 1.8.30; see *Rhetoric* 1.5-6); one's soul is characterized by wisdom, knowledge, courage, and temperance ("the golden mean"—arriving at the means by knowing the extremes) (*Ethics* 2.8-9); and one attains happiness of the mind—the highest good—in a contemplative life (*Ethics* 10.7). The good person in the *Nicomachean Ethics* is akin to the good speaker in the *Rhetoric* because both share common character traits and both must follow virtuous ends in their actions. Within the context of rhetoric, the good person possesses an ethos such that an audience would be especially persuaded. Even though Aristotle asserts that a speaker is judged on his or her ethos during a speech, the greater context of the good person in the *Nicomachean Ethics* clarifies Aristotle's stance in the *Rhetoric* on persuasion through ethos and the disposition of the speaker as a good person. By extension, public relations people should represent the "good organization speaking well" (Cheney, 1992; see Courtright & Slaughter, 2007).

Ethics in Message Design

For organizations to be perceived as good—to be perceived as, *and* to actually be, good corporate citizens—is central to epideictic discourse because audiences sit in moral judgment of epideictic messages and their sources (Mirhady, 1995). As a means of thinking about organizational character building, message design, and discursive action, based on D. L. Sullivan's

(1993) five components to the speaker's ethos in epideictic rhetoric, we suggest the following questions to address five imperatives of good public relations practice:

1. *Reputation*: What is the organization known for? What are its values (or what is its code of ethics)? What factors do different publics use in assessing that reputation (see Fombrun & van Riel, 2004)? How are these demonstrated through the discourse conventions they use? Is the organization allowing for a reasonable level of transparency through its communication?

2. *Vision*: What are the organization's goals? What appear to be its purposes in using a particular discourse convention (or set of them) as part of a larger campaign? In conjunction with the previous characteristic, how are genre conventions used to establish or maintain the organization's reputation as visionary (i.e., as a leader or innovator)?

3. *Authority*: Does the organization have legitimacy to speak on a particular subject using discourse conventions that make sense? Are the genres appropriate for the organization? (For example, the second author, while temporarily overseeing a radio station's community service announcements, learned that some for-profit companies assume that a special event qualifies as a public service, even if it clearly is a product sale that happens to be held on the premises of a local nonprofit.) Is the organization speaking authentically?

4. *Presentation of good reasons* (Fisher, 1987; Wallace, 1963): How sound is the argumentation used within the chosen genre(s)? Which genres allow for traditional reasoning to be used? Which ones work better (or worse) in supporting the organization's purposes, whether they are to entertain, educate, inform, or persuade? If narrative is a better choice in shaping a message (e.g., in using features genres), how many good reasons should be presented, explicitly or implicitly, to support the organization's purposes?

5. *Creation of consubstantiality with the audience* (i.e., identification; see Burke, 1945/1969): What sensitivity to community or audience values does the organization demonstrate with its use of a particular discourse convention? To what degree do the genre conventions employed inspire cooperation and/or identification with the audience?

Messages and the discourse genres that convey them are literal reflections of the self and its relationship with others. For as much as public relations does for organizations, their audiences, and society, it does so with an accountability to those same bodies and itself as a profession. The foundation on which any field can build itself is ethics, and this point is borne out in the literature about the professionalism of public relations (see David, 2004; Hoffmann, Rottger, & Jarren, 2007; Kim & Reber, 2009; Pieczka & L'Etang, 2001). The importance of ethics as a matter concerning both self and others (organizations and their publics) calls into question its role with power. Indeed, we join together ethics and power because of public relations' potential impact on communities in size ranging from the local to the global (Goddard, 2005). Public relations must nurture power based on relationships among people and organizations.

Power

Power is a problematic concept in public relations research and practice, as it is in communication quite generally. It carries with it semantic baggage—largely negative—that leads many people to believe they understand the concept of power. An "armchair" view of power often brings to mind typical ideas of control, domination, and influence but also, for example, electricity, permission, rank, authority, responsibility, accountability, gender, race, social position, money, resources, affiliation, ethos, persuasiveness, and results. Yet even though power deals with more than any combination of these ideas, the problem is solvable through strategic thinking about its three dimensions: hierarchical, rhetorical, and social. In the end, power and public relations are compatible because of people's sensibilities about these three dimensions and abilities to plan for ways to inspire cooperation between the groups for which they work and their publics.

First, the hierarchical dimension of power concerns how it is conferred on people in organizations. The hierarchical nature of organizations is a natural place for power based on individuals' rank and position. In this way, power's hierarchical dimension is captured in such god terms as control, leader, and authority. In contrast, devil terms to power include oppression and domination. In the former case, power is much more neutral to positive in this sense because it merely refers to one's bailiwick. The problem comes in when power as control or authority is framed in negative terms congruent with those associated with the selfish aims of oppression and domination. In this way, power is associated with the political dynamics that ensue among people organizing with one another at micro- and macrolevels.

Second, the rhetorical dimension of power concerns the effects and effectiveness of one's ability to create, use, and misuse language and symbols, which is a uniquely human capability. This dimension is most associated with manipulative motives behind communication of authoritarian regimes. Again, the key is the selfish side to power as deception, lying, or even spin. On positive or neutral grounds, the rhetorical dimension of power is best associated with persuasion, results, and influence. The presumption here is that someone's or some organization's message making is done on ethical grounds in the first place.

Third and last, the social dimension of power concerns relationships among people. This final dimension is one that most binds together the other two: Organizations and societies are made up of people who act with each other principally through communication. People gather together and invite others to join (or cast others away) because of the common ground they share (e.g., values, goals, worldview, etc.). Especially inherent in this dimension is ethics: People accept and abide by rules of individual and collective good thinking and behavior. The social dimension of power relies on people conferring on other people certain "powerful" attributes from above and below. In this way, then, the social dimension intersects with power's hierarchical dimension as it acknowledges micropolitical (i.e., individual to individual) and macropolitical (i.e., individual to group to organization and back) factors. The social dimension also intersects with power's rhetorical dimension because of the natural human capability to use language and symbols to appeal to one's intellect, emotions, and behaviors—and to inspire cooperation.

When taken together, however, all three of power's dimensions actually occur simultaneously, which is why power is problematic and valued. People tend to focus on one of the dimensions more than the others as, perhaps, a matter of convenience or importance. Clouding one's view of power, too, can be the frame in which one sees power—as a negative (selfish) phenomenon or as a neutral to positive (selfless) means for correction to the status quo. Power's multidimensionality makes it naturally difficult to apprehend while making it curiously attractive to apply. The most effective application of power, however, comes from an understanding of these three dimensions. Corporate contexts, whether social, political, economic, technological, or cultural, add further factors to be considered.

All together, power is not something that public relations possesses so much as it is something it exercises through relationships. Therefore, we believe power is a community-based phenomenon that people confer on each other through their relationships with one another. This conferring of power is based on hierarchical positions they hold, the rhetorical manifestation and recognition of relationships and positions through communicative acts, and the social implications these dimensions have on individual and, especially, communal views of the system of relationships that exist and evolve among people (see Smudde & Courtright, 2010). Indeed, publics may exercise more power than they realize (and that organizations may be loathe to recognize). Granted, because of their training, public relations practitioners have more extensive levels of communication competence in the matters discussed in this book than the average person. Do not forget, however, that the "average" person also recognizes, at least implicitly, when discourse conventions do not conform to expectations, even at perhaps a subconscious level, when she or he has the feeling that something "just isn't right" with the message received. Practitioners also must realize that some people working or volunteering for nonprofit organizations, engaging in activism, or organizing grassroots efforts develop more of a knack for using public relations genres with formal training.

The key to power and public relations is therefore looking at power's strategic implications. Strategy means applying an understanding of power's multidimensionality for what it has been in the past (i.e., to learn from it) and, most important, formulating future ways (i.e., to anticipate applications) to inspire cooperation within and outside an organization through public relations efforts. Such strategizing is possible through ethical practices involved in coalition building internally and externally, strategy development for an organization's overall business and individual operations' plans, message design that focuses on the relationships between organizations and their publics, genre choices that balance an organization's needs and wants for communication with the publics' needs and wants in communication, and program execution and evaluation that measures how well a public relations program or project worked for both the target publics and the organization through systematic and appropriate measurement methods.

Strategy

As we have asked in each chapter, a key question to answer is, "Now what?" More specifically, as we conclude our introduction, how can the general epideictic nature of public relations be translated into strategy? Each chapter presents specific implications of genre families on public relations strategy. But on a holistic level, we propose a simple framework for developing a broad-based public relations strategy that leans on the epideictic functions along with traditional business strategy matters. This framework can be applied across the range of public relations work, from individual campaigns or projects to annual operating plans for the public relations function.

Any effective strategic plan, whether for a one-time project or a long-term program, must include certain information. Core areas for that information include an opportunity summary, stakeholders/audiences, key messages, objectives, strategies, tactics, a timetable, budget/resources, and evaluation methods. Figure 10.2 outlines these and other areas that are essential in effective strategic plans (Smudde, 2007, 2011).

- ■ **Executive summary**
- ■ **Vision** (optional; concisely say a long-term future state for the organization)
- ■ **Mission** (optional; concisely say why an organization exists & how it does its business)
- ■ **Opportunity/Problem in context** (a.k.a. thorough situation analysis; employ the problem-solving process; the first five steps are key and the sixth begins with objectives)
- ■ **Key message platform** (optional; vital for communications)
- ■ **Audiences/Stakeholders** (internal & external)
- ■ **Objectives** (big-picture accomplishments sought; must include effect sought, audience targeted, and deadline; should include goals)
- ■ **Goals** (quantitative target for the effect sought in each objective; should be combined within objectives but could be listed separately if preferred)
- ■ **Strategies** (statements that systematize tactics toward one or more objectives & goals; organizational strategies become operational objectives)
- ■ **Tactics** (specific actions to be taken to meet/exceed goals & fulfill objectives)
- ■ **Critical success factors** (things/events that could help or hurt success; why is knowing these things valuable)
- ■ **Key performance indicators** (milestone measurements taken along the way to track progress toward goals; why is knowing these things valuable)
- ■ **Timeline** (overall and by phase; relate to objectives/goals and metrics)
- ■ **Budget & resources** (give data as specifically as possible; explain what's needed and why; ROI and value-added for the change are key)
- ■ **Evaluation method** (post hoc measurements & analysis of outputs, outtakes, outcomes, and outgrowths)
- ■ **Appendices** (any additional evidence specifically needed in other sections to support plan)

Figure 10.2. Basic strategic plan outline.

For our purposes in this book, the epideictic nature of public relations opens a new and potent dimension to the strategic planning of public relations. The keys are the four functions of epideictic discourse, the questions they pose, and the strategic implications that answer them. Table 10.1 shows a breakdown of the intersection of epideictic and strategy for public relations by showing what questions must be answered and how they affect the prospective, strategic business planning for public relations.

In Table 10.1, the column "Key Questions" has a particular context: the future. The reason for this is simple: Planning is all about what we want to happen, not what already happened. Planning, then, is prospective, not retrospective. Although there is much to learn from past experiences, those lessons and any supporting knowledge must be applied with an eye toward creating messages based on solid research and objectives. Epideictically speaking, strategic planning for public relations concerns the management of resources—from raw information to evaluation—that invite audiences to cooperate with an organization, celebrate it, and embrace shared values. In this way Table 10.1's column "Strategic Implications" shows how resource management is directly linked through the formal components of a proper strategic plan to the epideictic matters that arise from the answers to the "key questions." Through Table 10.1 and Figure 10.2, then, we show the real, practical relevance of the theoretical dimensions of public relations as epideictic discourse. Jumping to tactics, again, is shown to be a terribly wrong move. Understanding the epideictic functions of public relations better enables practitioners to engage in strategic thinking and decision making because it puts the emphasis on the most salient matters at the intersection of audience, the organization, message design, planning, discourse, and evaluation. This holistic approach to strategic planning for public relations of course would easily accommodate the genres, message design matters, and strategic implications that we explained in the preceding chapters about discourse families.

Closing Thoughts

So this is the beginning of a longer conversation. From what we covered in this volume, it is apparent that public relations is far more purposefully potent and strong than many people believe. Public relations is a kind of "industrial-strength rhetoric" that is much more ethically attuned to inspiring cooperation and celebrating organizations than merely spinning a good story. Our approach has been one of analysis (taking apart to see inside) and synthesis (putting together things in new, insightful ways), even to the point to suggest that analysis of public relations is important for learning from the past, but synthesis is just as vital because it con-

Table 10.1. Epideictic Matters Affecting Public Relations Strategic Planning

Epideictic Function	Key Questions (Dimensions)	Strategic Implications
Celebratory (concerns the effective presentation of ideas)	■ What might be the established, accepted patterns of language and action for praising things we value and/or decrying things we're against? (ritualistic)	■ Opportunity/problem analysis; key messages; objectives; goals; strategies; tactics; budget/resources
	■ What are the values we want to address in the message, explicitly or implicitly? (axiological)	■ Opportunity/problem analysis; key message platform
Performative (establishes how an organization is & how it develops relationships with audiences)	■ Is the message intended to advocate a particular cause, and, if so, how overtly does the position need to be stated? (political)	■ Opportunity/problem analysis; audiences; key message platform; objectives; strategies; tactics
	■ How might corporate reputation or identity be built through ethos? (identity management)	■ Vision; mission; opportunity/problem analysis; audiences; key message platform;
	■ How do we want audiences to identify with and/or act on messages? (rhetorical)	■ Audiences; objectives; goals; critical success factors; key performance indicators; evaluation
Epistemic (focuses on knowledge-building capacity for speakers & audiences)	■ What are the values held by the audience that we want to appeal to? (educational)	■ Opportunity/problem analysis; audiences; key message platform
	■ How can we define/explain new information so that it is understood? (explanatory)	■ Audiences; key message platform; objectives; goals; strategies; tactics; critical success factors
Preservative (subsumes the conservation & reinforcement of community values)	■ How can the verbal content and its visual presentation work together, within individual messages and across the campaign? (cohesion)	■ Key message platform; tactics; evaluation; budget/resources; timeline
	■ How can organizational self-concept be upheld and audience self-persuasion be enabled? (reflexivity)	■ Vision; mission; opportunity/problem analysis; audiences; key message platform; objectives; strategies; tactics; key performance indicators; evaualtion
	■ Knowing that messages become part of the public record, what messages do you want accessible by anyone in the future immediate or long term? (repurposing)	■ Mission; key message platform; tactics; evaluation

cerns planning for the future. For example, our approach allows for the possibility of applying principles from one chapter to other genre families (e.g., the Johari window may be used in making showcase genres more conversational when the situation warrants it). This flexibility is important because communication in general is not restrictive of what can be used to analyze and synthesize matters of effective discourse conception, creation, cohesion, and comprehension. Additionally, we purposely have not focused on traditional genre concerns, such as how they change over time (see Jamieson, 1976) or how elements of two different genres may be adapted when the situation warrants. Jamieson and Campbell (1982) call such uses of genre conventions "rhetorical hybrids," which are temporary in nature and typically do not generate new genres or "crossbreeds." Discussion about hybrids of the genres that we chronicled in this volume may best be addressed henceforth.

Public relations requires discourse competence, which, together with ethics. power, and strategy, creates the four-point plane to initiate the deeper conversations we envision our book to generate. We covered 39 individual genres of public relations discourse in seven "families" (see Appendix 1) that practitioners at every level of expertise, accountability, and authority are expected to use effectively in their careers, and they may use some genres more than others. The combination of the rules for their individual use (i.e., discourse conventions) and the four functions of epideictic rhetoric make a potent approach for both message design and strategic communication for public relations purposes in business contexts, including profit, nonprofit, government, and nongovernment organizations. We believe our treatment of public relations in this volume is the first of its kind and offers practitioners, scholars, and students a valuable, unique, and useful approach for better organizational communication with any audience. From here, the conversation must continue to probe the dynamics of the intersecting discursive, message, and strategic dimensions of public relations that inspires cooperation between organizations and their publics. In the meantime, for the practice of public relations, *let the celebrations begin!*

Notes

1. In tune with what we mentioned in Chapter 2, the intersection of discourse genres and rhetorical genres apply here as well.

2. At this point, it is important to recognize that technological features of a communication medium can truly begin to resemble discourse conventions. In particular, we are thinking about the effects of Web 2.0 on public relations, which have been addressed in sources like Argenti and Barnes (2009), Breakenridge (2008), and Scott (2009). Indeed, within the context of our argument in this book it seems the

technological forms of social media (e.g., blogs, podcasts, wikis, etc.) intersect with the rhetorical function of user-generated content. For example, a social networking site such as Facebook allows people to create dedicated content about themselves, an idea, a product, an organization, or anything, and then that Facebook site becomes a place for people to gather, share content, and commune. Public relations professionals can use any social medium to their strategic advantage, provided that they post content that both fits the technological parameters (including data fields) of the medium and, especially, complements the interests, attitudes, and expectations of users. In this way, then, social media are much more idiosyncratic in their facilitation of discourse because of the combination of technological constraints and user/community norms about what is allowed and acceptable content.

References

Agnew, L. (2008). "The day belongs to the students": Expanding epideictic's civic function. *Rhetoric Review, 27,* 147–164.

Argenti, P. A., & Barnes, C. M. (2009). *Digital strategies for powerful corporate communications.* New York: McGraw-Hill.

Aristotle. (1947). *Ethica Nicomachea* (W. D. Ross, Trans.). In R. McKeon (Ed.), *Introduction to Aristotle.* New York: Modern Library.

Aristotle. (1991). *On rhetoric: A theory of civic discourse* (G. A. Kennedy, Trans.). New York: Oxford University Press.

Black, E. (1970). The second persona. *Quarterly Journal of Speech, 56,* 109–119.

Blakemore, D. (2003). Discourse and relevance theory. In D. Schiffrin, D. Tannen, & H. E. Hamilton (Eds.), *The handbook of discourse analysis* (pp. 100–118). Malden, MA: Blackwell.

Bois, J. S. (1978). *The art of awareness* (3rd ed.). Dubuque, IA: Wm. C. Brown.

Breakenridge, D. (2008). *PR 2.0: New media, new tools, new audiences.* Upper Saddle River, NJ: Pearson Education.

Brønn, P. S., & Berg, R. W. (Eds.). (2005). *Corporate communication: A strategic approach to building reputation* (2nd ed.). Oslo: Gyldendal.

Burkart, R. (2004). Intermezzo: Consensus-oriented public relations (COPR): A concept for planning and evaluating public relations. In B. van Ruler & D. Verčič (Eds.), *Public relations and communication management in Europe: A nation-by-nation introduction to public relations theory and practice* (pp. 459–465). Berlin, Germany: Mouton de Gruyter.

Burke, K. (1969). *A grammar of motives.* Berkeley: University of California Press. (Original work published 1945)

Caillois, R., & McKeon, N. (1963). Circular time, rectilinear time. *Diogenes, 11,* 1–13.

Campbell, K. K., & Jamieson, K. H. (1986). Introduction (special issue on genre criticism). *Southern Speech Communication Journal, 51,* 293–299.

Cheney, G. (1992). The corporate person (re)presents itself. In E. L. Toth & R. L. Heath (Eds.), *Rhetorical and critical approaches to public relations* (pp. 165–183). Hillsdale, NJ: Erlbaum.

Condit, C. M. (1985). The functions of epideictic: The Boston massacre orations as exemplar. *Communication Quarterly, 33,* 284–298.

Conrad, C. (Ed.). (1993). *The ethical nexus.* Norwood, NJ: Ablex.

Courtright, J. L., & Slaughter, G. Z. (2007). Remembering disaster: Since the media do, so must public relations. *Public Relations Review, 33,* 313–318.

Courtright, J. L., & Smudde, P. M. (2009). Leveraging organizational innovation for strategic reputation management. *Corporate Reputation Review, 12,* 245–269.

Crable, R. E., & Vibbert, S. L. (1986). *Public relations as communication management.* Edina, MN: Bellwether Press.

Curtin, P. A., & Boynton, L. A. (2001). Ethics in public relations: Theory and practice. In R. L. Heath (Ed.), *Handbook of public relations* (pp. 411–422). Thousand Oaks, CA: Sage.

David, P. (2004). Extending symmetry: Toward a convergence of professionalism, practice, and pragmatics in public relations. *Journal of Public Relations Research, 16,* 185–211.

Eggins, S., & Martin, J. R. (1997). Genres and registers of discourse. In T. A. van Dijk (Ed.), *Discourse as structure and process: Discourse studies: A multidisciplinary introduction* (Vol. 1, pp. 230–256). Thousand Oaks, CA: Sage.

Eisenberg, E. (1984). Ambiguity as strategy in organizational communication. *Communication Monographs, 51,* 227–242.

Fairclough, N. (1992). *Discourse and social change.* Cambridge, MA: Polity/Blackwell.

Fisher, W. R. (1987). *Human communication as narration: Toward a philosophy of reason, value, and action.* Columbia: University of South Carolina Press.

Fombrun, C. J., & van Riel, C. B. M. (2004). *Fame & fortune: How successful companies build winning reputations.* New York: Prentice-Hall.

Frankena, W. K. (1973). *Ethics* (2nd ed.). Englewood Cliffs, NJ: Prentice-Hall.

Goddard, T. (2005). Corporate citizenship and community relations: Contributing to the challenges of aid discourse. *Business and Society Review, 110,* 269–296.

Halliday, M. A. K., & Hasan, R. (1976). *Cohesion in English.* New York: Longman.

Hoffman, J., Röttger, U., & Jarren, O. Structural segregation and openness: Balanced professionalism for public relations. *Studies in Communication Sciences, 7*(1), 125–146.

Hudson, R. A. (1980). *Sociolinguistics.* New York: Cambridge University Press.

Hymes, D. H. (1972). On communicative competence. In. J. B. Pride & J. Holmes (Eds.), *Sociolinguistics: Selected readings* (pp. 269–293). Harmondsworth: Penguin.

Jablin, F. M., & Sias, P. M. (2001). Communication competence. In F. M. Jablin & L. L. Putnam (Eds.), *The new handbook of organizational communication: Advances in theory, research, and methods* (pp. 819–864). Thousand Oaks, CA: Sage.

Jamieson, K. H. (1976). Generic constraints and the rhetorical situation. *Philosophy and Rhetoric, 6,* 162–170.

Jamieson, K. H., & Campbell, K. K. (1982). Rhetorical hybrids: Fusions of generic elements. *Quarterly Journal of Speech, 68,* 146–157.

Jaworski, A., & Coupland, N. (2006). Introduction: Perspectives on discourse analysis. In A. Jaworski & N. Coupland (Eds.), *The discourse reader* (2nd ed., pp. 1–37). New York: Routledge.

Kiley, D., & Helm, B. (2009). 100 best global brands: The great trust offensive. *BusinessWeek*, *4148*, 38–42.

Kim, S.-Y., & Reber, B. H. (2008). Public relations' place in corporate social responsibility: Practitioners define their role. *Public Relations Review, 34*, 337–342.

Kinneavy, J. L. (1971). *A theory of discourse*. New York: Norton.

Korzybski, A. (1950). *Manhood of humanity*. Lakeville, CT: International Non-Aristotelian Library. (Original work published 1921)

Langer, S. K. (1979). *Philosophy in a new key: A study in the symbolism of reason, rite, and art*. Cambridge, MA: Harvard University Press. (Original work published 1942)

McLuhan, M. (1964). *Understanding media: The extensions of man* (2nd ed.). New York: Mentor/Penguin.

Mirhady, D. C. (1995). A note on Aristotle *Rhetoric* 1.3 1358b5-6. *Philosophy and Rhetoric, 28*, 405–409.

Moffitt, M. A. (1999). *Campaign strategies and message design: A practitioner's guide from start to finish*. Westport, CT: Praeger.

Oravec, C. (1976). "Observation" in Aristotle's theory of epideictic. *Philosophy & Rhetoric, 9*, 162–174.

Perelman, C., & Olbrechts-Tyteca, L. (1969). *The new rhetoric: A treatise on argumentation* (J. Wilkinson & P. Weaver, Trans.). Notre Dame, IN: Notre Dame University Press.

Pieczka, M., & L'Etang, J. (2001). Public relations and the question of professionalism. In R. L. Heath (Ed.), *Handbook of public relations* (pp. 223–237). Newbury Park, CA: Sage.

Redding, W. C. (1990, June 1). *Ethics and the study of organizational communication: A case of culpable neglect*. Paper presented at the SCA Communication Ethics conference, Gull Lake, MI.

Samsung Electronics. (2007). *2007 Samsung Electronics annual report*. Retrieved January 10, 2010, from http://www.samsung.com/us/aboutsamsung/corporateprofile/download/SECAR2007_Eng_Final.pdf

Schultz, M., Hatch, M. J., & Larsen, M. H. (Eds.). (2000). *The expressive organization: Linking identity, reputation, and the corporate brand*. London: Oxford University Press.

Scott, D. M. (2009). *The new rules of marketing & PR* (rev. & updated ed.). Hoboken, NJ: John Wiley & Sons.

Smudde, P. M. (2007). Public relations' power as based on knowledge, discourse, and ethics. In J. L. Courtright & P. M. Smudde (Eds.), *Power and public relations* (pp. 207–238). Cresskill, NJ: Hampton Press.

Smudde, P. M. (2011). *Public relations as dramatistic organizing: A case study bridging theory and practice*. Cresskill, NJ: Hampton Press.

Smudde, P. M., & Courtright, J. L. (2010). Public relations and power. In R. L. Heath (Ed.), *Handbook of public relations* (2nd ed., pp. 177–189). Thousand Oaks, CA: Sage.

Sullivan, D. L. (1993). The ethos of epideictic encounter. *Philosophy and Rhetoric, 26*, 113–133.

Sullivan, L. H. (1979). *Kindergarten chats and other writings*. New York: Dover. (Original work published 1918)

Toyota Motor Corporation. (2007). *Annual report 2007: Building a platform for growth.* [Annual report]. Retrieved January 10, 2010, from http://www.toyota.co.jp/en/ir/library/annual/pdf/2007/ar07_e.pdf

Wallace, K. R. (1963). The substance of rhetoric: Good reasons. *Quarterly Journal of Speech, 49,* 239–249.

Ware, B. L., & Linkugel, W. A. (1973). They spoke in defense of themselves: On the generic criticism of apologia. *Quarterly Journal of Speech, 59,* 273–283.

Weaver, C. K. (2010). Carnivalesque activism as a public relations genre: A case study of the New Zealand group Mothers Against Genetic Engineering. *Public Relations Review, 36,* 35–41.

Williams, S. L., & Moffitt, M. A. (1997). Corporate image as an impression formation process: Prioritizing personal, organizational, and environmental audience factors. *Journal of Public Relations Research, 9,* 237–258.

Appendix

Families of Public Relations
Discourse Genres

The functions are given in the order of your outline of them but prioritized by dominance per grouping. Functions' individual characteristics are also prioritized.

News (press releases, video news releases, audio news releases, photo news releases, media advisories, and prepared statements):

1. Performative—[1] rhetorical; [2] identity management; [3] political
2. Epistemic—[1] explanatory; [2] educational
3. Preservative—cohesion; reflexivity; repurposing [these three characteristics are ever-present]
4. Celebratory—[1] axiological; [2] ritualistic

Summaries (fact sheets, fliers, posters, tip sheets, FAQs, and bios):

1. Epistemic—[1] explanatory; [2] educational
2. Performative—[1] rhetorical; [2] identity management; [3] political
3. Preservative—cohesion; reflexivity; repurposing [these three characteristics are ever-present]
4. Celebratory—[1] axiological; [2] ritualistic

Features (backgrounders, white papers, case studies, articles and matte releases):

1. Performative—[1] rhetorical; [2] political; [3] identity management
2. Celebratory—[1] axiological; [2] ritualistic
3. Epistemic—[1] educational; [2] explanatory

4. Preservative—cohesion; reflexivity; repurposing [these three
characteristics are ever-present]

Conversations (oral: conversations, pitch calls, interviews, meetings,
speeches, and podcasts; oral-based: pitch letters, written correspondence,
blogs and wikis):
1. Celebratory—[1] ritualistic; [2] axiological
2. Performative—[1] rhetorical; [2] identity management; [3] political
3. Epistemic—[1] explanatory; [2] educational
4. Preservative—cohesion; reflexivity; repurposing [these three
characteristics are ever-present]

Showcases (advertorials, public service announcements, press
conferences, press kits, and satellite media tours):
1. Celebratory—[1] ritualistic; [2] axiological
2. Preservative—cohesion; reflexivity; repurposing [these three
characteristics are ever-present]
3. Epistemic—[1] educational; [2] explanatory
4. Performative—[1] rhetorical; [2] identity management; [3] political

Collections (newsletters, video news programs and magazines):
1. Performative—[1] rhetorical; [2] political; [3] identity management;
2. Epistemic—[1] explanatory; [2] educational
3. Celebratory—[1] axiological; [2] ritualistic
4. Preservative—cohesion; reflexivity; repurposing [these three
characteristics are ever-present]

Reports (annual reports, issue reports, brochures/pamphlets, websites, and
advertisements):
1. Preservative—cohesion; reflexivity; repurposing [these three
characteristics are ever-present]
2. Celebratory—[1] ritualistic; [2] axiological
3. Performative—[1] identity management; [2] political; [3] rhetorical;
4. Epistemic—[1] explanatory; [2] educational

This breakdown presents a composite view of message design
approaches for the genres in each grouping, and it allows us to state individual
examples of each genre to support the composite view. This is much like
the discussion section of quantitative studies—pragmatic "messaging rules"
for making the most of discourse genres and their conventions. Our final
section in Chapter 10 on strategy implications contains our conclusions and
recommendations for strategic planning with these tactics.

Author Index

Subject Index

"cybercommunity" (online community), 103 fn., 119–120

dialogic communication, 121, 128
discourse
    community (*see* community, discourse)
    conventions (*see* conventions, discourse)
    genre (*see* genre, discourse)
dynamism, 143

eloquence, 128
entertainer's stance, 142–143, 146, 149
enthymeme, 2, 54, 187
enthymeme, organizational, 187
ethics, 24, 26, 34, 97, 103, 111, 113, 126, 128, 173, 178, 180, 185, 205–208, 209, 210, 212, 214
    and propaganda, 63 fn.4
    and video news releases (VNRs), 49
ethos (*see also* credibility), 30–31, 35, 47, 60, 116, 121, 146, 182, 204–205, 206, 213; *see also* 139
    and power, 208
    for good public relations practice, five components of, 206–207
expectations, audience (*see* audience—expectations)
exposure, selective, 74

form
    and function, 11 fn.1, 17, 22, 55, 59, 74, 81, 87, 108, 115, 196. 197, 198–200
    appeal to (*see also* genre classification schemes), 4, 46, 73, 91, 100, 101, 102, 118
    atrophy of, 77
formulary devices or materials, 108
frames, framing (rhetorical), 16, 17, 26, 45, 48, 70, 73, 74–75, 77, 78, 81, 82, 99, 142, 180, 181, 196
function
    of genres (*see* genre[s]—function)

of public relations, 1, 10, 150, 195, 202, 210
of reputation equity, 204
of rhetoric, 32, 200, 214–215 fn.2
of symbols, 118

gatekeepers, media, 47, 69
generic approach, 3, 4–5, 7, 20, 35
genre(s)
    and structure (*see* form)
    Aristotle and, 2, 16, 20, 27, 34, 117, 119, 131, 186
    classification schemes, 199
    corporate discourse, 18, 20
    definition, 3, 4, 5, 17, 20, 23, 196
    discourse, 3, 10, 11, 15, 17, 19–20, 21–22, 24–25, 35 fn.1, 40, 45, 59, 60, 61, 69–70, 75, 90, 92, 107, 126, 128, 133, 139, 158, 168, 176, 190, 191, 195, 199–200, 204, 208, 214 fn.1
    function, 6, 15, 133, 136, 155, 166, 201
    life cycle, 21, 26, 150, 158
    literary, 91, 101
    public relations, 28, 33, 35
    rhetorical, 35 fn.1
    apocalyptic, 3, 19
    apologia (see *apologia[e]*, corporate)
    diatribe, 3, 24
    eulogies, eulogy, 3, 16–17, 20, 26, 29
    hybrids (*see* hybrids, genre)
    jeremiad, 3, 19
    utopian, 19, 200
gratification, 58
    instant, 56, 81–82
    levels of audience, 56–57
    in Uses and Gratifications Theory, 63 fn.2

hybrids, genre, 115, 214

identification (*see also* consubstantiality), 34, 45, 54–55, 79, 80, 81, 83, 118, 119, 120, 122, 124, 127, 148, 201, 213
    defined, 78
    types of, 78